T3-BSD-629

Thoreau's Wild Rhetoric

Thoreau's Wild Rhetoric

HENRY GOLEMBA

NEW YORK UNIVERSITY PRESS
NEW YORK & LONDON

Copyright © 1990 by New York University
All rights reserved
Manufactured in the United States of America

Library of Congress Cataloging-in-Publication Data
Golemba, Henry L.
Thoreau's wild rhetoric / Henry Golemba.
p. cm.
Includes bibliographical references.
Includes index.
ISBN 0-8147-3036-1 (alk. paper)
 1. Thoreau, Henry David, 1817–1862—Technique. 2. Romanticism—
United States. 3. Rhetoric. I. Title.
PS3058.G6 1990   90—37578
                        CIP

New York University Press books are printed on acid-free paper,
and their binding materials are chosen for strength and durability.

Book design by Ken Venezio

Contents

Abbreviations

Corr   *The Correspondence of Henry David Thoreau,* ed. Walter Harding and Carl Bode. New York: New York University Press, 1985; reprint 1974.

EE   *Early Essays and Miscellanies,* ed. Joseph J. Moldenhauer and Edwin Moser, with Alexander Kern. Princeton: Princeton University Press, 1975.

J   *The Journal of Henry David Thoreau,* ed. Bradford Torrey and Francis H. Allen. 14 vols. Boston: Houghton Mifflin, 1906.

Life   Robert D. Richardson, *Henry Thoreau: A Life of the Mind.* Berkeley: University of California Press, 1986.

MW   *The Maine Woods,* ed. Joseph J. Moldenhauer. Princeton: Princeton University Press, 1972.

PJ1   *Journal, Volume 1: 1837–1844,* ed. John C. Broderick et al. Princeton: Princeton University Press, 1981.

PJ2   *Journal, Volume 2: 1842–1848,* ed. John C. Broderick et al. Princeton: Princeton University Press, 1984.

RP   *Reform Papers,* ed. Wendell Glick. Princeton: Princeton University Press, 1973.

W   *Walden,* ed. J. Lyndon Shanley. Princeton: Princeton University Press, 1971.

Week   *A Week on the Concord and Merrimack Rivers,* ed. Carl F. Hovde et al. Princeton: Princeton University Press, 1980.

Writings   *The Writings of Henry D. Thoreau.* Walden edition. Boston: Houghton Mifflin, 1906.

Preface

No one doubts Henry David Thoreau's dedication to writing. No one can question the commitment of an author for whom ten years spent perfecting a book was a mere tick of time. Nor can anyone miss Thoreau's quarrel with language. Throughout his three million published words, the craftsman's impatience with his tools frequently erupts. He complains that composition is like "the taking of a scalp" whereby the self is diminished when expressed. He laments that through writing as a form of memory, "We remember how we itched, not how our hearts beat." He expresses his frustration that no matter how carefully he writes, words bring him "never nearer to the source."

Nevertheless, he remains true to his early conviction that language is "the most perfect work of art" and that "a word is wiser than any man." In studying his obsession, he will in *Walden* break language down into its basic etymologies, even into its fundamental syllables. His poems will often defer to poetic theory. His prose will freely wander off on long digressions upon language, digressions so long and obvious that one wonders whether the "digression" or its stated topic is the true impulse of his composition. He is so fixated on language that some of his writings make better sense as descriptions of communication acts rather than as articulations of their purported themes, as when "Friendship" is more intelligible as an analysis of the reading process than as advice on personal friendships. Throughout his various genres, one obsession dominates: his fascination with the uses and limitations of language, particularly the phenomenon of meaning and its relationship to a text.

Thoreau's Wild Rhetoric clarifies what Thoreau calls his "friendship" with language, giving special attention to the frustration and uncertainty his love entailed. It examines specific literary devices, images, techniques, and organizing principles as they accent his broader concerns with language, writing, communication, and meaning. It centers especially on passages like the *Journal* entry for 9 November 1851:

> Facts should only be as the frame to my pictures; they should be material to the mythology which I am writing; not facts to assist men to make money, farmers to farm profitably, in any common sense; facts to tell who I am, and where I have been or what I have thought. ... I would so state facts that they shall be significant, shall be myths or mythologic. Facts which the mind perceived, thoughts which the body thought,—with these I deal. I, too, cherish vague and misty forms, the vaguest when the cloud at which I gaze is dissipated quite and naught but the skyey depths are seen.

Thoreau had great skill with a language of facts, a descriptive language that communicated how to live profitably or simply, what social evils to rage against, the beauties of nature to enjoy, autobiographical reports, or even the facts about "what I have thought." For more than a century, he has been valued chiefly for this language of "facts."

Thoreau gained satisfaction from factual language, from writing, like his Theophrastus from "Wild Apples," in precise, deliberate, and forceful prose whose meaning was explicit and clear. Yet he was also lured by a language of desire that he felt to be more challenging, more potent, more portentous. This language of desire is imaged in the Homer anecdote, also from "Wild Apples," where words are like apples "which Tantalus could not pluck," and the reading experience is like "the wind ever blowing their boughs away from him." He would use factual language to fashion a frame whose picture would dissolve into "skyey depths." Sometimes he did so because language expressing "Coleridgean thoughts," as he once put it, was the style of his era. At other times he firmly believed that an indeterminate language of desire was the only linguistic mode that could communicate his transcendental visions without debasing their complexity to the level of moral or slogan. Even when he suspected that these transcendental visions and idealistic truths may have no existence in the world except in the web of words, he comforted himself that a tantalizing writing at least engages readers strongly and makes them participate in the creation of meaning. Rather than a style that merely fed readers facts, a language of desire could whet appetite powerfully.

Thoreau was enamored "of vague and misty forms." He was intrigued by a "mythologic" language where his "facts" would evaporate like the cloud he gazed upon, where his statements would become "significant" (or seem to be significant) as they dissolved before his readers' eyes while they strove to describe what they thought had been glimpsed in the vanishing words. Although he would become best known as a writer of facts, he desired to create a wild rhetoric whose meaning always remains elusive and untameable, while its facts provoke readers to interpret, to decode, and thus to domesticate his sentences. *Thoreau's Wild Rhetoric* clarifies what Thoreau meant by a mythologic language. It contemplates why he should seek to perfect a rhetoric that means to run wild, why he chose to fill his texts with gaps, contradictions, oxymorons, self-erasing statements, and dissolving images. It studies how he experimented with rhetorical situations and strategies that would use facts and explicit language in order to create "vague and misty" forms full of indefiniteness and indeterminacies.

Wild Rhetoric emphasizes the most significant language problems that Thoreau discovered, problems that he articulated and "embodied" but did not resolve, because he felt that resolving them would demean their mystery and debase their significance. Of course, Thoreau's embodiment of communication problems is germane to all writers. As he pushed beyond specific technical questions to confront problems writ large as "Writing" and "Language," he encountered the ultimate, eternal enigmas that affect writers of any age. Although his discoveries are cast in the words of his American Romantic era, a Flaubert or a Borges would recognize the sphinx-like riddles of his furthest linguistic explorations.

I have many people to thank for their help in the preparation of this book. Elizabeth Hall Witherell not only helped with manuscripts, but she also provided many insights, particularly with respect to Thoreau's poetry. Joseph J. Moldenhauer answered several of my research questions, and Arnold Goldsmith provided much encouragement. Philip F. Gura and Wendell Glick offered useful advice about scholarship and revision. Leonard Neufeldt, Steven Fink, and Evan Carton shared ideas about their current work through correspondence. Of unique value were the responses from Dan Cottom, Ross Pudaloff, and Michael Scrivener when this project was in its infancy. I particularly appreciate their willingness to let me talk through ideas before setting them on paper.

I am also grateful for readings from individuals whose specialties lay outside American Romanticism. John Reed, Suzanne Ferguson, and Alan Raucher are three whom I owe special thanks. I am also indebted for stylistic suggestions from the editors of *American Literature, ESQ,* and *Essays in Literature,* where sections of *Thoreau's Wild Rhetoric* appeared in early versions. Although these editors and advisors are usually anonymous, some whom I can name include Thomas Joswick, Kathleen MacLean, and Louis J. Budd. Of course, I owe a debt too vast for description to my wife, Adine, particularly during those years when life was simplified as either uninteresting or potentially relevant to my book.

Wayne State University awarded me two research grants and a sabbatical in order to research and to write *Thoreau's Wild Rhetoric.* The following institutions allowed me to examine their Thoreau holdings: The Berg Collection of the New York Public Library, the Huntington Library in San Marino, the Massachusetts Historical Society in Boston, the Pierpont Morgan Library in New York, and the Center for The Writings of Henry David Thoreau in Santa Barbara.

Problems

One of Thoreau's most empathetic readers was Harrison Gray Otis Blake, whose letter in the middle of March 1848 initiated a voluminous correspondence (*Corr*, 214). Long after his friend's death, Blake reported that he had read and reread Thoreau's twenty-five letters all his life and was "still warmed and instructed by them, with more force occasionally than ever before; so that in a sense they are still in the mail, have not altogether reached me yet, and will not probably before I die" (*Life*, 328). Blake's succinct description highlights three distinct reading experiences. Thoreau's texts provoke "warmth," whether the friendly feeling that can sometimes extend to discipleship, or the angry response from outraged or irritated readers. Thoreau's texts also seem extremely instructive, full of practical advice and idealistic exhortation.

For the century following Thoreau's death, his letters—both the literal letters to his friends, and the letters of his creative writings—have been studied primarily for their warmth and instruction, but this book's principal focus is the third special reading experience that Blake recommends: Thoreau's letters, no matter how often read, always seem "in the mail." They seem always about to be delivered but never finally arrive. Their meaning seems to be perpetually reaching toward us. *Thoreau's Wild Rhetoric* thus builds upon the scholarly emphasis of the last two decades, which views Thoreau primarily as a writer for whom language was his primary concern, and its main objective is to clarify how Thoreau refined his special rhetorical ability to achieve the effect of meaning's perpetual immanence, to create the reading experience that his letters are ever en route, to develop a style that includes gaps, dissolves, and contradictions, creating rhetorical situations wherein readers are forced to participate as coauthors in creating his letters' meaning.

Obviously Thoreau's sentences can be clear and inspiring and can impressively communicate explicit ideas in superbly crafted, memorable phrasing. No one can plausibly deny that his message-oriented writings have had profound impact on readers. The influence of his "Resistance to Civil Government" on heroes like Gandhi, Leo Tolstoy, and Martin Luther King, Jr., is inarguable. *Walden* has inspired an untold number of longings for and many actual experiments in living simply and harmoniously with nature. For vastly different purposes, organizations as serious as the Sierra Club and Greenpeace or as commercial as giftbook publishers and calendar vendors have found his texts to be an invaluable resource. His *Maine Woods* and other excursion pieces have caused readers, even as early as 1876 and as seemingly uncongenial to Thoreau's thought as the editors of *The National Baptist,* to value his advice on forest lore and to call him "that king of all woodcraft" (*Corr,* 624). His general criticisms of American culture and his jeremiads against his country's lapses have been prized as highly in the 1980s as in the 1890s, at times even in identical words; when, for example, Taylor Stoehr insists in his recent book that we need to listen to Thoreau's criticism "now more than ever," his language echoes that of Joseph Wood Krutch in 1962 and Samuel Arthur Jones in 1899.[1]

However, Jones, like scholars before and after, further acknowledges that to read *Walden* properly, to obtain its full meaning, one must "read it," as he warns, "between the lines." The inspirational message of Thoreau's maxims should not eclipse the magical evanescence of his prose; while hearing Thoreau urge readers to step boldly to the music that they hear, they should have one ear cocked for the prose that is as subtle and transient as are musical notes. Jones punningly subtitles his collection of letters a "still-born book," both in the sense of a collection not previously published and—as though an echo of Blake—a kind of writing that seems always new, never quite delivered, still being born. In like manner, I concentrate on the shadow lands and border areas, the gaps and obscurities, the qualifications, erasures, and silences in Thoreau's texts—those rhetorical effects that perhaps have caused Thoreau's writings to be the object of much intense study while more explicit, clearer naturalists, social reformers, idealists, and polemicists have, in Thoreau's words, "attained to obscurity."

Thoreau sought to write clearly, forcefully, and solidly, but he also developed what in "Walking, or The Wild" he called *"Gramatica parda,* a tawny grammar," a concept that might with good cause be phrased in more modern terms as a "language of desire," a language whose meaning seems to evaporate as the reader's eye follows Thoreau's words, enticing the reader to fill the gaps with his or her own meaning, transforming the reader into a coauthor of the text. Hence, while other scholars might highlight passages that pertain to political, idealistic, biographical, scientific, or historical theses, or other explicit messages, I tend to select samples that seem carefully crafted to invite yet defy reduction to such messages.

In other words, this book concentrates on that peculiar kind of communication that Thoreau mentions in his *Journal* for 23 June 1840, and that he later incorporated into his first published book: "Yes and No are lies—A true answer will not aim to establish anything, but rather to set all well afloat" (*PJ1*, 139). *Thoreau's Wild Rhetoric* focuses on those textual situations where both positive and negative assertions are disestablished, where seemingly explicit statements are made to hover and float. With *Walden,* for example, I am less concerned about how it emerges from the tradition of the conduct book, a centuries-old genre by the time of *Walden*'s publication, than I am with *Walden* as a magic show, a presentation of patterns that are made to seem real only to be dissolved.[2] If forced to select a muse from one author Thoreau took to Walden, I would nominate Homer's Penelope, whose perpetual weaving and unweaving in order to forestall disaster is a more appropriate trope than Mentor's practical wisdom. "Ravel" is a useful verb, for it can simultaneously mean both weaving and unweaving.

Thoreau's "language of desire" is evident in primitive rhetorical forms —that love of puns and double-meaning words, that tendency to oxymorons of which Emerson complained, that urge to "rewrite" popular slogans and cultural myths so that they acquire radically different meanings, as at the outset of "Resistance to Civil Government," or that penchant for curious etymologies that make readers doubt precisely which of many possible meanings is intended—but I am more interested in Thoreau's more elaborate rhetorical experiments. Others have already elucidated

Thoreau's mastery of standard rhetorical devices, explaining that "there is hardly a trick of the writing trade that Thoreau does not use."[3]

One of the clearest statements Thoreau made on the elusive subject of a language of desire appears in his *Journal* for 7 March 1852:

> As I look down the rail-road, standing on the W[est] brink of the deep cut—I seem to see in the manner in which the moon is reflected from the W[estern] slope covered with snow in the sort of misty light as if a fine vapor were rising from it—a *promise* or sign of spring. This stillness is more impressive than any sound. The moon the stars—the trees—the snow—the sand where bare—a monumental stillness—whose void must be supplied by thought— It extracts thought from the beholder, as the void under a cupping glass? raises a swelling. How much a silent mankind might suggest! There is no snow on the trees— The moon appears to have waned a little—yet with this snow on the ground, I can plainly see the words I write— What a contrast there may be between this moon & the next![4]

This passage suggests that in Thoreau's wild rhetoric—a style that mirrored the "style" of nature—clear statements are used like a physician's cupping-glass to create a void that in turn forces a swelling thought from the reader. Believing that the mind of a reader abhors a vacuum as much as nature does, Thoreau plays upon this phenomenon in order to create a more enticing text, one that will place a reader in a relationship to Thoreau's text that mirrors Thoreau standing on the brink of the deep cut and reading the text of nature's landscape spread out unbounded before him. Through a language of desire that creates vacuums and erases statements as soon as they are made, Thoreau makes readers feel more intensely compelled to discover the text's "true meaning" and to experience a sense of communication, even communion, with its author. They will "discover," they will "experience," or, at least, they will take pleasure in the illusion that they have done so.

Thus, Thoreau takes pains to render definite statements indeterminate, to unsay sayings, to space out seemingly self-evident sentiments in order to achieve the rhetorical effect of "a monumental stillness." And, true to his own rhetorical belief, he concludes—or, more accurately, "inconcludes"—this passage about the attractive force of the void by saying that the moon that inspired these thoughts may not come again, at least not in the same form or phase. Even indeterminacy may be indeterminate. These rhetorical means, this withdrawing of an assertion as soon as it is proffered, makes Thoreau's writings seem perpetually "in the mail," re-

gardless how often his letters have been read. Perhaps it is this requirement of a perpetual reading and rereading that has caused readers like
Harrison Blake to imagine and appreciate Thoreau's writings "with more
force occasionally than ever before."

Yet Thoreau's reading of a beautiful landscape is not as idealistically
cheerful as might seem. In his description of nature's supreme rhetoric
lurks poignant anxiety. Thoreau's imagined vision of "a promise or sign
of spring" becomes immediately knotted with thoughts of disease, sick-
ness, and pain. The elated view from "the Deep Cut" instantly reminds
him of physical impurities and infections and of a medical treatment that
was rapidly becoming obsolete. Less obviously, these linked images of
the moon's misty light and the physician's cupping-glass expose Thoreau's
reluctance to imagine nature and writing without thinking of health;
instead of a "monumental stillness" and the aesthetic pleasure of experiencing an evaporating "fine vapor," health implies improvement, better-
ment, and myriad other value judgments. That is, for all his fine talk—
and fine talk it truly is—to the effect that the finest writing should "set
all well afloat" and transcend "Yes and No," he was still rooted in a
humanistic tradition, a tradition that had just begun its American transformation while Thoreau was at Harvard. This was Thoreau's principal
intellectual agony. He delighted in filling the void of nature with his own
thought, and he sought to create a kind of writing that would woo readers
into attempting to fill textural gaps with their own meanings, but he still
feared that a rhetoric that depended on vacuum might attain to nothing
more than vacuousness. Although his theory might often sound Derri-
dean, he balked at the thought that language may be nothing more than
Pyrrhic play.

Thoreau's agon reflects the anxiety of Romantic discourse. One desire
was to write, as Thoreau records in his *Journal* for 20 December 1851,
"Flights of Imagination, Coleridgean thoughts. So a man is said to soar in
his thought, ever to fresh woods and pastures new" (3:144). Yet an
equally strong influence of his times insisted humanistically that the
intellectual's office was "to cheer and to guide," and so Thoreau agonized
that his quest for a transcendent meaning beyond words might leave
communication lost in a void, and he could not console himself always
that being an aesthete was enough. In perfecting a rhetoric that left a
silence that readers would feel compelled to fill, Thoreau often doubted
an Emersonian confidence in an oversoul or a George Ripley's faith in

humanity's divine essence, which would fill his silence with truth; he feared that his vacuums might be stuffed merely with Hamlet's "words, words, words," or with Ishmael's cartloads of rubbish to fill the Milky Way.

Such agony haunts some of Thoreau's more startling, almost frightening passages, as it does his *Journal* entry for 17 October 1859:

> Why, a philosopher who soars higher than usual in his thoughts from time to time drops down into what is just such a wilderness to him as that was to La Mountain and Haddock, where he finds hardly one little frog gone into winter quarters to sustain him and runs screaming toward the climes of the sun. (12:398)

How swiftly the loftiest meditation erupts in fear, and the language of desire shouts in pain. At best, Thoreau's wild rhetoric encourages a dynamic process of perpetual rereading and interpretation, of always awaiting those letters finally to arrive; at worst, the result was unceasing frustration. On the dark side of a supreme rhetoric lurked the agonized dread that transcendent meaning merely meant meaninglessness, that language was not sufficient to communicate what Thoreau called the "highest truth" to others, that his magnificent "monumental stillness" may be a mask, as in *Moby-Dick,* for monumental emptiness.

Early in his career, on 5 March 1838, Thoreau wondered, "But what does all this scribbling amount to?" He complained that a passage that seemed satisfying in the act of composition soon became stale, that he could never quite pierce to the meat of the matter, that his writing was "unprofitable—in fine, is not, only its shell remains—like some red parboiled lobster-shell—which kicked aside never so often still stares at you in the path" (*PJ1,* 33–34). This unsatisfied desire never totally left Thoreau, even though he developed a wild rhetoric and a "natural" style in an attempt to transform this frustration into a satisfying rhetoric. Although he sometimes revealed his agony about being unable to communicate the meat of his meaning through words, he did succeed in exploiting that dissatisfaction to create forceful and memorable images. Readers would find it hard to forget his description of the red parboiled lobster-shell staring at them in the path. Modern readers might aver that fine writing is its own (even only) reward. The aesthetic satisfaction derived from the lobster trope that so effectively communicates Thoreau's sense of failed communication may be sufficient to those modern readers, but to Thoreau, locked in his times, such consolation was small.

Although "agony" has come to mean intense mental or spiritual stress, the word derives from the Greek *agonia* for "struggle" or "contest for a prize."[5] *Agonia* originally connoted celebration as well as anguish, and for Thoreau it was a source of creative power. It arose from problems sufficiently complex for his hungry mind to feast upon, an agony challenging enough for his considerable intellectual gifts. Hence, he indicated his appreciation for agony through many emblems: his frequent military imagery; his depiction in *Walden* of his own intellectual contest as a wrestling match between earthbound Antaeus and the demigod Hercules; his choice of Aeschylus's *Prometheus* for translation; his admiration for the soldier-explorer courtier-rebel Walter Raleigh; and his definition of friendship as an honest if painful confrontation between individuals. Agony is that moment in the text when readers sense that they are touching Thoreau's anxiety behind the masks of smiling optimism or cocksure satire, that moment when seemingly resolved issues dissolve into rhetorical mists, those textual moments when the author seems to have trespassed the boundary fences of what he can assuredly know or say. Agony is that moment when the author seems to be straining to grasp at a meaning that lies beyond; it is the linguistic embodiment of the Tantalus myth.

For those reasons, Thoreau's texts provide a fascinating field for studying a "wild rhetoric." The icon "Thoreau" seems the least appropriate choice for examining the "language of desire." Previous writers like Laurence Sterne or the later modernists would seem more apt; even contemporaries like Emily Dickinson and Ellery Channing would seem "better" choices. But the very fact that Thoreau seems so definite, so positive, sometimes even desperate about the urgency of his message and the explicitness of his meaning creates a formidable challenge and complex problem when examining his narrative dissolves. While Emerson had said that Thoreau's "riddles are worth the reading," he complained that Thoreau was an absolutist who articulated a chain of unarguable certainties. There were many more, extremely complex linguistic riddles in Thoreau than Emerson acknowledged.[6]

Surely Thoreau regretted the way people often waste their lives. Surely he believed business inimical to poetry. Surely he enjoyed nature. Surely he warned against materialism. Surely he insisted that America needs reform. Surely he valued conscience and consciousness. Surely he represented arch individualism. Surely he championed alternative modes of living. But just as surely he wrote texts that allowed, even demanded, alternate readings. Thus, Lawrence Buell can begin his chapter on Thoreau's relationship to Concord by citing two epigraphs from the *Journal* that contradict each other. Walter Harding and Leo Stoller can intelligently disagree on how committed Thoreau was to social action after his Walden experiment, and, more recently, Richard Bridgman and Mary Elkins Moller can offer radically different portraits of Thoreau as a social being. Editors can feel justified in presenting a Thoreau essay under different titles because of their differing interpretive persuasions. *Walden* can make readers feel confident in viewing it as a literal transcription of an experiment and an accurate autobiography, even though Thoreau warns in *Walden* that he has put "the best face on the matter."[7] Indeed, if one believes Thoreau spoke sincerely and truly in *A Week on the Concord and Merrimack Rivers* when he said, "It is necessary not to be Christian to appreciate the beauty and significance of the life of Christ," then it is logical to conclude that he requires his readers to be, as it were, unThoreauvian (*Week,* 67). He creates textual conditions that encourage readers to read beyond and against his statements in order to appreciate fully the beauty and significance of his texts.

Impelled by the perceived fragmentation if not decay of American culture, inheriting popular modes of rhetoric, both religious and political, which emphasized presenting a message forcefully, clearly, and persuasively, Thoreau is a problematic focal point for questions about the communicative quality of language: whether ultimately it achieves communion or entrapment in the experience of shared communication, whether it is a window through which one can gaze out at a supralinguistic reality, or whether it is ultimately more a mirror or a web. When attending to those passages created by Thoreau's linguistic cupping-glass, readers must be alert to the possibility that they may be—as Thoreau once described his own vision when looking out upon nature—"staring out at one's own eyes." In those textual passages where gaps are created and readers seem invited to become cocreators and fill the void with their own meaning, it is an understandable temptation to plug the gaps, to leave them blocked with a settled understanding that has been imported into the text.

This problem of looking out at one's own eyes is further compounded by the variety of Thoreau's "I's," the different voices that speak to us from the pages of Thoreau's texts. Emerson's voice tends to remain distinctively Emersonian regardless of the essay or journal passage one reads, as does Emily Dickinson's voice from poem to poem. Whitman's voice is so definite that it remains the same even when he shifts from one genre to another, whether he is writing prose or poetry. But Thoreau's voice varies from text to text. The speaker who fairly steams with a love of nature in *Walden* seems icebound or arid in *Cape Cod.* The writer who spends an entire chapter praising vegetarianism in *Walden* sits before a campfire in *The Maine Woods* dining on moose lips while the remains of the carcass are scattered about the campsite. The man who seems so cocky and self-assured in his essay "Life Without Principle" calls himself "a bundle of vain strivings" in a poem. Another short poem is frequently quoted: "My life has been the poem I would have writ, / But I could not both live and utter it." Thoreau placed this couplet praising life over writing in the final chapter of *A Week on the Rivers,* but attentive readers note that he inserts another poem ten pages later to contradict the famous complet's message:

> And what's a life? The flourishing array/
> Of the proud summer meadow, which to-day/
> Wears her green plush, and is to-morrow hay.
> (*Week,* 343, 353)

Readers tend to dismiss an early Thoreau essay like "The Landlord" on the curious grounds that it "does not sound like Thoreau" or, even more curiously, that this staunch antimaterialist "wrote it to sell." Despite recent efforts to promote Thoreau's *Journal* as his finest and most truly representative work, critical history has privileged *Walden* and "Resistance to Civil Government" as his major pieces despite their contrasting popular images of a withdrawal from society and a championing of social activism. Readers are forced to make choices about whether Thoreau is serious or satirical when he praises soldiers and militaristic conduct, with precious few textual clues to guide them.[8]

A most remarkable case occurred not long ago when psychologists asked twenty Thoreau specialists to fill out a Minnesota Multi-Phasic Personality Inventory as they believe Thoreau would have completed the survey had he taken it in 1854.[9] By specifying the year 1854, the psychologists clearly meant experts to imagine how the projected voice in *Walden* would have responded, but Thoreau typically developed disparate voices for different books at the same time. When he was creating the narrative persona for *Walden* he was simultaneously developing the contrasting voices of *Maine Woods* and *Cape Cod,* as well as other texts. After *Walden,* Thoreau was concurrently drafting "Life Without Principle" and "Moonlight," whose content, style, and voice are radically opposite (*Life,* 332; *PJ2,* 445–66). Specialists were being asked to look out upon their own eyes, to gaze at the critical and cultural tradition that (for its own reasons and because of its own internal structures and conventions) has privileged *Walden* as Thoreau's primary text, perhaps because *Walden* is his most public presentation of an American self.

Since this book aims to study more than Thoreau's aesthetic and linguistic theory, it must attend to these curiosities. Since it concentrates on the intended and actual rhetorical effects of his writings, it must acknowledge that "Thoreau" is much broader than the three million words contained in his "complete works." "Thoreau" entails not only Thoreau's writings but also the responses, receptions, and reactions that those writings have provoked. Since *Walden* has become a cultural icon, it will be necessary to look at those sentences that Thoreau experimented with but did not include in a final version, sentences that would have compelled readers to read the texts differently and to imagine a very different voice had those variations survived to publication. A more subtle approach is to study those passages that Thoreau *did* publish in some form but that are seldom invoked when readers describe their image of the author they are interpreting; the "I" in their eye.

The man who said he could not both live life and write about it also uttered a less famous statement on 17 December 1851: "Improve every opportunity to express yourself in writing, as if it were your last" (*J,* 3:140). With such devotion to language and with such seeming contrariety of mood, Thoreau's rhetoric must be approached by a method as pliant as those organizing principles he developed for his texts. When themes must be pursued, their exceptions and bounds must be admitted. Contradictions must be incorporated; insoluble problems must be respected. Textual anomalies must be valued as signs indicating that Thoreau has reached the outer perimeter of his linguistic exploration. "Anomalies" work in tandem with more accepted, standard patterns; together they define each other as the "eccentric" helps to set the "norm." *Thoreau's Wild Rhetoric* does not mean to rebut standard views of Thoreau, nor does it seek to "prove" that previously published interpretations are "wrong." Rather, it is concerned with how Thoreau's clear and dramatic images are launched upon a sea of contradictions, qualifications, and discrepancies. Like his principal image in *Cape Cod,* the muscular arm of his definite pronouncements always remains there despite being swept by swirling sands and deceived by illusions that loom on all horizons.

As should be evident by now, *Thoreau's Wild Rhetoric* is a problem-oriented book. Rather than seeking to resolve Thoreauvian ambiguities, it searches for unsolved problems as signs of his furthest linguistic explorations. No severe problem exists (as I define "problem") when Thoreau is saying yes, whether to nature or to a life of self-discovery; nor does a problem exist when Thoreau is speaking out against misspent lives or various forms of slavery. But a crucial problem arises when Thoreau makes statements like "Yes and No are lies," especially when that statement follows hard upon a yes or no he has just uttered. A more complex problem arises when inspecting those Thoreauvian statements that seem to speak yes and no simultaneously, causing one to wonder if statements that imply yes and no together are meant to suggest truth. In fine, the main bounds of Thoreau's wild rhetoric occur when his clarion yeas or nays interweave with his more floating, hovering, and ambivalent statements. Thoreau himself liked to pun upon the word "bounds," both specifically and philosophically. Bounds allowed him to bound; limits helped him leap.

I trust that my methodology has been tailored to suit. I must go on guard whenever it seems too successful, for that may be a sign that the rhetorical problems are being reduced. Remembering Thoreau's admonition, I wish my methodological coat to be sufficiently roomy so that its seams will not be stretched. Consequently, as one particular methodology begins to "succeed" in solving a problem, further problems will arise, calling for different approaches, which will in turn create further problems, demanding still other perspectives. Markedly different from eclecticism as well as from theory-bound criticism (whether new critical, structuralist, or deconstructionist), this problem-oriented approach seems germane to a writer like Thoreau who valued flux, flow, melt, and mist in nature and in language. It centers not only on problems about Thoreau but also about the various interpretations of Thoreau, about Romantic aesthetics and the discourse of Thoreau's time, about critical theories and their assumptions, as well as about my own theories and their assumptions.[10]

Before we launch ourselves into the book proper, let us take a moment

to orient one problem by pursuing the clothes imagery already established, especially since clothes imagery is a ready metaphor for the ways
an author dresses himself for reader reaction. Certainly Thoreau dressed
in simple clothes because of personal preference, and his choice of cordu-
roy pants linked him with the working man. But he was also well aware,
like Ben Franklin in the court of France, of plain dressing's narrative
value and audience appeal. As Thoreau admits in *A Yankee in Canada:*
"Probably there was not one among all the Yankees who was not more
splendidly dressed than I was. It would have been a poor story if I had
not enjoyed some distinction" (*Writings,* 5:28). Again, two versions are
extant about Thoreau's story of the Indian trying to sell hand-woven
baskets to a lawyer. In the *Journal,* he criticizes the Indian for failing to
create interest in the buyer, but in *Walden* he brags that he "studied
rather how to avoid the necessity of selling" his weavings of "delicate
texture," causing one to wonder about the extent to which his aloof,
anticommercial, plainly dressed pose is itself a saleable idea, especially
since his word-woven text more closely resembles a lawyer's argument
than an Indian basket (*J,* 2:83–84; *W,* 19).

When Bronson Alcott calls Thoreau "a Declaration of Independence
in himself," how much is he praising Thoreau for being independent,
"unique," and original and how much is he characterizing Thoreau as an
avatar of a cultural ideal as represented in its most famous public document? In like manner, the paradoxical problem of being original in America is highlighted by Whitman's comments on Thoreau in 1888: "One
thing about Thoreau keeps him very near to me: I refer to his lawlessness
—his dissent—his going his own absolute road let hell blaze all it chooses."
Apparently, dissent has powerful attractive power, and lawlessness can
forge firm bonds between reader and author. Definitely, Whitman saw no
contradiction in prefacing his praise for the binding power of lawlessness
by saying that Thoreau is also "one of the native forces—stands for a fact,
a movement, an upheaval: Thoreau belongs to America."[11]

The public presentation dressed as an original self with particular
attention to readers' receptions of those presentations was one of Thoreau's
most significant rhetorical concerns. I would not go so far as to say, as
some have, that Thoreau was a "compleat aesthete" like an Edgar Allan
Poe or an Oscar Wilde, but I do agree that Thoreau's fascination with
language was intense. For him, language had become life's most compelling activity. He was quite serious when he said in his most pure travel-

ogue, "I want nothing better than a good word. The name of a thing may easily be more than the thing itself to me."[12] Language had become a stronger commitment than his need to understand nature, society, reality, or even truth. As he states in the next to last paragraph of "Life Without Principle": "I love literature and *to some extent* the truth also . . ." (emphasis added).

Were this book concerned only with Thoreau's presentations of his various selves and ideas, its proper title would be "Thoreau's Aesthetic," but Thoreau's paramount problem was meaning, and meaning meant not just what he said but what was heard. Hence, he was crucially concerned with readers' responses, and so this book focuses more on his rhetoric: the impact, the effect upon, the anticipation and invention of reading experiences. Thus, after Thoreau has stated in "A Yankee in Canada" that he wants "nothing better than a good word," he follows the assertion by justifying its worth and desirability in terms of the communion effected by the reading experience: "Inexpressibly beautiful appears the recognition by man of the least natural fact, and the allying his life to it. All the world reiterating this slender truth, that aspens once grew there; and the swift inference is that men were there to see them."

Thoreau did not solve all the problems he posed, nor did he intend to solve them. He had little difficulty in resolving the kind of "problem" that should more accurately be termed a technical device: the organization of a narrative around the cycle of a week or four seasons as one example, a pattern of light imagery as another. The kind of problem that interested Thoreau most was like that self he describes in *Walden*'s conclusion, one that requires perpetual exploration. The kind of problem he sought also resembled his language of desire; only a language of desire could begin to suggest the complexity and vastness of the problem. Only through a language of desire could truth's dimensions be suggested, and its definition would always remain elusive, thereby creating a greater sense of its desirability and tantalizing power. Thoreau was intensely concerned about rhetorical guidelines and general rhetorical rules, often beginning sentences in his *Journal* with constructions like, "If a writer would interest a reader . . ." Frequently, he would frame his goals as a writer in terms of his expectations as a reader, sometimes blurring the distinction between the two categories and conceiving a readerly writer or an authoring reader, similar to the way he was glad to discover that a linguist had argued that "willed" and "wild" were etymologically related.

Thoreau liked to include maps, charts, budgets, lists, and other forms of calculations in his publications, and he liked to approach language in a scientific and rational fashion, but he delighted most in rhetorical problems that defied easy definition, linguistic borderlands that slid past supposed boundaries, eluded too tidy categorizations. He most enjoyed those moments when his meticulously crafted rhetoric ran wild. After all, this is the author who enjoyed incorporating white spaces into his linguistic maps like those cartographers of old, the man who revised his life's principal goal from "know thyself" to the more open-ended "explore thyself" in a late emendation of *Walden*. In fact, one of the most gleeful episodes in Thoreau's writings relates how Emerson had planted a lengthy hedge along what he presumed to be his property line only to find out from Thoreau years later that he had unintentionally appropriated a large chunk of his neighbor's land. In like fashion, Thoreau pleasured in language most when its boundary lines strayed, faded, or dissolved.

Thoreau surveyed many rhetorical boundary lines, including such problems as the Romantic era's passion to "make it new," erupting in that eerie compendium of literary styles called *Moby-Dick* and in the vastly different experimental forms of Whitman's and Dickinson's poetry, as well as in more general issues such as dilemmas about genre demands and distinctions. Or, as John Carlos Rowe has stated the problem, "What major work of nineteenth-century American literature belongs to any recognizable genre?"[13] Other significant problems involve how to read nature as a text, how to present a personal self through the vehicle of public language, and how to develop a writing style that gives the reader a sense of freshness and spontaneity in a printed book. How might this writer reconcile his assertion that huckleberries are never truly tasted when bought in the marketplace with his criticism of friend Ellery Channing's poetry as "sublimo-slipshod"?

Perhaps the most significant problem Thoreau "fronted" was a refined version of what his age would call a "natural style." As Thoreau read nature, he found that it sometimes spoke in moral tones, as many others had also said; but he also discovered that nature spoke in many voices, showed many faces, and revealed many facets of its ever-changing and infinite essence. Sometimes nature was most powerful when not speaking at all, when being like a physician's cupping-glass. As Thoreau said in "The Service," "All sounds, and more than all, silence, do fife and drum for us." As I might say, all crucial problems with respect to rhetoric, language, and literature appear to coalesce in this set of writings that we call "Thoreau's works." One might recall that Emerson's only complaint about Thoreau as a writer, a complaint he registered in a letter to Thoreau and repeated in his eulogy twenty years later, was his stylistic mannerism of using oxymorons, of calling "a cold place sultry, a solitude public, a wilderness *domestic* (a favorite word)." One can understand Emerson's irritation, and the examples he specifies are particularly illuminating, since they might have struck him as a parody of his own attempts to articulate a bipolar unity. But rather than executing stylistic tricks or rhetorical gimmicks, Thoreau attempted a daring language experiment in style that mirrored his reading of nature, using oxymorons as but one of his many techniques. Any solitude we know about *is* public, "wilderness" *is* the word our culture-bound "domestic" language gives to one part of nature, and all values we ascribe to reality may be but elements of language. By experimenting with a natural style, Thoreau would explore those boundaries between qualities and things and attempt to erase the spaces between words to reveal the ultimate space of language.

In radical departure from Hegelian thought, Thoreau believed that the more gnarly problems of language could not achieve synthesis and that silence's rhetorical role must be respected.[14] Thus, in a quick paragraph in his *Journal,* Thoreau addresses three varieties of language:

> The halloo is the creature of walls and mason work—the whisper is fittest in the depths of the wood—or by the shore of the lake—but silence is best adapted to the acoustics of space. (*PJ1,* 61)

The "halloo" appears in Thoreau's style when he issues ringing statements of definite sentiments and explicit meaning; when he bangs critiques and affirmations off the "walls and mason work" of society. His "whisper" surfaces as those powerfully suggestive metaphors, often paradoxical, sometimes aching with the weight of associations they are intended to bear—the sun as morning star, the bug in the table as an emblem of man's potential spiritual awakening.

Previous Thoreau scholarship has done admirable service in elucidating these two forms of Thoreau's language, but this book seeks to study "silence" within language as those textural moments when the words have created a vacuum that the reader is provoked to fill. The crucial point is the interweaving of different styles to produce a rhetoric, the seemingly free but in fact deliberately crafted interplay of various voices, personae, and styles in the creation of Thoreau's wild rhetoric. At the same time, Thoreau's agonies must be respected, those problems he believed were urgent but did not deign to resolve. He encodes this dynamic struggle in his free translation of Plato from "The Service," a rendering that he also included in his first published book:

> I read that "Plato thinks the gods never gave men music, the science of melody and harmony, for mere delectation or to tickle the ear; but that the discordant parts of the circulations, and beauteous fabric of the soul, and that of it that roves about the body, and many times for want of tune and air, breaks forth into many extravagances and excesses, might be sweetly recalled and artfully wound up to their former consent and agreement."

The smooth if not glib resolution that Thoreau attributes to Plato is not one that Thoreau can share. Instead he will say in his most famous book, "I am convinced that I cannot exaggerate enough even to lay the foundation of a true expression," leaving readers to decide whether the statement is meant as a justification of his wild rhetoric or as an admission that language, even in exaggerated or tantalizing form, cannot do what he desires. Language fails to communicate truth; it can only create the illusion that elusive truth could be communicated if only words were adequate to a transcendental vision. This book centers on those white spaces cartographers of old entered on their maps to indicate the unknown areas of their knowledge, white spaces that Thoreau took care to enter into his own texts, alluding specifically to the practice in his conclusion to *Walden,* alluding to the spaces at the precise point at which he had revised his advice on life's principal goal from "know thyself" to the more open-ended—and seemingly more narcissistic, if not more bourgeois—"explore thyself."

A similar bound exists beyond the interweaving of statements within Thoreau's texts. One example involves the perception of Thoreau's uniqueness vis-à-vis other writers of his period. From the time he first published, Thoreau has suffered from his characterization as Emerson's disciple, as one who merely seconded Emersonian ideas, even parroting Emerson's style in lecture and writing presentations. Authors as dissimilar as James Russell Lowell and Herman Melville depicted Thoreau as Emerson's intellectual and stylistic gofer. In the last dozen years, however, a movement has been afoot that claims that one could just as reasonably demonstrate that Thoreau's writings resemble more closely the ambiguous, ironic style of a Hawthorne or a Melville. Attractive as this recent movement is—in particular, its emphasis on Thoreau's literary relationship with Hawthorne, who came to live in Concord at the influential time following Thoreau's brother's death—it still is piecemeal. A fuller approach would be to examine the discourse of Thoreau's times as the comparative standard, to give a sense of that shared language of the period that emerges in the writings of a linguist, a preacher, a politician, and an impresario, as well as an Emerson or a Hawthorne.

For that reason I begin this book by presenting Thoreau's language in the context of his era's discourse. Although Thoreau cautioned that a writer should not be *pro tempore*, he admitted that all writers are *ex tempore*, that their ideas and their language emerge from the cultural envelope that surrounds them. Critics like James Armstrong and Taylor Stoehr have shown that Thoreau's opinions on sexuality and reform are less extreme when seen against the background of Thoreau's times. This book begins by attempting to do the same with Thoreau's language, attempting to give a sense of the way power, anxiety, ignorance, eros, and politics (in the broadest sense) surface in the language of Thoreau's era. The opening chapter could not possibly include every aspect of the discourse of Thoreau's age without inviting chaos. While it offers examples from both popular and erudite levels—so that P. T. Barnum is found in curious company with S. T. Coleridge and Davy Crockett with Kant—its controlling rubric is the conflation of public and private language reflected particularly in political discourse, popular discourse, and the linguistic theories of ministers and professors about the problem of self-expression through the public presentation called language in its various rhetorical modes and genres.

CHAPTER ONE

Thoreau in Time

I. TRANSCENDENT TRANSLATION

One way to begin a study of Thoreau's relationship to his times is with the three important letters he wrote to his alma mater. Although ridiculed in *Walden*, Harvard was also the place where "what I was learning in College was chiefly, I think, to express myself," or so he told Richard Fuller, his companion on their walk to Wachusett, as Fuller was about to matriculate in 1843 (*Corr*, 94). The first letter, written in 1847, responds to a college survey in that tone of whimsy and defiance that has endeared Thoreau's style to so many readers. Describing himself as a jack-of-all-trades, Thoreau boasts of his life, even though he is aware that his classmates might view him as an unsuccessful alumnus (*Corr*, 185–86). In a less famous letter, Thoreau modestly answers a request in 1859 for donations to the Harvard library by quietly remitting a sum that, though probably small in comparison with other donations, amounts, he says, to all his income for the past four months (*Corr*, 545).

Thus far no interpretive complexity exists. Thoreau's relationship to his times as reflected in his attitude toward Harvard can be considered positive, as in his advice to Fuller and his library donation, or negative, as in his *Walden* satire and his 1847 letter. But an intriguingly complex problem arises when one refers to the letter he wrote to Jared Sparks on 17 September 1849 (*Corr*, 249). Attempting to persuade Sparks to permit him certain library privileges, Thoreau justifies his request by arguing that he should be accorded these privileges "*because I have chosen letters for my profession,* and so am one of the clergy embraced by the spirit at least of her rule." The italicized portion of this line, the only part Thoreau underlined in the entire letter, is of course important because it demonstrates that he has chosen to present himself no longer as a jack-of-all-trades, but as a dedicated writer who has committed himself to literature—at least, so it seems in this diplomatic petition. But the more interesting problem is contained in the part that follows the stressed portion.

In describing himself as "one of the clergy" in spirit, Thoreau raises a keen paradox. On one hand, he often complains of the clergy: their mechanical lecture style, their cowardice in the face of crucial social issues, and their collusion with other cultural institutions whose main fault was not so much their conservativeness but their ineffectiveness. On the other hand, Thoreau often linked himself with this group, comparing his role as a companion on a moose-hunting expedition in *The Maine Woods* to that of a chaplain in the army, frequently using conventional religious language, as many scholars have noted, and sometimes offering his own discourse as an improved variety of sermon, as when he says, "I hope that I am not so poor a shot, like most clergymen, as to fire into a crowd of a thousand men without hitting somebody—though I do not aim at any one." In "Slavery in Massachusetts," Thoreau might criticize the clergy and his times for their "worship of Mammon, both school and state and church," but he would also cast his social criticism in a much different mode, as when, railing against materialism, he paused to explain, "I do not say this by way of complaining of the custom in particular, which is beginning to prevail—not that I love Caesar less but Rome more. It is my own way of living that I complain of as well as yours—and therefore I trust that my remarks will come home to you."

In this love for the Roman ideal of America that obliged him to play the role of an angry Juvenal, Thoreau seems similar to that group of Unitarian ministers like George Ripley and Theodore Parker, who believed that they were merely extending logically the premises of their religion only to hear their fellow Unitarian clergymen call them heretics, Transcendentalists, or worse. With respect to Harvard, Thoreau might go so far as to name names and to criticize "Story, and Warren, and Ware," but he would also offer himself as a wiser teacher, a professor with something truly worth professing.[1] In the three million words of

Thoreau's extant writings, the clergy often comes under attack. Almost as often, Thoreau presents himself as a better version of clergyman than those who are employed by institutions. As both the enemy and the fulfillment of the spirit of the clergy, he sometimes presents the issue parodically, making it impossible to determine whether the parodic pose is a joke or a very serious statement.

Beyond the frame of the Harvard Divinity School, the same problem emerges: How much does Thoreau pose against his times and how much does he represent them? In his *Journal,* he once wrote a line that was later published in a political essay but that appears more forcefully in the *Journal,* where it was written as a one-sentence paragraph. The sentence begins, "I rejoice that I live in this age," and concludes, "that I am his contemporary" (12:421). The first part is more extreme than his more famous statement that he is glad that he lives in "the nick of time," for its use of "age" expands the concept beyond Concord and nature to embrace his cultural era. But the complexity of the problem increases as one considers whom he meant by his "contemporary," a man he admired much more than Daniel Webster and more than Horace Mann, Emerson, and, it would seem, even himself.

The man who makes Thoreau rejoice to be his contemporary is John Brown, and the sentence concludes a paragraph in "A Plea for Captain John Brown." The man he celebrates as the contemporary who makes Thoreau proud to live in his era is one being denounced from the pulpit, in the courts, and by the press; his actions are being disavowed by supposed sympathizers, and his life is about to be taken by the federal government. Nevertheless, Thoreau presents Brown as the individual who best represents his times, even though those times seem rather displeased with him. His sentence sounds like Plato saying that he rejoices at being an Athenian, that he is Socrates' contemporary, that he lives in 399 B.C. on the eve of Socrates' execution.[2]

The sentence is typical of one of Thoreau's more complex styles: "I rejoice that I live in this age, that I am [the] contemporary [of a man whom the age condemns.]" In order to make the two parts of that single sentence fit together, one must see Thoreau positing Brown as a "representative" American of the 1850s, even though the America of the 1850s would reject that representation, would later prefer to select as its representative the man who would be elected to the presidency the year after Brown's execution, the man whose famous 1858 speech on the theme that "a house divided against itself cannot stand" Thoreau flatly dismissed, saying instead in his 1859 "A Plea for Captain John Brown" that "there is hardly a house but is divided against itself, for our foe is the all but universal woodenness of both head and heart."

At least when Emerson presented his six *Representative Men* in 1850, five of them had been canonized as great men by his culture. Thoreau proffered instead a martyr, one less clearly a cultural hero than even a Socrates or a Joan of Arc. Emerson would discuss his representative men in terms of "divine essence," and Thoreau would champion Brown for what Thoreau called his "vitality," which escaped the "universal woodenness of both head and heart," but the interesting connection between the two is their idea of representativeness, which entails viewing heroes as simultaneously representative yet transcendent of their cultural matrices.

Melville's Ishmael may recommend that one live "in the world without being of it," but Thoreau represents himself—rather, he represents one "I," or one of his many selves—as both in and of, yet against the world. Hence, he writes what might be a parodic prayer in his *Journal:*

> I thank God that the cheapness which appears in time and the world—the trivialness of the whole scheme of things—is in my own cheap and trivial moment.
> I am time and the world.
> I assert no independence.
> In me are summer and winter—village life and commercial routine—Pestilence and famine and refreshing breezes—joy and sadness—life & death. (*PJ1,* 392)

One is further reminded of Thoreau's pun on recommending *ex tempore* speech, that a writer should speak against, outside, and despite his times, yet he must speak from and of his era (*PJ1,* 158).

However, the entire heart of the problem has not yet been addressed. The representativeness of Thoreau's hero is further complicated by three significant factors. One involves a fairly standard technique of political rhetoric. As with Melville's Billy Budd, who, although a fulfillment of his culture's ideals and aspirations, will be destroyed by his times, Thoreau casts the rebel Brown as an avatar of America's most inspired moments as culturally agreed upon by America. In the concluding paragraph to "A Plea," Thoreau associates him with "the Landing of the Pilgrims and the Declaration of Independence," as he had earlier imaged Brown as a Christ figure, an imagery that would be more emphatically created in Thoreau's lecture for Independence Day, 1860, called "The Last Days of John Brown." The language Thoreau uses to praise this extreme cultural radical is extremely conventional, fraught with cultural icons and accepted national symbols.

A second technique is more complex, less conventional. In elevating Brown to heroic heights, Thoreau creates the rhetorical effect of simultaneously presenting Brown as a mirror of Thoreau's own values while also using Brown to reveal how close Thoreau is to his culture and complicitous with his times. Thoreau depicts himself as Brown's spiritual comrade both in desiring to clear the temple of vice yet also in being among those who should be scourged and driven out. Thoreau might simply state his allegiance in the shortest sentence of "A Plea": "I agree with him," meaning *agreement* as spiritual, political, and intellectual identification. Still, he would say in his *Journal,* despite the thrust of his argument, which seeks to defend Brown against charges of insanity, that, "At any rate, I do not think it is sane to spend one's whole life talking or writing about this matter, and I have not done so. A man may have other affairs to attend to" (12:430).

In his *Journal* draft of "A Plea," he also wrote a more problematic passage, one that he deleted from the published essay—and one could speculate endlessly on the reasons for the deletion and whether it was included in his lecture. This passage interrupted his depiction of Brown as a Christ figure by saying, "I need not describe him. He has stood where I now stand; you have all seen him." Thoreau's stand with respect to Brown and their era, the outlaw and the law, the accused and his executioner, is complex. It is not a positioning like the apocryphal anecdote of Thoreau in prison gazing out through a window from one side of a wall at society on the other. Rhetorically, it is more like a revolving see-saw, with Thoreau and his culture sitting at opposite extremes yet sharing the same ride. It is like a chorus in which Thoreau sings not another tune from the rest, but a contrapuntal harmony. The lecturer the Concord audience sees before them stands where Brown once stood and identifies with Brown but is not quite like Brown. How often the essay interweaves an "I" representing Thoreau and a "he" standing for Brown with a "we" that meant Thoreau and his times. Perhaps the most dramatic use of this technique occurs in "A Plea" when Thoreau says:

When a man stands up serenely against the condemnation and vengeance of mankind, rising above them literally *by a whole body,*—even though he were of late the vilest murderer, who has settled that matter with himself,—the spectacle is a sublime one,—didn't ye know it, ye *Liberators,* ye *Tribunes,* ye *Republicans?* —and we become criminal in comparison.

Thoreau might be more radical than the liberal newspapers cited in this essay, but the "we" links him more firmly with them than with the man who once stood where Thoreau now stands, the man who had taken his stand at Harpers Ferry, a stand similar to one that Thoreau insinuates he too might be compelled to take—someday.

But this day, this one day in his times, Thoreau deploys the contaminating "we," which is also the editorial and royal and democratic "we," to say,

> We preserve the so-called peace of our community by deeds of petty violence every day. Look at the policeman's billy and handcuffs! Look at the jail! Look at the gallows! Look at the chaplain of the regiment! We are hoping only to live safely on the outskirts of *this* provisional army. So we defend ourselves and our hen-roosts, and maintain slavery.

The voice that speaks from "the outskirts" in this essay remains closer as a rhetorical subject to the center of violence and society than it is to the complete freedom of the wilderness beyond Kansas or to the violent action at Harpers Ferry. If one doubts Thoreau's rhetorical self-association with the army, the chaplains, and other policemen of society, one has only to confront his confession near the midpoint of "A Plea for Brown": "I hear many condemn these men [of Brown's] because they were so few. When were the good and the brave ever in a majority? Would you have had him wait till that time came?—*till you and I came over* to him?" (emphasis mine).[3]

Thoreau further emphasizes the contrast between himself and his hero —between the speaker and his text—by drawing many similarities between Brown's life and his. Describing Brown's "Spartan habits" and his "rare common sense and directness of speech" highlights the fact that while Thoreau shared these qualities he was not literally "in his camp," himself placing quotation marks around the phrase. The most revealing biographical detail he includes is that Brown, like Thoreau, was a surveyor and made "many original observations" about natural phenomena and should have "made a book of his observations," presumably along the lines of "Autumnal Tints" or "The Succession of Forest Trees." This detail is revealing for its very gratuitousness. It does nothing to further the essay's argument, and it slows down an otherwise impassioned narrative. Even more than the reference to Brown's grandfather who, like Thoreau's, had fought in the American Revolution, it draws atttention to facts that emphasize the differences between these similar individuals. The closer identification through historical and biographical detail stresses a wider differentiation. Similarities accent difference.

I am not approaching these passages as proof of Thoreau's guilty feeling about not being more aggressive, about not taking more direct action against slavery, which he considered evil in itself and which he despised even more intensely as the egregious emblem of the state's tyranny over the individual. Perhaps Thoreau did feel guilty, but my aim is his rhetorical strategies. The voice that speaks from this essay is many voices. Sometimes it whispers confidences into our ears. At other moments, it shouts criticisms at the audience from behind the lectern up on the stage, distanced from us, both spatially and metaphorically "above" the audience. At still other times, the voice seems to be speaking from the seat next to us, including himself within the huddle of failed Americans. These multiple voices within a text's voice will also sound in his other writings despite their extreme differences in texture, mood, and aim.

In *Walden,* the thrust of the book might be to present Thoreau's mode of life as a contrast to civilization, materialism, and technology, but in one chapter Thoreau also presents himself as an employee of that very railroad that he says rides upon us. Just as he associates himself with the railroad, America's fond emblem of progress and civilization, he also links himself with hunters, at the opposite extreme to civilized activity. He includes himself in the picture when, ruminating upon people hunting musquash, he asks, "Am I not a trapper too, . . . setting my traps in solitude, and baiting them as well as I know how, that I might catch life and light, that my intellectual part may taste some vension and be invigorated, that my nakedness may be clad in some wild, furry warmth?" (*J,* 12:82). Whether wearing a railroad engineer's cap or a hunter's fur coat, Thoreau tried on many of his culture's fashions, and the effect could be sincere or parodic. Rhetorically, he liked to dress his naked speech in many guises, often wearing many different suits of clothes in a single essay, sometimes in a single page of an essay.

Likeness seems to be the operative term involving this technique of voice. Whereas Whitman speaks in terms of *is*—he *is* the prisoner in the jail window, he *is* with the martyred soldiers in Texas—Thoreau in "A

Plea" presents himself as *like* Brown, like the "criminals" who are complicitous in his hanging, yet also *like* the lecturer who dares take the stage to lecture passive bystanders in the audience, even though Thoreau admits he is much *like* them as well.

The same tactic of likeness is evidenced in this essay's third technique: even Brown is *like* "Brown." The living man is *like* Thoreau's ideal hero. As a representation of the true American, Brown is an avatar, an actual likeness of abstract beliefs that elude actuality and language—a "transcendentalist above all," as Thoreau says. Brown is a contrast to that extreme and growing pressure to conform to a language and a value system that speaks only in cliches, a pressure blatantly represented by the "press"—meaning not only the literal newspaper press, but lawyers, politicians, ministers, schoolteachers, and businessmen as well, all those public word-users who constitute the "press" of language.

The one theme along with slavery that runs persistently through this essay, the earlier "Slavery in Massachusetts," and "The Last Days of John Brown" is the theme of the "press" of society. The "ship of state" celebrated by Longfellow, Holmes, and Whitman has in "A Plea" become "the slave-ship," tyrannizing over the individual's capacity for independent thought. The most awful example of state tyranny was the continued existence of slavery as an institution, a point Thoreau belabors in the bitter nicety that America's population at the time of its war for independence and freedom was the same as the number of slaves in the 1850s.

This "press" that prefers to print "pleasant things" instead of the truth, that sings "an obscene song, in order to draw a crowd," creates heroes that are "mere figure-heads upon a hulk." Ironically, this essay, which presents Brown as a true hero, warns against hero-worship: "The curse is the worship of idols, which at length changes the worshiper into a stone image himself." Those men whom America had established as their cultural heroes ceased to be heroic as soon as they had become established, had become transformed into floating signifiers or stereotypes. To express this concept, Thoreau ransacks both nature and civilization for appropriate images. He says that totemic icons rot like old mushrooms, that they "deliquesce like fungi." Switching from natural to man-made tropes, he complains that the power of the revolutionary heroes has been sapped as they become icons: "The best of them fairly ran down like a clock. Franklin,—Washington,—they were let off without dying; they were merely missing one day" (*RP*, 120, 134).

The problem, then, is how to promote Brown as a true hero, one who has "got enough life" in him so as not to be made into a stone image. The treatment is through likeness, and *likeness,* as I will soon show, was a crucial term in the religious discourse of Thoreau's day. In this political essay, however, Thoreau begins by presenting Brown as "not a politician or an Indian," neither as one entrapped within the center of his culture and speaking in set speeches to please the crowd, nor as a powerless Indian speaking from beyond society's outskirts in a language that mainstream America would not listen to or comprehend. Thoreau continues by praising Brown for speaking a language and performing deeds with which one can empathize and imagine an understanding, but the explicit message of Brown's actions and words lies just beyond our grasp, remains elusive from the net of our comprehension. He is offered as a true hero in that he is "such a man as it takes ages to make, and ages to understand." If the time should come when Brown is in fact finally understood, he will then cease to be a true hero, will then become a national treasure, and his statue "will be the ornament of some future national gallery." At that time, Brown will become as famous—and as ineffectual, if not as meaningless—as those other cultural icons like "the Landing of the Pilgrims and the Declaration of Independence."

As the essay concludes, the crucial phrase warns that Brown will become famous and understood, will eventually be embraced as a cultural hero, "when at least the present form of slavery shall be no more here." The qualifying phrase "at least" seems to promise that when the institution of chattel slavery is abolished, other, more subtle forms of slavery will supplant it, and Americans will remain in thrall to a public language whose sentences are formulaic, whose words are meaningless, whose signs are empty. At that time of what Thoreau calls Brown's "translation," America will continue to indulge in hero-worship of stone images, including the stone image of Brown. "We shall then be at liberty to weep for Captain Brown" without being inspired to independent thought, without feeling compelled to take original action.

That is not what "A Plea" seems to say, certainly not upon a first, quick reading. Initially, the essay seems a clear denunciation of slavery and America's cowardice to face this social evil, and it is certainly that; it can still raise hairs on the backs of readers' necks, especially when "A Plea" is read aloud. Thoreau provides only the faintest of clues that his inspirational message has a dark countervoice. We do not know if he emphasized the phrase "at least the present form of slavery" when he delivered the lecture, but he chose not to italicize the passage upon publication. Nevertheless, his warning about how very difficult it is to have an original thought or to express it in the overwhelming presence of a cliché-ridden public language emerges forcefully when these three related essays on slavery are seen as a piece.

In "The Last Days of John Brown," Thoreau put the matter most succinctly. Brown's deeds may not have galvanized America to action and may not have achieved their intended effects, but they did succeed in exposing the vacuity of public language. Because of Brown, people could now see "that what was called order was confusion, what was called justice, injustice, and that the best was deemed the worst." As Thoreau translates Brown's actions, he believes they expose the noncommunicative nature of public language as it is generally spoken and received, the fact that words do not actually mean what they are popularly thought to mean. In his *Journal,* Thoreau considers public language to be comprised of "made words" and finds them a barrier to the communication of thought and its honest expression not only in the public language of the press, the ministry, the schools, and the political arena, but also in personal relations where "manners" are required. However, he does not issue a wholesale condemnation of public language. In attempting to understand why some still despise Brown, he says in "Last Days," "Show me a man who feels bitterly toward John Brown, and let me hear what noble verse he can repeat. He'll be as dumb as if his lips were stone."

Ironically, Thoreau posits this ability to memorize and recite as a test not of rote skills, but of both ethereality and inward nobility. He has condemned the "old formulas" and "made words" of public language as found in newspapers, political speeches, and religious sermons, yet he extols another variety of public language. He has asserted that words do not mean what they say—that order is confusion, justice injustice, the best the worst—yet he insists upon a meaning that can be read through and beyond words. Indeed, he argues that those who read language literally are not reading at all: "They are true to their *sight,* but when they look this way they *see* nothing, they are blind" (*RP,* 148).

To create meaning, reading must operate as translation, must read in collusion with and simultaneously in opposition to the words that instigate the activity of reading in the first place. Just as "Brown's words" have "an authority, superior to our laws," the meaning of "Brown" has an authority superior to the words that have sparked the quest for meaning. To read rightly, one must read transcendentally of the laws, the established formulas, and the literalness of words; one must go "behind the human law," "behind the apparent failure," and fracture the communicative codes in order to sense the unstated message, to intuit the spirit of the meaning behind its letters, and create "kindred sentiments"; finally, one must use the letters of public language to mark the experience in—of all places!—one's "commonplace book" (*RP,* 148). From the reservoir of language, with its dictionaried words and common usages, Thoreau demands a transcendent reading that reaches toward the ineffable spirit of explicit statements, only to return such transcendent readings to the necessary realm of the commonplace book, the repository of essential yet universal intimations, of private understandings encoded by time in public language, the only language accessible to a journal of such experiences unless one decides to go "Indian" and, like Emily Dickinson, employ a private language that no publisher could ever print.[4]

Transcendental reading is perpetual translation, or so Thoreau seems to argue in his purportedly political essays on slavery and John Brown. *Translation* is a tricky word also because of its religious connotations, which Thoreau invoked on diverse occasions. In the religious discourse of Thoreau's day, one was "translated" when one passed from an earthly to a presumably more spiritual existence. Three months after his death, his sister, Sophia, wrote in a letter that her brother was not dead; he was merely in the process of being "translated" in both a spiritual and a literary sense.[5] On the literary plane, even his choice for translation is telling. One of his earliest efforts was Aeschylus's *Prometheus Bound* with its doubled main characters of Prometheus, bound because defiant, who is conflicted with Io, eternally bounding because victimized by both Zeus and his jealous consort. This doubly entwined conflict of articulations figures in a series of communicative images: the wrestling match between the demigod Hercules and the earth-rooted Antaeus in *Walden;* Thoreau's hubris at having forced the earth to "say beans" when it was content to say grass. No less than seven miles of beans did Thoreau cultivate, consuming none in accordance with Pythagoras's injunction to his disciples against flatulence. All these bushels of beans were lovingly and laboriously grown to be traded. His beans were bartered. The principal physical activity of *Walden,* often received as a document on how to live independently, would lead to public markets.

Just as independent living is a negotiation with the public market as represented in *Walden,* so translational reading is a negotiation between public and private language. Thoreau skewers the kind of reading and public language that results in repetition, formula, denotation, and explicit statement, but his texts are certainly constructed to invite if not to demand close and careful reading, even if in reading deliberately one is "de-liberated," a pun Thoreau makes when explaining why he will not marry, making one less sure exactly what he means when he says in *Walden* that he sought to "live deliberately" (*Corr,* 191). Yet, clearly Thoreau can use words quite precisely to lodge his complaints forcefully. His manuscript drafts prove what care and pains he took to communicate an idea using dictionary words, even when the meaning of those ideas was meant to transcend dictionary definitions.

The paradox of using public language in order to create a reading experience that is essentially translational can be more sharply understood by reference to Thoreau's description of transcendental reading in "The Last Days of John Brown." In that exposition, Thoreau's transcendental reader receives a significant work from the public domain—whether the Bible, history, a noble verse, or Brown's simple speech—and studies its words carefully until the point is attained where the reader can read beyond the words, behind its literal statements, and intuit its implicit and unstated messages. Readers must understand that they are coauthors of meaning. Their own imaginations, inspired to thought by the author's words, fracture the formulas and laws of the letters—an achievement, Thoreau argues, that the purely public language of the newspapers and other conventional forms of address cannot achieve. Readers then should return to record their own "kindred sentiments" in a "commonplace book," leaving records of their vision for other readers to come across, beginning the process of transcendental translation all over again (*RP,* 147–49).

This description of transcendental reading is paralleled by Thoreau's depiction of John Brown as an exemplum. In "Last Days," Thoreau's audience represents those Americans who have been awakened enough by Brown's example to come to the meeting. The man lecturing them presumes to represent an even more awakened state, but he remains closer to the audience than to Brown. Brown is lauded for his heroic gesture, but Brown's gesture remains just that—a gesture, a sign pointing to a still more heroic possibility that finally has no statement in the public language of the real world. Ultimately, the man called Brown, the hero's heroic gesture, the lecturer, the audience, and the lecture itself, are all unified as symbols of an ineffable ideal whose true meaning lies always beyond its various manifestations. In fact, it is meaning's very ineffability that provokes and inspires (and, yes, "tricks") readers to strain toward that meaning whose absolute truth will constantly elude their grasp. This rhetorical form that develops a language of desire can, like desire, be painful. It can inspire, and it can frustrate. As an act not of possession but of a perpetual reaching toward meaning, the language of desire can make readers as achingly aware of loss and disappointment as they are of promise and possibility. It can call attention to the gap, the void, the vacuum of the text. It can stress the discrepancy, as Jefferson Humphries has written, "between what is being sought—and what is being read— and the object itself."[6] Humphries' definition is not far removed from Thoreau's *Journal* meditation for 11 June 1851. Musing upon the gulf between memory and experience, between an idea and its expression in language, he writes: "We remember how we itched, not how our hearts beat" (2:237–38).

In "Last Days," Thoreau characterizes newspapers as the language of desire's rhetorical other. Representing the hegemony of America's grow- ing mass culture, newspapers use public language as propaganda in the original sense of *propaganda,* as clear and persuasive exposition of ortho- doxy. Their language does not provoke readers to read behind or beyond the words. A form of propaganda, newspapers presume the voice clearly sounded in the twentieth century by Walter Cronkite. In deep, confident tones controlled to stop just short of pomposity, this famous anchorman would conclude each of his television newscasts by proclaiming, "And that's the way it is." The rhetorical intention of journalists is to make readers feel that newspaper accounts are "real," that they reveal "the way it is" for any given day.

In other essays, Thoreau would compare the literal pose of what would come to be called "mass media" with other less influential vehicles of public language: the clergy, schools, politicians, reformers, and so forth. Thoreau himself would make ample use of public language, for the private enterprise of transcendental translation is predicated on it. He will, for example, pretend to offer merely a more "systematic" version of the motto from one of the most influential newspapers of his day to begin "Resistance to Civil Government." He concludes *Walden* with some of the tritest proverbs, such as "A living dog is better than a dead lion."

Thoreau was careful to include what he referred to as the "made words" of public language, both actual words and culture's revered images, as the basis for his more transcendental rhetoric of, as it were, "unmade words." By creating gaps in his language, by dissolving statements, by erasing assertions as soon as they are made, by using paradoxes, puns, oxymorons, and contradictions, he would create a rhetoric that would be sure to provoke or even to necessitate a reading that translates, a reading that must take place against the words read. In his texts, Thoreau would provide a kind of public language in the sense that he would offer literal matter—extremely precise measurements of Walden Pond; bold, confident assertions offering severe criticisms of American culture; fond affection for nature's glory—but he would also be sure to develop a more "wild rhetoric" that would encourage a more private reading, a process of transcendental translation.

To some, Thoreau's wild rhetoric with its requirement of transcendent translation may seem an elaborate game of cat's cradle, a perpetual weaving of patterns that are given names that dimly resemble their referents. His texts frequently are a perpetual weaving of one pattern that dissolves as soon as it is created in order to begin creating another pattern, which also quickly ravels. Thoreau often plays Penelope, weaving and raveling her shroud in order to keep hope alive, weaving and unweaving to forestall the corrupt demands of her degenerate culture. One of the degeneracies of Thoreau's culture was expressed in the "press" of its public language.

The motivation for this rhetorical weaving and unweaving came as much from an agreement with his times as from an objection to the press of public language. As literary craftsman, Thoreau strove to reflect what he called "the Protean nature of things." While he was alluding to reality at large, the urge was intensified by a protean "America" whose facts were changing rapidly and drastically. His wild rhetoric arose in part from an America that was different from day to day, even with respect to the most basic factors such as where it was and who lived in it. Even the crudest statistics were being revised almost daily. Like Redburn in Melville's novel, Thoreau is constantly pointing out the instant obsolescence of guidebooks and maps, especially in works like *Maine Woods* and *Cape Cod*. In like fashion, the map of his America had to be redrawn constantly.

Scholars have done excellent work describing the vertiginous change that occurred during Thoreau's lifetime. More specifically, scholarship has demonstrated how Concord was changing as rapidly as any town.[7] Thoreau could easily stroll from his Walden cabin to visit an enormous factory, or make Boston and back in a day on the new railroad link. Pages could be spent detailing these changes, but one poignant example may serve as effectively as reams of statistics: while sitting in his room, writing about his "Life in the Woods," he could hear axès chopping down Walden woods. That anecdote may explain why in 1859 he proposed that Concord adopt a plan like Frederick Law Olmstead's and designate the woods a city park. Walden's changing woods may be what lay behind his instruction to his publishers to drop the subtitle "Or, Life in the Woods" from *Walden*'s next edition. In a mere five years, the locale for what some have read as a hermit-like existence could have become the city park.

Research has also shown that many of Thoreau's reform and political ideas, seemingly radical to moderns, would not have been considered extreme to his contemporaries. Similarly, Thoreau's rhetorical ambitions should be contextualized within the discourse of his times. And so, this chapter will now examine what might be called the cultural origins of Thoreau's originality, performing for Thoreau's rhetoric what other scholars have done for his themes of reform, sexuality, technology, and so forth, ballasting the natural temptation to see him as *sui generis,* as though a writer's originality could be considered apart from his cultural matrix and the discourse of his age.[8] Of the many possibilities, religious discourse is a fruitful starting point, particularly as it is concerned with problems about communication, the nature of language, the varieties of reading experience, the relationship of the reader to an author and to a given text, and the creation and location of meaning.

2. LIKENESS TO GOD

Religious arguments that raged during the four decades before the Civil War centered on no less an issue than the nature of the soul and the salvation of humanity, and in this debate on divinity and its manifestations, much provocative thought was expended on language. While highly educated and articulate divines were striving mainly to describe the best way to comprehend God, they developed a religious discourse whose cruxes involved definitions of reading, epistemological concerns about how a sense of meaning is attained, and the interrelationship of reader, author, and text. This voluminous debate comprised a true discourse, baring anxieties and crises while attempting to achieve synthesis. Often a writer, criticizing a flaw in another's system, would inadvertently reveal a corresponding flaw in his own. Frequently, a theologian would develop a radical idea only to be shocked at the implications others would make of his development.

This complex discourse had three significant pulses starting in the 1820s. In the first, the controversy centered on the definition of the soul, particularly with respect to the biblical passage that claimed that mankind was made in God's image. By the 1830s, the activity of reading became the crucial topic, and confrontations such as the "Norton-Ripley Controversy" argued about the reader's proper relationship to God and His Word. In the next two decades, linguistic theories, such as those of Horace Bushnell and Charles Kraitsir, refined formidable conjectures about precisely what language is and how it makes meaning possible. The debate's original orientation toward God and His Word quickly broadened to involve any creator of words who intends to convey meaning, especially as Coleridge's concept of "clerisy" began to be debated and as writers began to view themselves as ministers to the people.[1] This broader linguistic and epistemological dimension is the focus on the following pages.

In 1823, Samuel Miller, professor of theology at Princeton, declared, "It is evident that Unitarianism . . . consists of NOT BELIEVING." A Congregational publication later echoed that "the fire of unbelief has been the ruling principle of your [Unitarian] system." Throughout the 1820s, ministers like Moses Stuart and Leonard Woods lamented what had become tagged as "new views" about the word of God and blamed what they considered heretical ideas on a pernicious "Germanizing" influence.[2] These men were both right and wrong. Impelled by a xenophobic distrust of continental thought that persists into the present, these ministers erred in blaming Germany alone. As René Wellek and others have demonstrated, foreign influences were vast. Even a casual reading of the pamphlets of the day discovers a galaxy of references—Pestalozzi in Switzerland, Cousin in France, Schleiermacher in Germany, Spinoza in Holland, and a multitude of others, including Samuel Taylor Coleridge in England, whose *Aids to Reflection* James Marsh presented to America in his edition of 1829. These men were also right, as one can say with the confidence of hindsight, because these "new views" were obviously heretical as judged by any paradigms of systematized theology. These new views were drastically more radical than the Copernican theory that the earth revolves around the sun or Galileo's speculations about the moon. They struck right at the core of whether mankind can be sure that there is an objective sun or moon at all.[3]

It is quite possible that debates over language have never been more intense in this country than they were during these four decades, and it all started seemingly simply.[4] By 1819 divines at the Harvard Divinity School had begun to wonder whether the biblical assertion that man was made in the "image of God"—or in "likeness to God," some translators would insist—should be taken in a physical or spiritual sense. If physical, then the sentence meant that humanity resembled God in appearance. If *likeness* or *image* meant a spiritual identity, however, then all heaven and hell broke loose. If humanity were "like" God spiritually, then the entire Calvinistic system that had attempted to make sense of the world and man's place in it collapsed as definitely and spontaneously as Oliver Wendell Holmes described in "The Deacon's Masterpiece: Or, The Wonderful 'One-Hoss Shay' " (1858).

Two people in particular were representative of these "new views" of the 1820s. James Walker had become editor of the influential organ called *The Christian Examiner,* and he insisted that the pages of his journal should be open to any responsible views. Walker foreshadowed that plethora of journalistic enterprises whose intent would be immediately recognized by their names—*The Dial, The Harbinger, The Spirit of the Times.* William Ellery Channing, the elder, was an even more problematic individual. In sermons such as his "Likeness to God" and "The Ordination of Jared Sparks," he argued that God was within, and he rejected the Calvinist belief that humanity was essentially depraved. On the basis of these theological premises. Channing provided mirror imagery that would be echoed by subsequent theorists, such as in the assertion that "as face answereth to face in a mirror, so the divine in man responds to the divine of God."[5]

The radical implications of this thought are readily apparent. By claiming that "likeness" meant spirituality instead of physicality, theologians were also instructing readers to read metaphorically rather than literally. By asserting that man, because divine, can reliably read God's text—whether the text of the Bible or of creation—by trusting to man's own interpretations and translations, these theologians were suggesting that readers did not need the matrix of theological frameworks, commentaries, and dogma. A careful reader, by logical extension, did not need God. Or, rather, since the texts of the Bible and the world were like a mirror in which readers could see their own divinity reflected, there was no need to attempt to peer through the textual mirrors as though they were windows in an effort to glimpse a divinity beyond the realms of the self and the world. In modern critical terms, God, the presumed ultimate and original author, was decentered. The reader, or more precisely the reading experience, the interactive relationship between the reader and text, became the dominant phenomenon. To paraphrase Alexander Pope, the proper study of truth became the activity of reading.

This reader-centered approach to literature would emerge as one of the leading characteristics of American Romanticism. Romantic writers would fix their readers with as riveting a gaze as the ancient mariner does the bridal guest. Poe would challenge his readers to determine whether his narrators were mad, and Hawthorne's eternal cat-and-mouse game with his readers is well known. Whitman may close canto 20 of *Song of Myself* by claiming, "I exist as I am—that is enough; / If no other in the world be aware, I sit content"; but despite this assertion of authorial self-sufficiency, he begins canto 20 by articulating the urgent necessity of a reader-centered literary experience: "All I mark as my own, you shall offset it with your own; / Else it were time lost listening to me."

A fifth of Thoreau's first published book focuses on books and how to read them, and *Walden* devotes an entire chapter, as well as its first two dozen paragraphs, to the issue of reading. One of Emerson's classic utterances on this topic concludes the opening section of *Nature* (1836): "Yet it is certain that the power to produce this delight does not reside in nature but in man, or in a harmony of both." Although the certainty that opens this sentence is hedged before it ends, it is clear that Emerson, while centering man or nature, has excluded the presumed Author or Creator of nature. Cast as a communication model, Emerson's statement would read: the power to produce beauty—aesthetic delight, truth, meaning, a Transcendental vision, or a religious experience—resides not in the text but in the reader or in the relationship between reader and text.

This sentence is representative of the communication crises of the 1830s, when Thoreau was studying at Harvard. Theodore Parker's auto-

biography, *Theodore Parker's Experience as a Minister* (1859), is an instructive example. Parker records his surprise at discovering that biblical
studies did not merely entail careful reading and thorough knowledge of
what books and words comprise biblical studies; he was also expected to
interpret the Bible, to ask, "What does the Bible mean—what sentiments
and ideas do its words contain?" Sounding like a bright and knowledge-
able modern English major confronting the most recent critical theories
for the first time, Parker narrates how he soon learned

> that the Bible is a collection of quite heterogeneous books, most of them
> anonymous or bearing names of doubtful authors, collected none knows how, or
> when, or by whom, united more by caprice than any philosophic or historic
> method, so that it is not easy to see why one ancient book is kept in the canon and
> another kept out. I found no unity of doctrine in the several parts; the Old
> Testament "reveals" one from of religion, and the New Testament one directly its
> opposite; and in the New Testament itself, I found each writer had his own
> individuality, which appears not only in the style, the form of thought, but quite
> as much in the doctrines, the substance of thought, where no two are well agreed.[6]

Upon graduating from Harvard Divinity School in 1836, Parker would
find that others would present ideas similar to Channing's, and their
presentation would include even more radical terms. One of the most
extreme versions appeared in George Ripley's *Discourses on the Philosophy of Religion Addressed to Doubters Who Wish to Believe,* published the
same years as *Nature,* containing sentiments such as, "The sun might
exist as the fountain of light . . . and pour forth its streams over the earth,
but [without] the inward nature of man . . . the beauties of nature would
be a lifeless blank, the variety of colors, of forms, of motions in the
universe would be without significance, and the lavish bounty of Providence apparently bestowed in vain."[7] A modern critical theorist would
not be shocked at this statement. Translated as a communication model,
it simply asserts that characters on a page remain undecoded hieroglyph-
ics until they are read as words; meaning is created by the reader's
interaction with the text.

One can easily comprehend why such expressions were considered
heretical in the 1830s. While exponents of the new views were often
castigated as pantheists, they were in fact even more radical, as Ripley's
imagery suggests. The sun itself, holy icon and powerfully charged religious symbol of both pagan and modern religions, of Thoreau and Ahab
alike, is rendered cold and lifeless in Ripley's passage. Unless the "inward

spirit" of man transforms the sun's rays into a glorious warmth, they remain mere "streams." Enlightenment comes from the reader; from the sun, only light by which to read. An author may provide words, but the reader creates meaning. God may be seen as a Creator, and nature or the Bible His text, but humankind is the meaning maker, the creator of truth.

Ripley's extreme position arose from unusual circumstances. On 5 November 1836, Andrews Norton, Ripley's former mentor at Harvard, attacked him in the public arena for what he called infidelity. Forced into the difficult position of defending liberal Unitarianism against both conservative assaults and radical defections, Norton used Ripley as a whipping-boy to stand for the growing number of "new views" disciples. The details and nuances of this Norton-Ripley Controversy, as it soon came to be called, are too complicated to enter here, but the crucial point of this argument soon centered on how biblical miracles should be received.

Norton believed they were literal, that miracles were signs from God, proof of His Son's divinity. Ripley, Orestes Brownson, and others argued that miracles were rhetorical devices, not spiritual proof. Any skilled magician could seem to walk on water; a confidence-man could appear to raise the dead. Miracles were attention-getting tactics and narrative strategies to draw readers' interest to the text and to its possible truths. Miracles were not in themselves messages or meaningful; they were signs that said "heed the following" or "watch this space." Meaning was created when a reader of the Bible read beyond the signs and intuited the spiritual truths that were in his or her "inward nature" as these truths were provoked by the text. The magnum opus of Norton's career was entitled *Evidence of the Genuineness of the Four Gospels* (1838), which Brownson blithely dismissed as irrelevant in his *Quarterly Review* for January 1839. To exponents of the new views, miracles were not "evidence" at all, only textual markers or signals to the reader.

In the 1820s, then, the most dramatic shift in linguistic concerns involved privileging the reader while decentering the creator/author, and it is interesting that even those standard textbooks on composition that Thoreau studied at Harvard—by Blair, Campbell, Whately (Thoreau was examined on Whately by Emerson)—are remarkable for the importance they grant the reader, at times even esteeming the reader as the main controlling force over what the writer has to say and how he or she says it.[8] By the 1830s, this question had expanded to focus on precisely what was this newly elevated reader's relationship to the text, whether a text of words or of nature. In the 1840s, a third development occurred, fixing on language in general, particularly with respect to the special rhetorical possibilities available through a language of ambiguity, metaphor, and paradox.

Over the past decade, scholars have done much to explain the intense discussion in the 1840s of language's role, especially with respect to biblical exegesis, and the evolution of linguistic concerns from James Marsh to Horace Bushnell and Charles Kraitsir has been impressively described.[9] Horace Bushnell is an especially interesting case, not only because his *The Age of Homespun* (1851) is a literary cousin to *Walden* but also because his career shows how inadequate labels like "radical" and "conservative" are in this age of intellectual turmoil; Bushnell's *God in Christ* was considered radical in 1849, but his *Nature and the Supernatural* (1858) attacked the radical views of the Transcendentalists. But Bushnell's primary importance derives from his attention to the supreme rhetorical function of paradox and inexplicit language. Philip F. Gura explains that Bushnell considered writing to be *"the making of a language, and not a going to the dictionaries"* (Gura's italics). "Feeling a new exhilaration in the choice and use of his vocabulary, [Bushnell] became aware of how, as he put it, 'the second, third, the thirteenth sense of words—all but the physical first sense—belong to the empyrean, and are given, as we see in the prophets, to be inspired by.' "[10]

Bushnell was one of several who developed a movement that redefined the priorities of linguistic communication, shifting emphasis from the literal to the figurative, from the exact to the metaphorical, from the explicit to the suggestive. Opposed to Hegel, who perceived a fusion of antithetical postulates, these philosophical linguists stressed a "liquidation," a flowing together of opposites into a suspended truth, a philosophy and imagery that can be seen reflected in Thoreau's writings. Or, as Bushnell says, according to Gura's interpretation:

> The creative use of language involved a powerful dialectic process: "as form battles form, and one [word] neutralizes another, all [their] insufficiencies are filled out" and "the contrarieties liquidated," allowing the mind to "settle into a full and just apprehension of the pure spiritual truth." Man never comes as close to absolute truth, Bushnell declared, "as when it is offered paradoxically," under "contradictions"; that is, "under two or more dictions, which taken as dictions, are contrary one to the other."

Only through paradox can language approach an absolute truth, only through linguistic expression of contrary dictions can a sense of "sincerity" be conveyed, only through a series of harmonies that neutralize each other like the harmonic motion of waves can a writer approach that fullest expression of sound and sense wherein the grandest sense of sound is silence.

Publishing their most influential books in 1846 and 1849, respectively, Kraitsir and Bushnell may have reinforced and stimulated Thoreau's own linguistic developments as he paused for several months before undertaking the final three revisions of *Walden;* however, as I will demonstrate when addressing *Walden* more particularly, Thoreau's language was more radical than Bushnell's and Kraitsir's, and his similar theory antedates theirs. He had already settled many of their crucial issues for himself by 1842, when he published "Natural History of Massachusetts" in *The Dial,* writing that "Nature is mythical and mystical always, and works with the license and extravagance of genius" (*Writings,* 5:125). Wary of institutionalized discourse, whether in religion or the rising discipline of science (the word "scientist" was first coined in 1844), Thoreau would fall back on what he saw as the language of nature and its "natural style" to justify what he most valued in literature. And so, by the 1850s when he was preparing "Walking, or The Wild," he insists, "In literature it is only the wild that attracts us. . . . It is the uncivilized free and wild thinking in Hamlet and the Iliad, in all the scriptures and mythologies, not learned in the schools, that delights us" (*Writings,* 5:231).

Interestingly enough in terms of the discourse of the age, Thoreau and Bushnell both would recognize the similar sentiments in Whitman, who, working independently of Thoreau and Harvard, would begin canto 44 of *Song of Myself* by saying, "It is time to explain myself—Let us stand up." When he does stand to explain his language experiment, its ultimate rhetorical end resembles Bushnell's "liquidation" and Thoreau's wildness: "What is known I strip away; / I launch all men and women forward with me into THE UNKNOWN." The unknown, of course, is not a place but a rhetorical strategy involving deliberately constructed spaces or gaps in the text. If it did not sound so awkward, it could be called "the unning of the known," an erasure of a statement as soon as it is made, a stripping away of assuredness. In one variety, the unknown is created when the author has his text contradict itself or speak in irreconcilable "contradictions," thereby forcing the reader to attempt to fill in the gaps or to imagine coherence in the text. The reader is thereby made key in the triangular relationship among reader, author, and text, and this centered reader is made the focal point in the attempt to create meaning.

While Thoreau might proclaim the virtues of a wild rhetoric, and while Whitman might boast of how his "I" launches his readers into "THE UNKNOWN," and while Bushnell might argue that liquidation is a supreme form of language, one should not be deceived by their optimism; one who has seen the failings of the humanism that makes such optimism possible cannot be deceived. The fact is that their apparent confidence arose from a mass of unresolved problems, from a bundle of vain strivings, as Thoreau said of himself in his famous poem. Centuries of midrash and commentaries may not have made the Bible more explicit or more persuasive, and the decades-long controversy over religion and reading during Thoreau's lifetime had not truly resolved any crucial issue. At times the debate degenerated into name calling. Conservatives accused radicals of infidelity and unbelief; radicals retaliated by complaining of the conservatives' "creed-bound religion" and snidely labeled Andrews Norton "Pope Norton."

One exception is Ripley's *Discourses on the Philosophy of Religion,* whose full title is revealing—*Addressed to Doubters Who Wish to Believe.* "Doubters" could accurately apply to any of the discordant groups: agnostics desiring to be converted, people from conservative religions yearning for a dynamic interpretive relationship to religion. Morever, "doubters" could also include exponents of the new views themselves, since they proclaimed that they perpetually doubt the meanings they have tentatively garnered from their reading of creation and other texts. They made a virtue of doubt, often admitting that they had deliberately created texts that defy absolute, universal, or single interpretation.

When concluding the first section of *Nature* by claiming that the power to produce delight resides in readers or in their relationship to the text, Emerson goes on to point out that reading is very easily overdetermined by the reader's moods, that the very "same scene which yesterday breathed perfume and glittered as for the frolic of the nymphs is overspread with melancholy to-day." In his *Discourses,* Ripley stated the identical problem in more prosaic words: "By changes in our inward condition, a corresponding change is produced in the objects with which we are surrounded." Ultimately there is no reconciliation of creed and chaos, of belief and doubt. No way was found to balance Ahab's monomaniacal certainty with Ishmael's impulse to "try all things."

Bushnell believed that a rhetoric of paradox and contradiction was the best way to approach absolute truth, but his phrasings are fraught with problems. Language such as an "approximate absolute" or even "*an* absolute truth" creates paradoxes as thorny as any of the biblical problems Bushnell hoped to solve. All too often what sounds like an inspirational solution becomes upon inspection almost an admission of defeat. The voyage toward a language of liquidation can be snagged on the hard reefs of words. Exhortation toward a lofty goal can easily deflate when its specific framing is inspected. The problems inherent in Bushnell's language are typical of the discourse employed by all those who valued the new views, and his rhetoric reflects the discourse of his era. As with Bushnell, so Emerson begins his famous passage in "Self-Reliance" (1841) by claiming that "nothing is at last sacred but the integrity of your own mind." But when his "friend" suggests that his impulses may originate from the Devil instead of from Divinity, a reader, even a friendly one, feels disappointed at Emerson's tepid reply. As one of America's most superb epigrammaticists, Emerson is capable of producing an inspirational, memorable response to this crucial question about the origin of intuitive truth. Instead, he mildly responds, "They do not seem to me to be such." Readers are right to wonder why this master stylist should choose to present his reply so lamely. Rather than providing a forceful rejoinder, he proffers a limp, almost tired sigh.

Emerson's tameness is particularly puzzling since he had had plenty of time to formulate a rebuttal. He had faced the objection at least since his aunt, Mary Moody Emerson, raised it nine years before in her letter of 24 February 1832.[11] In "The Poet" (1844), Emerson wishes to take both sides of the language debate, pretends both to have and to eat his philological cake. On one page, he sides with the radicals and says, "But the highest minds of the world have never ceased to explore the double meaning, or shall I say the quadruple or the centuple or much more manifold meaning, of every sensuous fact." But before a page goes by he needs to promise "balance," reconciliation, and resolution: "The poet is the person in whom these powers are in balance, the man without impediment, who sees and handles that which others dream of, traverses the whole scale of experience, and is representative of man, in virtue of being the largest power to receive and to impart."

In his *Essays Before A Sonata,* Charles Ives praises Emerson for slipping the bonds of dogmatic theology, saying, "Emerson's transcendentalism was based on the wider search for the unknowable, unlimited in any way or by anything except the vast bounds of innate goodness." While this has become a fairly traditional reading of Emerson, it is also typical that a vast qualifier like "except" be inserted. The text called "Emerson" seems to value the unknowable, and yet it also seems to promise something solid and set and steady; his impulse towards chaos remains anchored to a humanistic belief in "innate goodness." In like fashion, Thoreau would proclaim in *A Week on the Concord and Merrimack Rivers* that "even virtue is no longer such if it be stagnant" (132). At one and the same time, Thoreau's sentence seems to be championing a flux or liquidation while also respecting a state of virtue. It is desirable to become virtuous, and it is imperative to change as soon as one has.

In rejecting a creed-bound theology, the radicals nonetheless feared chaos. In denying dogmatism, they still felt obliged to express a belief in spiritual laws. In objecting to the assertion by Norton and others that there was but one true way to read or to know God, they would champion the possibility of many ways, but they were reluctant to think that any way was as valid as any other. They might agree with Bushnell that a supreme language was one of contra-dictions, but they also inherited a need to have something to say, some imperative to convey. They might despise those who set themselves up as intellectual popes, but they were equally wary of amoral aesthetes. They could appreciate Poe's complaint about the "heresy of the didactic," but they were just as appreciative of a Goethean ideal of self-culture. They might promise with Emerson "to live then from the Devil" if that were indeed the nature of one's inward being, and they might with Thoreau vow to "get the whole and genuine meanness of [life], and publish its meanness to the world" wherever discovered. But they hoped that they would not have to do so. They believed just as strongly that their office as poets and intellectuals was "to cheer and to guide" their fellow man. They were aware that taking a position instantly involves limitations, yet they felt strongly obliged to take stands, or to seem to take stands, at least as an initial requirement of dedicated writers who desired to be read. To be read ultimately as "liquidation" or "silence," they understood that they would first have to be read more conventionally for a message, for an explicit meaning their letters would seem to convey.

The radicals of the new views faced dozens of other crucial problems, and they are most impressive when they articulate these problems without resorting to facile resolution. Emerson might write in his *Journals and Miscellaneous Notebooks* (18 May 1840) that, "criticism must be transcendental, that is, must consider literature ephemeral and easily entertain the supposition of its entire disappearance" (7:352). But how can a writer believe that and still take such pains with his writing? What is the purpose in spending ten years in revising *Walden,* for one example, if it is ultimately to disappear?

Other problems involve the oxymoronic quality of originality and the impersonality of the author, which, in the very aspect of self-erasure, draws attention to the self as a performative presence,[12] not to mention the rather cavalier lumping together of different perceptual and reading processes. It would seem that an individual's relationship to natural phenomena or "sensuous facts," and to a book created by a single author, and to a text like the Bible written by many people over a long period of time would indicate three distinctly different reading activities, and yet the radicals often treat them as though they were all one.

Sometimes the most interesting discussions of these problems came from contemporaries who did not consider themselves radicals, but were earnestly attempting to understand what was meant by these "new views." Among these may be counted Mary Moody Emerson's letters to her famous nephew and Francis Bowen's review "Emerson's *Nature*" in the *Christian Examiner* (January 1837). A less-known writer is the Reverend William Batchelder Greene, a friend of Orestes Brownson, who had caught on to one Transcendentalist stylistic strategy and realized that "to follow a transcendental writer, we must not endeavor to find the logical connection of his sentences, for there is no such logical connection, and the writer himself never intended there should be."

In 1849 Greene tried to explain "why so many, notwithstanding their desire, have been unable to read the writings of the new school." His answer was that "they have tried to find a system of doctrines where they ought to have looked for a point of view. . . . A transcendentalist never reasons; he describes what he sees from his own point of view. We ought rather to transcend space and time (if indeed we can,) and follow him there." Greene could not, would not do so. His genuine fear was that were he to transcend space and time and trust only to the subjectivity of his inward spirit, he would have to "deny both God and the universe, putting some chimera, which does find its reason in man, in their place and stead." Greene could understand this new rhetoric that relied on paradox, "liquidation," "silence," and "THE UNKNOWN," but he dreaded its implications, and took refuge in saying pejoratively that "transcendentalism is, therefore, a sort of human Pantheism, requiring a conception of contradictions in the same subject."[13]

Yet a Transcendental rhetoric proved most effective in enticing readers like Greene to struggle to understand where they were being led. This rhetorical effectiveness arose to a great extent from the Transcendentalist practice of encoding problems and anticipating objections within their prose. *Nature* can serve as a quick example of two techniques. In its concluding paragraph, the text promises, "All that Adam had, all that Caesar could, you have and can do."—a statement that has prompted Richard Poirier to ask:

> Is anyone supposed to believe this? Should we act upon the conviction that it is true? He does not really expect us to, and his careless combination of references ought to indicate as much. Anyone who has "all that Adam had" would be utterly indifferent to all that Caesar did. And neither figure is being proposed as a model. He is dismissing both of them in favor of whatever version of their "genius" may exist in each of us, now.[14]

But Emerson has not said this; the text has, but not its author. The radicalness of the passage has been buffered by earlier references to songs that "a certain poet" sang, Emerson's "Orphic poet." The extreme promise regarding Adam and Caesar is protected by quotation marks. It is not a promise Emerson has dared to utter, but one he has ventured to quote from "what my poet said." The reader is left to interpret, without hope of ever arriving at a final translation, whether the poet's voice is Emerson's wilder persona, an allusion to a specific poet like Alcott, or a transcendent song that originates from an inward self that, because universal, is the reader's own voice.

This is a form of quotation widely used by the American romantics, although for other purposes. In Hawthorne's "Young Goodman Brown," for example, it is not Hawthorne exactly but rather Satan who makes the speech whose burden is that "evil is the nature of mankind." When reading Whitman, one quickly learns to be on the alert for statements made in parentheses because these parenthetical remarks often contradict what seems the main point of the poem. Whitman stands "very pleas'd and joyous" at the end of "Facing West from California's Shore," except that a two-line parenthesis wistfully queries: "(But where is what I started for, so long ago? / And why is it yet unfound?)" In "All Is Truth," the leading idea seems to be that "there are really no liars or lies after all," but the reader cannot forget Whitman's confession in an earlier parenthesis that "I feel in myself that I represent falsehoods equally with the rest, / And that the universe does."

Early in *Nature,* Emerson uses parentheses to create gaps that allow for infinite contra-diction. A famous example is the passage that boasts, "In the woods, we return to reason and faith. There I feel that nothing can befall me in life—no disgrace, no calamity (leaving me my eyes), which nature cannot repair." The parenthetical remark pokes a vast hole in the text through which any number of interpretations can be driven. Nature's healing powers are not absolute; there is an exception. If one exception exists, then so do any number of possible exceptions. Different readers are free to insert whatever they feel is irreparable into the sentence's parentheses.

The same rhetorical effect is produced by a writer often presented as Emerson's antithesis. In Edgar Allan Poe's "The Pit and the Pendulum," readers can place whatever they most fear into the pit; so it is with Emerson's parentheses. Some may most fear the loss of sight, while others' worst fear may be a different physical loss. To readers like Greene, what they would have most to lose by filling in Emerson's parentheses would be their souls.

Emerson's proverb would have a sounder ring had he omitted the parentheses. Its presence opens his statement to a multitude of possible meanings and transforms a confident assertion into chaos. I have too much respect for Emerson as a writer to think this was accident. When coupled with the myriad other examples of how the text is opened with gaps, the technique comes to seem deliberate. The tactic seems representative of Transcendental agony. Romantics like Emerson would have liked to be able to offer unqualified proverbs, but their intellectual honesty would not allow them to leave their texts aphoristically pure, and they welcomed the elaborate linguistic theories that provided a humanistic base to justify their use of self-erasing rhetoric.

No matter how much I admire his argument, I cannot concur with Richard Poirier's *The Renewal of Literature.* I do agree that Emerson greatly pleasured in what Poirier calls "the turning of tropes," and I see Emerson's need to cast doubt upon a truism as soon as he has created it as a reflection of the linguistic controversy of his days. But I cannot agree that Emerson used humanistic intentions simply as flirtatious come-ons (90). The Transcendentalists created remarkably open texts, "open" in that they lend themselves to many interpretations. A Jonathan Bishop or a Stephen Whicher can read the texts thematically and present humanistic interpretations that, textually, are as valid as the portrait of Emerson as word-player that Poirier depicts. One can read *Walden* and picture an angry rebel railing against society, or one can envision a loving, gentle man serenely hoeing his beans and communing with nature.

It is otiose to argue which interpretation is "best" or "most correct." Transcendental texts allow, encourage, even demand multiple interpretation and endless translation. Posing as confident optimists and cheerful idealists, their authors did not use obvious signals to the readers such as subtitling a novel "The Ambiguities" or running the letter *A* through its various transmutations, but their texts are as open as Melville's and Hawthorne's. However, the difference is that the Transcendentalists offered a series of truths or pictures that would then be dissolved. For Emerson to claim that every thought is also a prison, he must first convince us of that thought or that prison. For Thoreau to assert that even virtue can become stagnant, he must first give his readers a firm sense of what virtue is, what evils must be resisted.

A standard joke about Poe's stories is that they can easily be reduced to maxims. The moral of "The Black Cat" is "Be kind to animals." Of "The Pit and the Pendulum," "Never give up hope." Of "The Tell-Tale heart," "Murder will out," or "Crime does not pay." The joke is funny because it would be clearly an egregious oversimplification to do this to Poe's works. A Transcendental rhetoric works somewhat differently. A promise is held out, a truism is asserted, then dissolved with the higher promise that a greater truth is being created by the reader. In "Self-Reliance," the reader is urged to "trust thyself," but plenty of textual markers warn that in trusting himself or herself the reader may be indulging in nothing more than *"Whim,"* and may never push through to the other italicized word in the essay: *"Being."*

But Emerson goes on, endowing the reader with authority to explain what he means, forcing the responsibility for interpretive meaning upon his readers: "I hope it is somewhat better than whim at last, but we cannot spend the day in explanation." In Melville's *Mardi,* a chief commands his philosophers to try to find "the one true root" of a multitrunked banyan tree. *Mardi* suggests it would be presumptuous of anyone to try; a Transcendental text seems to command its philosopher-readers to attempt the endeavor.

Hawthorne's famous characterization of Melville has been taken to be a self-characterization as well. But it would seem appropriate to extend the characterization to symbolize one of the most crucial language problems in the discourse of Thoreau's times. Melville reasoned "of Providence and futurity, and of everything that lies beyond human ken," Hawthorne averred. "He can neither believe, nor be comfortable in his unbelief; and he is too honest and courageous not to try to do one or the other." In religion as in art, antebellum intellectuals attempted a rhetoric that interwove belief with unbelief. They created texts that mirrored their most intense reading experiences, which involved an interplay of certainty and silence, and these texts created paradoxes, ambiguities, and "liquidations" that would encourage, provoke, or entice future readers to attempt the "one or the other" of which Hawthorne spoke.

After reading several essays on Thoreau by James Russell Lowell, Charles Ives once said that Mr. Lowell's Thoreau was not his Thoreau. "You know your Thoreau, but not my Thoreau."[15] Ives was obviously right, for their two readings are as different as can be, as different as belief and unbelief, faith and skepticism. Each had been provoked to grasp one trunk of the banyan tree of Thoreau's wild rhetoric and to proclaim it to be the one true root. Ives' Thoreau is not Lowell's Thoreau, but Thoreau would claim—and disavow—both.

3. A CONSTITUTIONAL LANGUAGE

America remembers that Franklin Roosevelt proclaimed, "We have nothing to fear but fear itself." However, those were not his words. His *First Inaugural Address* (4 March 1933) reads, "The only thing we have to fear is fear itself." Thoreau is usually cited as the source of Roosevelt's famous quotation. However, Thoreau's proverb is quite different. His *Journal* says, "Nothing is so much to be feared as fear."[1] These three quotations introduce several significant questions about language and the activity of reading. The first is an example of what Thoreau's era fondly called a "memory quotation," the type of quotation that has salvaged Emerson's proverb about building a better mousetrap, since Emerson never put that maxim in writing. If a "memory quotation" does not accurately remember what was said, it "remembers" what should have been said. Or, as in the Roosevelt case, the spirit of the remark is preserved in more memorable phrasing. Memory quotations articulate, *pace* Alexander Pope, "What's oft been thought, but ne'er so well expressed."

The memory quotation reinforces one of Thoreau's assumptions: that readers read beyond the words to the spirit that the words suggest. Since reading "beyond" is a natural phenomenon, Thoreau incorporates that fact into his rhetorical strategies. Moreover, a "memory quotation" can be a microcosm for a much larger problem. The authenticity and the accuracy of a "memory quotation" of a single line can be checked, but what happens with a longer text? After one reads Thoreau's three million words and ten million words of commentary and then issues an interpretation, has not one offered a kind of "memory quotation" on a vaster scale? Indeed, are not the acts of remembering and interpreting simultaneously a tribute and an insult to the author's words—tribute since they have provoked us into this labor of love, insult because we feel his meaning needs to be expressed more clearly and more accurately?

Secondly, although a "memory quotation" shows readers reading *beyond* an author's words, it does not satisfy Thoreau's rhetorical demand that they read *against* his words. Both Roosevelt's proverb and its memory quotation involve a language completely different from Thoreau's. Roosevelt allows readers to know precisely what he means. They may not agree with the president, they may quibble about casting an emotion as a "thing," or they may point to the fact that the entire nation in 1933 was indeed full of fear, but they have no problem resolving exactly what Roosevelt intended. The author of the president's text, writing to the public in a time of national crisis, has carefully presented a message that allows for the narrowest range of interpretation. Its intended meaning is as precise as those Thoreauvian maxims that "patriotism is a maggot" and "we do not ride upon the railroad; it rides upon us." America and its president have used "closed language," whereas Thoreau's text is "open."

"Nothing is so much to be feared as fear" is more open. The author had placed fear at the top of a vague list of unspecified items. Readers can only guess whether the list is long or short, finite or infinite. A willful reader might even argue that "nothingness" is as fearful as fear, and cite Thoreau's "Ktaadn" for support. The open text seems to call for a memory quotation of both its phrasing and its spirit. Its margin for interpretation is deliberately wider, so wide as to permit misinterpretation or idiosyncratic reading. This "open" language is not quite the language of liquidation discussed in the previous section of this chapter. Rather than emphasize gaps, paradox, and contra-dictions, this "open" language does seem to have a clear leading idea. In fact, its intention seems so enticing as to invite us to close the sentence and transform it into an aphorism. Readers are tempted to make it be the source for Roosevelt's proverb, make it crisper, like Benjamin Franklin's Poor Richard sayings, make it satisfy America's penchant for capsulized wisdom, which John Bartlett answered in 1855, the year after *Walden,* with his *Familiar Quotations.*

As an example of an "open" text, Thoreau's quotation seems closer to Roosevelt's political statement. It is certainly not as wild as, for example, his beautifully elusive imagery in the hound, bayhorse, turtledove parable, nor as inscrutable as utterances like, "Give me a sentence which no intelligence can understand." Open as his fear proverb may be, it is linguistically less wild than the sentence immediately following it: "Atheism may comparatively be popular with God himself." No politician would dare attempt to transmute *that* statement into a maxim for public consumption! Public consumption is key in differentiating these languages. Thoreau's wildest pronouncements may seem "democratic" in that they allow readers to think their own thoughts and create their own meanings using the author's text as a guide. They are also undemocratic, elitest in that they make readers doubt whether they have grasped the author's intended meaning or have missed the point entirely. Thoreau promises that he will never paint "No Admittance" over his gate, but *Walden* also warns undemocratically that not every John or Jonathan will understand him.

Less wild than liquidation or a language of desire, Thoreau's open language is more political, more keyed to public consumption. They are more "political" in the sense that the author's personal thoughts are more intensely negotiated with public concerns. An open language involves a series of negotiations between the writer and his times, the self and the state. In negotiating the boundaries between individual *virtu* and civic virtue, it develops the sense of one's personal constitution as a communal body and investigates the political nature of the literary process. An open text explores the parallels between literary authorship and cultural authority, the interplay of literary power and political power, and the similarity between a writer's control over readers and a society's governance of its citizens. It also lays bare the complex question of the degree to which a personal, subjective reading of nature—supposedly "apolitical" and hence "ideal"—is in fact a political interpretation.

Political language has three main varieties: empty, explicit, and open or constitutional. The first two are self-evident. Empty rhetoric launches floating signifiers, those icons that a culture cherishes but that do not provoke thought. We have seen Thoreau invoke Bunker Hill and Plymouth Rock in his John Brown essays. Explicit language is called upon to word a law as specifically and carefully as possible or to persuade an audience to a specific course of action, to convert citizens to a particular reform program. Constitutional language is a form of open language that is less clear, less specific, and less static. Thoreau parallels constitutional language with the slang expression, "taking a constitutional." It is a language whose meaning is exercised, which gives tone to the political body. It is a language which, as it were, "lives and breathes." Like the human organism, a constitutional language represents those tensions, balances, and evolving, shifting dynamics of the cultural organism.

Although the preceding description groans from an overabundance of simile, the rest of this section will give a more substantial description of constitutional language, particularly as defined by those professional readers known as legal scholars, judges and justices. First, however, I will pay more attention to that remarkable *Journal* entry for 7 September 1851 in which appears Thoreau's proverb about fear. That long entry has much to say about public consumption and readers' tolerance. It also studies the degree to which his wild rhetoric can be considered "supreme," and it demonstrates that Thoreau's rhetoric depends upon a blending of languages, an interweaving of linguistic modes ranging from the closed to the open to the wildest versions of literacy.

The entry's spark was intensely political. Literary reviewers had just scalded Harriet Martineau's latest book on the grounds of whiggery and heresy. Thematically, Thoreau's response may be a jumble, but it is linguistically controlled. He glides from an explicit language complaining of narrow-minded repression, to the open text of his fear proverb, to the wilder language of his sentence about God endorsing atheism. Finally, the entry culminates in a long discussion praising a supreme rhetoric of a language of desire. Moreover, his praise is written in a language of desire. That is, his explicit praise includes images and phrasing that undercut, qualify, and liquefy his specific message.

The loftiest moments of inspiration, Thoreau avers, can only be suggested through language after "their truth subsides, and in cooler moments we can use them as paint to gild and adorn our prose." These ineffable moments of inspiration are "like a pot of pure ether. They lend the writer when the moment comes a certain superfluity of wealth, making his expression to overrun and float itself." The theme is clear praise for a language that avoids explicit communication and suggests a meaning that overruns its words, that floats above its prose, but note how the vehicle contradicts the message. Instead of airy, ethereal imagery, inspirational truth, represented as "pure ether," is put into a pot. Elsewhere Thoreau's poet is also a seer, but here the roles are disjunctive. The dedicated writer must cease to be a seer in order to write. His "expression" must "overrun itself" because he is only recollecting a truth, only presenting a facsimile of the event. Language only "paints" the experience.

Dismayed that his countrymen had rejected Harriet Martineau's latest book on the grounds of heresy, he records his anger at small-mindedness and propaganda:

> What shall we say of these timid folk who carry the principle of thinking nothing and doing nothing and being nothing to such an extreme? As if, in the absence of thought, that vast yearning of their natures for something to fill the vacuum made the least traditionary expression and shadow of thought to be clung to with instinctive tenacity. They atone for their producing nothing by a brutish respect for something. They are as simple as oxen, and as guiltless of thought and reflection. Their reflections are reflected from other minds. The creature of institutions, bigoted and a conservatist, can say nothing hearty.

The problem is that everything he says against stupid readings and "traditionary expression" also applies to his own supreme rhetoric. The phrase "vast yearning of their natures for something to fill the vacuum" can easily be used to stand for his explanation of the power of a language of desire. The images he uses to criticize propaganda and rote reading are almost identical to those from the *Journal* passage about the vision highlighted in *Wild Rhetoric*'s introduction as one of his most forceful descriptions of his supreme rhetoric. The yearning he felt to fill the void of nature at the west cut that he figured as the physician's cupping-glass sounds all too close to the oxen-like reading that disgusts him here.

How does a Transcendental writer convey thoughts that are not "clung to with instinctive tenacity"? How can the institution of literature discourage bigoted and "conservatist" readings? How does a writer in a democratic culture offer truths that readers will meditate upon without confusing their reflections with Lockean imprints "from other minds"? If it shuns explicit messages, then how does a language of desire differ from an empty language of floating signifiers that also capitalizes on gaps, vacuums, and "vast yearnings"? These rhetorical problems inspired Thoreau to one of the earliest versions of his now famous dictum, "Let him step to the music which he hears, however measured or far away." In 1851, the idea read, "It is not so much the music as the marching to the music which I feel." Not the music, but the marching is privileged, not the text's message but the activity of reading, not the thought but the experience of thinking. The music is more enticing, so the passage suggests, the less seemingly measured and the least far away, when its melody becomes so rooted in the muscles and sinews of the body that it becomes something felt, not understood.

By *Walden*'s publication, this proverb would become less airy and less physical, less abstract and less bodily oriented. In its published version polished for public consumption, the imagery would become more militaristic, presenting a crisp picture of a soldier-idealist. Its 1851 *Journal* version is more wild. Its power is located imagistically in the reader's own private body, not figured in a public uniform. Its expression arises from the specific political issue of America's informal censorship of authors, and its context concerns the dire implications of his idealistic rhetoric in a democratic culture. A supreme rhetoric deployed gaps, contradictions, paradoxes, and oxymorons to create textual vacuums that readers, intent upon arriving at meaning, would be provoked into filling with their own original thoughts. Thoreau hoped that this rhetoric would forestall the "brutish respect for something" that resulted in the bovine readings that had rejected Martineau's book. But to avoid exchanging a brutish adoration of icons for a hearty respect for anything, he blended his supreme rhetoric with explicit language and the rhetorical strategy of an open text.

We saw how he interwove languages in his John Brown essays. The spirit of Brown may be far removed from his deeds, but the narrative voice weaves through all the narrative locations—on the lectern, in the guilty audience, at Brown's side, far inferior to Brown, and so forth. Switching the metaphor from politics to art, Thoreau made the same point about the interdependence of language modes. Shortly before going to Walden, he wrote in his *Journal:*

Not only has the foreground of a picture its glass of transparent crystal spread over it, but the picture itself is a glass or transparent medium to a remoter background. . . . It is not the fringed foreground of the desert—nor the intermediate oases that detain the eye and the imagination—but the infinite, level, and roomy horizon, where the sky meets the sand, and heavens and earth—the ideal and actual, are coincident.—The back ground into which leads the path of the pilgrim. (*PJ2*, 101)

All parts of the picture are as "coincident" as the ideal and the actual. Glass leads on to picture, which itself is glass leading on to further vision; a mode of language leads to other modes that call forth still others.

Whether the art of words or the art of paints, one meaning leads to another, which in turn suggests a still further meaning. In his parable of the cave, Plato might image the sun as the source of truth, but in *Walden* even the sun itself is depicted as "but a morning star." The George Ripleys and Theodore Parkers might offer specific political reforms, but Thoreau's "more perfect and glorious State" at the end of "Resistance to Civil Government" is one he has only imagined "but not yet anywhere seen." His supreme rhetoric offers "shadows of thoughts," employing a style that uses the "least traditionary expression," but how can he guarantee that readers will receive these texts as linguistic buoys and balloons that can set their readers' thoughts afloat without fooling readers into clinging to the texts' ideas tenaciously? Moreover, if Thoreau forces readers to read a certain way, has he not succeeded in being like propagandists, whose principal aim is to manipulate audiences? Democracy works only when its citizens vote "their own minds," as the cliché goes. But how can a transcendental writer be democratic when he seems to have no choice but to serve one of two devils: either control readers' responses or persuade them that true thoughts are never settled, that every settled thought is a prison? How does an author reconcile his "authority" over his readers with his desire also to be a "liberating god"? These are only some of the serious, broadly political problems that Thoreau would develop a rhetoric to confront.

Thoreau issued many explicit statements on specific political and social issues. In "Resistance to Civil Government," he interwove slavery, the treatment of Indians, and the Mexican War as examples to lay bare the flaws of a government based on majority or minority rule, the only possible bases for any government. Later in life, he cited the division of labor, the rise of monopolies, and America's rapid population growth as three chief threats to the social fabric.[2] Myriad scholars have analyzed Thoreau's specific political thought; along with nature, it is his most discussed topic. Taylor Stoehr and Anne Rose, among others, have argued that Thoreau's political thought is valuable, while critics like Edward H. Madden complain that Thoreau was too naive and anarchistic for his reform ideas to be of much worth.[3]

Some, like Michael Meyer, suspend judgment, preferring to describe how others have interpreted Thoreau. One of the most provocative statements on this issue remains Walter Harding's:

> Unfortunately altogether too many students of Thoreau have not been willing to accept the fact that Thoreau did not formulate and unify his thinking. Approaching his writings with a preconceived notion that there was a unity to his ideas, they have attempted to impose a consistency where no consistency existed. They have accepted those ideas of his that fitted their own particular orthodoxy and silently rejected the rest. Thus they have been able to "prove" that Thoreau was a stoic or an epicurean, a pacifist or a militarist, a pessimist or an optimist, an individualist or a communist. There is hardly an ism of our times that has not attempted to adopt Thoreau.[4]

I would not say that those who "adopt" Thoreau are "wrong." Thoreau's open texts do encourage readings that discover bold, urgent, coherent, and explicit messages. Nor is Harding's position incorrect; rather, he features the one form of Thoreau's language: the wildness of his rhetoric, the wildness that would surface in such *Journal* proclamations as, "An honest misunderstanding is often the ground of future intercourse" (*PJ1*, 229).

When we focus on Thoreau's concern with the broader notion of "Government," particularly rhetorical governance, three issues become paramount: the development of a "constitutional language" that encourages "an honest minunderstanding" of its text, the exploitation of nature in order to create that text, and the vexing question of authority for a writer like Thoreau, who conceived himself as living during what some considered America's last chance to transform itself into a true democracy.[5]

Two major forms of political language influenced antebellum America. One is famous: the age of oratory. Daniel Webster, Henry Clay, Frederick Douglass, John C. Calhoun, William Seward, Sojourner Truth, and hosts of other speakers could move large groups to adopt specific views. Theodore Parker's lecture audiences reputedly numbered in the thousands, and he once cowed a lynch mob. Orators were celebrities. A popular children's game was to gather in the woods and take turns while one child after another mounted a tree stump and imitated the grandiose oratory of celebrated elders.[6] Although the political aims of these orators could not be more diverse, their language was similar. Their discourse was essentially closed. They had specific intentions in mind, and they used traditional rhetorical techniques to persuade listeners. The term *suasion* was invoked to describe this rhetorical situation, a term that became obsolete by the end of the century.

The closed language of suasion was already losing its force in 1850s America. After the Civil War, Mark Twain would ridicule such speech in his "Whittier's Birthday Address," but its decay can be marked as early as the 1830s, when Davy Crockett ran for Congress. The success of his lecture format depended on mocking the golden orators. After a rival office seeker orated in the grand style, Crockett would rise to his turn and simply announce "free drinks." On those occasions when he was to speak first, he would deliver his opponent's speech, memorized word for word, leaving his rival without anything prepared to say.[7] With his criticism of "made words" and prepared speeches, Thoreau probably would not be above recommending that only one speech need be memorized to mimic all the others.

Crockett's parody is not very far from Thoreau's ridicule of fat politicians whose corpulence was exceeded only by their fat themes. In "Huckleberries," Thoreau singles out politicians like William Seward and Caleb Cushing (Attorney General, 1853–1857), who represent obese public figures whose performances could be measured only with "a ten-foot pole."[8] Thoreau spoke harshly even about Frederick Douglass, complaining that his fiery oratory only made his hearers all the more timid. In 1849, Thoreau had handled Webster gently in "Resistance to Civil Government," praising him above all other political orators for his "comparative wisdom," saying, "we thank Heaven for him." But by 1854, after the Anthony Burns and Thomas Sims cases, Thoreau would characterize America's famed orator as a "venomous reptile" and dung-beetle—"a dirt-bug and its ball"—allowing the dirt-ball to stand equally for the law and for the closed speech of political suasion.[9]

Whatever psychological attraction Thoreau may have felt toward John Brown as a surrogate father figure, he was also attracted to his plain style, a spare rhetoric that avoided the oratorical splendor of a Webster, a

Cushing, or a Seward. Thoreau insisted on honest speech, even should it devolve upon a reader's "honest misunderstanding" of that speech. He also insisted on a defiant reading, a creative reading wherein readers presumed themselves to be wiser than the author or the text. The Constitution, for example, was not merely to be memorized and its authors revered as icons. Rather, he approves an adversarial relationship to the text. He applauds Wendell Phillips' reading when Phillips asserts he is "wiser than" the framers of the Constitution, and when he transforms the empty icon of the traditional Thanksgiving proclamation from "God save the Commonwealth of Massachusetts" to "God dash it into a thousand pieces." With such a reading relationship, Thoreau insists, the original document called "The Constitution" "has improved these sixty years' experience of its working." A defiant, creative reading can improve the meaning of the text (RP, 60).

In 1850, Thoreau told Harrison Blake that he was sure the Constitution was a living document, its meaning as organic as the body out for a stimulating walk: "If there is anything more glorious than a congress of men a-framing or amending of a constitution going on, which I suspect there is, I desire to see the morning papers" (Corr, 258). A more active reading experience than to be "a-framing or amending" was to smash the frame to pieces and read defiantly. After all, that is how the founding fathers themselves had read their textual sources when composing their rereading as the Declaration of Independence. They changed John Locke's goals of "life, liberty, and property" to read, "life, liberty, and the pursuit of happiness." Their revision transformed something definite into an indefinite concept, made a specific goal vague. In substituting an idea that can vary for each reader, they created a more open text.[10]

While the Declaration is usually seen as America's more transcendental utterance, and the Constitution its realistic compromise, even the Constitution has been valued for its open language. As Lincoln Caplan has elucidated:

> Over the years, liberal and conservative scholars have agreed that the framers of the Constitution deliberately chose ambiguous language as a form of compromise on many important questions. "No Constitution is the same on Paper and in Life," wrote Gouverneur Morris, who was one of the authors of the text, and who, along with other framers, began to debate the meaning of the document almost as soon as it was adopted. Liberal and conservative [Supreme Court] Justices have declared that the words of the Constitution are capable of well-

tempered growth, and that the Supreme Court must continually reinterpret the text, with its ambiguities, compromises, and internal tensions, in the light of new conditions. The most consistently honored declaration about the law as a living character—John Marshall's warning that we must never forget that it is a constitution we are expounding—has been taken as a given since at least 1819.[11]

This was the variety of rhetoric that fascinated Thoreau, a form of language that was open, living, fluid. When he says at one point that he wants words that would "bleed if you cut them," he is referring to a language that seems, like nature, real, and he is also calling for a language that is like the body: never static, always changing, growing.

This form of language is an open text whose crucial terms are protean. Different readings, different framings would change their meanings. Indeed, Proteus would not have had to change his forms had not Odysseus tried to seize him. Emerson complained that Thoreau's chief fault as a writer was his overuse of oxymorons, but Michael Kammen has demonstrated that one form of nineteenth-century political language was essentially oxymoronic. For example, coupling *liberty* with *order,* Kammen explains, "would not have seemed a paradoxical oxymoron to Americans of that era." Americans who might claim to be mystified by Keats's "negative capability" could easily bracket *liberty* variously with *property, justice, happiness, independence, union, equality, peace, Protestantism,* and *the law.*[12]

Modern Americans, particularly those trained readers called Supreme Court Justices, are keenly aware that the Constitution is an open text. In 1959, Justice Tom Clark said that liberty is "a mighty word," also "an abstract one—having such meanings as one injects into it. Thus, its significance tends to change from person to person and from time to time." In 1930, Felix Frankfurter emphasized the reader-centered nature of the Constitution: "The meaning of 'due process' and the context of terms like 'liberty' are not revealed by the Constitution. It is the Justices who make the meaning." Nineteen years later, nothing had changed Frankfurter's opinion. In words that echo Thoreau's assertion that even virtue can become stagnant, Frankfurter insisted that "great concepts . . . were purposely left [by the founders] to gather meaning from experience. For they relate to the whole domain of social and economic fact, and the statesmen who founded this Nation knew too well that only a stagnant society remains unchanged."[13]

Thoreau's frequent use of bodily images and his stated preference for what he called a "hearty language" (like the body's constantly pulsating heart) are connected with a Constitutional language. He sought a rhetoric that was open, that allowed meaning to breathe. Caught in a time of severe crisis in the body politic, Thoreau offered a rhetoric that seemed alive. His rhetoric matched the idealistic claims and lofty aspirations of the Declaration of Independence while inviting readers to read him as Jefferson read Locke, to participate in rendering the true import of his phrases, to read like Frankfurter and create the text.[14]

He had little choice. What topic could he honestly describe that did not open to differing interpretations, even misreadings? Even the clearest, most obvious choice was problematic. Nature itself was oxymoronic, as invaded as the Maine wilderness. Nature is posited as the antithesis of civilization, the opposite of society, whereas politics, of course, is the art of social interaction. But in Thoreau's day, the split was not that neat. Nature was being constantly read, interpreted, and translated for political purposes. It was persistently exploited for political metaphors. The Puritans, starting with John Winthrop's sermon "A Modell of Christian Charity" (1630), may have argued that the natural world was separate from the social-political realm, but Tom Paine completed what Cotton Mather and Jonathan Edwards had begun: using nature to explain and to justify political and philosophical positions.

In Thoreau's time, nature was exploited for any political position on any given topic. Slavery was the most dramatic of these topics. Young William Seward argued against slavery, basing his case on John Locke's position that "natural law was superior to all man-made law." Conversely, some interpreted Blackstone to mean that "the right of property . . . is founded in the way of nature, and is antecedent to all civil regulation," and thus slavery was justified on natural grounds, as "unnatural" as that argument sounded to Seward.[15] Finally, as Brook Thomas has made clear, the legalistic rhetoric of lawyers played free and loose with nature, shaping nature to substantiate any courtroom claim, occasionally producing the spectacle of rival lawyers in a civil suit each invoking what was "natural" to support their conflicting arguments.[16]

By the time Thoreau went to college, it had become a stock slogan for Americans to refer to their country as "Nature's Nation."[17] "Natural rights" within a political system had become an established appeal, and Montesquieu's belief that custom was superior to contrived systems because it was more "natural" had become axiomatic. Perhaps the most radical point about Emerson's *Nature* in 1836 was that he separated nature from consciousness, setting nature along with culture apart from "the ME," a separation of powers from which later Transcendentalists like Whitman, Dickinson, and Thoreau would depart. In the next generation, nature would not seem so ambivalent, and debates over nature gave way to controversy over natural selection. As James Russell Lowell said in 1886, "In a last analysis, there is but one natural right; and that is the right of superior force."[18] In the 1840s, nature still wore a many-colored coat, and its tints were colored by the observer. As Hawthorne specified in "The New Adam and Eve," we "can never adequately know how little in our present state and circumstances is natural and how much is merely the interpolation of the perverted mind and heart of man."

Thoreau would not postulate man's perverted heart, but he concurred when Hawthorne claimed that through creative reading and "through the medium of the imagination we can lessen those iron fetters, which we call truth and reality." While one of Thoreau's friends, Emerson, averred that an imaginative reading could free us from our prisons, another friend, Hawthorne, opined that such an achievement only made us aware "what prisoners we are." Living in an era when a constitutional language was valued, Thoreau enjoyed—or perhaps "suffered" is the more operative verb—a clear sense that nature was crucial. It was also capable of being interpreted at will. However he argued the pleasures of nature, regardless of the freedom he allowed his readers, Thoreau was rooted in the discourse of his age on slavery, nature, and other current topics. Even when he appears to oppose his times and to dig in his heels, he is very much part of his era. Scholars like Taylor Stoehr and James Armstrong have shown that Thoreau is not so radical when viewed in the context of contemporary reform programs. Nowhere is that point demonstrated more firmly than by the single, most popularly accepted "fact" about the icon "Thoreau": that he went to live a hermit-like existence in a cabin in the woods far from the madding crowd.

When Thoreau went to his cabin, the oxymoron of the "famous hermit" was a long established and respected tradition in America. Thoreau was no hermit, but he depended upon the cultural myth of withdrawal to develop his famous work, much as he used the travelogue to produce his excursion pieces. There were woman-hating hermits like John McQuain, and man-fearing hermits like Sarah Bishop. The autobiographies of Francis Phyle (*The Hermit,* 1788) and Robert the Hermit (1829) were popular. By the 1840s, the cave-dweller Benjamin Lay, whose tracts Benjamin Franklin had published, was widely recognized for his stands on vegetarianism and abolition. His picture could be found in any Quaker house, and John Greenleaf Whittier celebrated him in verse. Albert Large was already a folk hero because of his twenty-year seclusion from about 1840 to 1860. One might also mention that when *Walden* was published, America's "First Lady" was known as "The Shadow in the White House" because Jane Means Pierce lived as reclusively as Emily Dickinson.[19]

In 1840s America, living in a hut outside the mainstream of American society was not uncommon. Taylor Stoehr has an entire chapter concerned with the Emersonian statement that "huts are safe." Four years before he went to Walden, Margaret Fuller had recommended that Thoreau temporarily retire to "some lonely hut" (*Corr,* 57). His friend, Charles Stearns Wheeler, had conducted his hut experiment at Flint's Pond, not far from Walden, years before Thoreau built his cabin. After he read *Walden,* Daniel Ricketson told Thoreau that he had already been living his version of *Walden* for several years in "a rough board shanty 12 × 14 three miles from New Bedford in a quiet and secluded spot" (*Corr,* 332). William H. Goetzmann provides perhaps the most remarkable account of quasi-Thoreauvian hut-dwelling; "Thoreauvian" because it so closely resembles *Walden*'s account, "quasi" because independent of Thoreau's influence. In an age when German philosophy clubs could be found across the United States, people like Henry C. Brokmeyer, a Hegelian and self-made millionaire from St. Louis, Missouri, chose to meditate upon reform issues and to commune with nature from his hut in 1854, the same year *Walden* was published. As a crowning touch, German Missouri Hegelians like Brokmeyer would later come to Concord, Massachusetts, to rescue Bronson Alcott's failing Concord School of Philosophy. There they would publish what they claimed was the first edition of Thoreau's "The Service."[20]

Hut-dwelling and experiments in seclusion were an emblem in antebellum America for individualism, another culturally desirable myth, an emblem that presumed intentions of spiritual and political rejuvenation, a symbol of individual freedom as the power to do what one ought to do. As such, the symbol was more active and more socially oriented than depictions of America as an "asylum" by Joseph Stansbury, Hector St. John de Crevecoeur, and others. American intellectuals intensely felt the need for and the power of withdrawal, whether they were aware of the

implications or whether they were fulfilling culturally established arche-
types. Georg Lukacs faults the Romantics, saying that they never understood "the deep nature of this withdrawal and its complex relations."
Joseph J. Ellis, on the other hand, claims that the voluntary withdrawal
of American artists and intellectuals into a separate sphere was not peculiar; it was merely a part of a major fragmentation as America became
modern.[21]

Be that as it may, there is a fascinating association of withdrawal, hut-
dwelling, and experiments in geographical individualism with a language
of paradox, oxymoron, and open texts. As the age of hut-dwelling and
communal experiments subsided into the genteel tradition after the Civil
War, as the Romantic language of ambiguities shifted to the Realistic
presentation of experience, so the language tended to close. Kammen
reports that the Civil War "prompted large numbers of Americans to
reconsider the ideal of achieving *a balance* between liberty and order in
favor of *subordinating* the former to the latter." George Frederickson
argues that prewar individualism and openness provoked more institu-
tional and closed views, and John Higham sees the same shift from
boundlessness to closed order.[22]

Thoreau's hut-dwelling and his cultivation of two and a half acres of
bean rows were at once more radical and more traditional than other
experiments in terms of its political statement. By the 1840s, the American political imagination had firmly linked together the plough, republican virtue, and freedom. In 1855, Congress would commission Constan-
tino Brumidi to prepare two frescoes for the Capitol: *Calling of Cincinnatus
from the Plow* and *Calling of Putnam from the Plow to the Revolution*. In
1856, Henry Wise would emphasize that in Houdon's statue of Washington, the father of his country "stands on the mother earth, the plough
share placed on the left by his foot. These signify the idea of 'Country.' "
Thoreau was fond of citing Cato in his writings, particularly in *Walden,*
and America had come to refer to Samuel Adams, one of the most radical
of the founding fathers, as "the American Cato." Much has been made of
the fact that Thoreau went to live at Walden on the Fourth of July, and,
as Michael Kammen points out, "actually there is no more effective way
to fault a nation than by means of its most familiar icons and cherished
clichés." Thoreau's move to Walden on Independence Day parallels the
tactic of the historically important shoeworkers' strike at Lynn, Massachusetts, on George Washington's birthday, 1860.[23] Nevertheless, Tho-

reau, valuing more open statements, would insert the iconized date and then claim that it was "by accident."

Eventually *Walden* and its author would themselves become cultural icons, and the transformation should come as no surprise given Thoreau's embroilment with the cultural, political, and linguistic issues of his day. After all, Thoreau had once clearly proclaimed that he asserted no independence, that he was time and the world, that village life and business routine met in him. As William L. Howarth has shown, upon *Walden*'s completion Thoreau plunged deep into two projects as diametrically opposed as time and the world. One was a political essay on the Anthony Burns case; the other was an ambitious project called "Night and Moonlight" (also "Moonlight" and "The Moon"), a course of lectures whose rhetorical strategy was wilder. Moonlight language Thoreau called a Sanskrit, "world of poetry, [with] its weird teachings, its oracular suggestions," as opposed to the more explicit language of his Burns manuscripts. One project inspired others. Plunging into a specific political issue would inspire a concomitant flight into the ethereal reaches of spiritual meditation. As a reflection of the political discourse of his age, one language rages against a political situation as clearly as possible, while the other develops a more open text through a language of desire. Perhaps the most graphic illustration of this yoking of contrary topics and rhetorics is his holograph for "The Dispersion of Seeds," several pages of which are written on the backs of broadsides announcing John Brown's martyrdom.[24]

Experimenting with two different language projects at the same time was Thoreau's routine rhetorical practice, but "routine" is an eely word. A form of politics in its broadest sense, routine is essential to negotiate originality. In his *Journal* entry for 23 January 1841, Thoreau discusses the "solidity and apparent necessity" of routine and links it remarkably with nature.

If there were but one erect and solid standing tree in the woods, all creatures would go to rub against it, and make sure of their footing. Routine is a ground to stand on, a wall to retreat to; we cannot draw on our boots without bracing ourselves against *it*. It is the fence over which neighbors lean when they talk. All this cockcrowing and hawing and geeing, and business in the streets, is like the spring board on which tumblers perform, and develope [sic] their elasticity. (*PJ1*, 229)

If Daniel Webster is celebrated as The Great Compromiser of antebellum America, Thoreau can be taken as a Great Negotiator. After all, he tells readers in the first paragraph of *Walden*'s "The Village," "As I walked to the woods to see the birds and squirrels, so I walked in the village [every day or two] to see the men and boys"; and he found that the gossip about town affairs and newspaper articles "was really as refreshing in its way as the rustle of leaves and the peeping of frogs." In another *Journal* entry, Thoreau records how he had once supposed that "the red-bird which I saw on my companion's string on election days I thought but the outmost sentinel of the wild, immortal camp,—of the wild and dazzling infantry of the wilderness,—that the deeper woods abounded with redder birds still," but he had since come to think that politics and nature were correspondent, that the wildest red bird and the tamest political emblem were integral (*J,* 6:293).[25]

In personal life, Thoreau might proffer portraits of himself as an eccentric, but he was saddened by a friend's insanity. Although he presented himself as a supreme individualist with the loftiest idealistic visions, he regretted that James Clark had to be put in "the Poor House—insane with too large views, so that he cannot support himself," a fate he felt was "more tragic than death" (*Corr,* 200). In poetry, he sought originality of expression, but he criticized his friend Ellery Channing's style for being what Thoreau disdained as "sublimo-slipshod." He might rail against money-grubbing, but his antimaterialist statements would be couched in monetary phrases and financial images, and the language of social and political power would thus be interfused with a language of desire.

From a political and cultural perspective, the reason *Walden* and "Resistance to Civil Government" have come to be considered Thoreau's most important works—indeed, the reason the authorial voice called "Thoreau" is equated with these two works—is because *Walden* and "Resistance" are his most "public" performances, his most generous compromises and liberal negotiations with cultural demands. In one of his first published pieces, "The Landlord," he had aimed too low. Having gone to New York in 1843 to break into the publishing market, he had written an essay that has embarrassed Thoreau aficionados as being too commercial, too pleasant, too politically tame. With respect to form and style, *Walden* seems more original than "The Landlord," but it is not as eccentric nor as innovative as his first book, *A Week on the Concord and*

Merrimack Rivers, which had failed so drastically in the marketplace that it plunged Thoreau into debt for years.

With respect to politics, "Resistance" is certainly provocative and has been greatly influential, but it is not as politically radical as his John Brown essays, and certainly not as extreme as "Slavery in Massachusetts," with its incendiary insinuation about "what match I would touch, what system endeavor to blow up" (102). Perhaps its success as a public negotiation explains why people, even those who know otherwise, still feel at liberty to call "Resistance" by its incorrect titles, "Civil Disobedience" or "On the Duty of Civil Disobedience"—the phrase Thoreau borrowed from the Declaration of Independence, one of America's most public political documents.

Going public, of course, is politic, not only for the pedestrian aims of becoming published but also for effecting negotiation. After all, some of Thoreau's greatest respect for John Brown derived from the fact that "he is no longer working in secret. He works in public, and in the clearest light that shines on this land." Thoreau felt that writers as well as revolutionaries needed to work in public with public language. To be sure, a spur to Thoreau's recommendation came from his confidence that he could work in public and still (perhaps "therefore") work "in the clearest light." One of the two extracts from *Walden* published prior to the book was "A Poet Buys a Farm." The most notable aspect of this essay from a political/rhetorical point of view is how it enables the reader to remain liberated while making its message clear. Obviously, the essay's leading idea is that one can see more with a poetic eye than from a proprietary view; the poet's vision skims the cream, while the farmer reaps only the crop. However, Thoreau manages to introduce sufficient self-parody into his persona of The Poet so that the reader is left feeling free to decide just how seriously to take the essay's advice. Readers can view the persona's attitude as right but somewhat ridiculous, as sublime but a bit silly, as sincere but perhaps tongue-in-cheek. Through an open language, the author has succeeded in making his points while avoiding dictatorial governance. He has offered sentiments in "a constitutional language" that are allowed to breathe.

4. "THE ASTONISHED EYE"

Analyzing popular discourse beyond the level of anecdote or generalization is a tricky enterprise. Lacking are the established foci and internal structures of disciplines like politics and religion. Also absent is a sense of boundary; one senses when one is passing beyond the specific definition of politics into the broader range, but popular culture is vast and its borders obscure. In addition, specific phenomena have many manifestations. Folklore would have Daniel Boone a pioneering loner like Natty Bumppo, but biography has him agent for a land corporation. Popular history wants Davy Crockett to be a democrat, but his politics were Whig. The patron saint of ecologists may have revered nature, but John James Audubon slew hundreds of a single specimen to acquire models for his drawings. Perhaps the severest problem is coping with stereotype and generalization.

Cultural plurality is one illustration. On one hand, it seems safe to say that antebellum America was an age of teeming multiplicity. In religion, Catholicism was still exotic, new religions like Mormonism were springing up, established religions like the Quakers were changing radically, and curious phenomena like the Millerites were rife. In politics, one of the two major political powers was disintegrating, and another would be born in the 1850s; factions and parties like the Loco-focos, the Know-Nothings, and others were legion. Even a specific reform group like the antislavery society contained a vast variety of persuasions. When Whitman created his persona as the poetic embodiment of America, he could express this single personification only through contradiction and diversity. "Do I contradict myself? / Very well then I contradict myself. / (I am large, I contain multitudes.)"[1]

Consequently, it seems trite to mention vast multiplicity as the hallmark of this era. One of the most difficult tasks for a late twentieth-century mind—conditioned by *its* hallmarks of mass market and mass media, with their confident assumptions of a "mainstream" culture—is to try to grasp the teeming, fluctuating diversity of Thoreau's age. Yet, having made that seemingly safe statement, one must also admit that many in Thoreau's age would belie that diversity. They would claim that a mass culture was already in place, even before the term "mass culture" had been invented to describe the phenomenon. In *Douglass' Monthly* for October 1859, for example, Frederick Douglass wrote that:

The contact into which men are brought by those means of communication [i.e., public schools, newspapers, interstate commerce, transportation, rapid settlement], is one of the most powerful promoters of general and uniform culture; and in vain would one look here for the isolated, secluded places which a traveler will frequently meet with even in the middle of the most cultivated countries of Europe, where a small population is found entirely isolated, cut off from the rest of the world, speaking their own peculiar dialect, . . . forming a little world by themselves, . . . whose mental horizon does not reach farther than the extent of the acres they cultivate. Here, on the contrary, everywhere, in the middle of deserts, on nearly inaccessible mountains we hear our own language almost uncorruptedly spoken, and meet with people hardly different from ourselves in manners, notions and knowledge. Even foreigners soon show the influence of that general leveling civilization.[2]

Similarly, a very different orator like Daniel Webster would agree, saying in his Independence Day Address for 1851, "To whatever region an American citizen carries himself, he takes with him, fully developed in his own understanding and experience, our American principles and opinions, and becomes ready at once, in co-operation with others, to apply them to the formation of new governments."[3]

A vast multiplicity may very well be the hallmark of the age, and yet it may actually be a reaction to the growing and inevitable cultural uniformity. Language that insists upon America's diversity may be merely a symptom of "that general leveling civilization." In Thoreau's "Wild Apples," one strong theme is that individuals are giving way to "unoriginal men" as fast as wild apples are disappearing and varieties are dwindling. Soon "we shall be compelled to look for our apples," our thoughts and words, "in a barrel" or some other commercial package. By the next generation, "masses of men" will be shortened to "masses." Language will flatten as America moves from the Romantic to the Realistic period, paralleling the cultural centralization of authority into mass media. As James Russell Lowell said, by 1886 the newspaper editor had subsumed the offices of church, university, and court; the press of the Press had become complete.[4]

As a word-artifact of its age, *Walden* can be read as a nostalgic pastoral depicting the bygone dream of Jeffersonian democracy, an imaged experience close to Douglass's description of the old European world. This kind of reading is reinforced by *Walden*'s frequent allusions to its local New England audience and to old New England, left behind by the ambitious seeking their fortunes in cities or California gold fields. However, it can also be read as a useful corrective to its age, a phillipic whose meaning becomes all the more valuable as mass culture becomes more pervasive. Douglass mentions how quickly foreigners are assimilated, and the grandson of an immigrant from France would write a book that would soon become a principal document of American civilization. Alcott would describe him as "a Declaration of Independence in himself"; the arch-individualist would personify a cultural archetype. Thoreau would complain about the influence of mass media as represented by the newspapers, yet in an early essay he would express his pleasure that, upon ascending a mountain with his companion, there was sufficient light from the heavens to read the newspapers they had brought with them. He frequently complained about received ideas and stereotyped thinking, but in his *Journal* for 14 March 1838 Thoreau expressed his belief that "every proverb in the newspapers originally stood for a truth." One obligation of the writer, then, is "to preserve [a proverb's] significance, to write it anew" (*PJ1*, 35).

Such problems are an indication of true discourse. A language may be explicit, saying clearly what it intends, but discourse immediately suggests its contradictions. A language can attempt to resolve meaning into its narrowest scope—like signs that say "No Trespassing" or "No Admittance." Discourse is more dynamic, preferring signs that read "Enter At Your Own Risk," which simultaneously ward off and tempt trespassers. Thoreau can be oriented to his age's popular discourse by streamlining this complex problem to two phenomena. Both are cultural events, but one is directly linked with Thoreau's published work while the other lies at the opposite extreme from his literary efforts: the magazine presentation of Thoreau's "Ktaadn" and the cultural phenomenon of Phineas T. Barnum.

The usual scholarly approach to an author is to study his manuscript extracted from its appearance. That is to say, a scholarly edition of an author's works faithfully represents an accurate, complete text independent of its debut format. However, if one attempts to locate an author in his time, such formats become valuable. Therefore, Thoreau's "Ktaadn, and the Maine Woods," an especially interesting piece because of its depiction of an alien nature of "chaos and old night," becomes even more significant in terms of its public presentation, particularly since it is an early publication, antedating Thoreau's first book and marking one of his first appearances as an American author. The nature of its public appearance is more than of antiquarian interest; rather, it demonstrates Thoreau's early cultural reception, a reception he had to attend to in order to remain in demand with publishers.

"Ktaadn," its awkward spelling immediately intimating wildness, was published in editor Caroline Kirkland's *The Union Magazine of Literature and Art* in five installments beginning in July 1848. In the first installment, Thoreau characterizes his expedition as an Adamic experience in the uncivilized wilds of nature. He interweaves specificity with universality, narrating how "on the thirty-first of August, 1846, I left Concord" with the locution, "as Adam did." But *The Union Magazine* automatically did its utmost to domesticate Thoreau's text, a domestication Thoreau would incorporate into his other works. The first installment is immediately followed by three lachrymose poems, complete with sobbing angels; the second by H. H. Clements's praise of John Quincy Adams as a Representative Man (two years before Emerson's famous series of essays on that theme) who is "scholar, sage, poet, and statesman."

The third installment introduces Anne C. Lynch's melodrama about aristocrats who hide out from the French Revolution, called "The Solitary of Saint Renan." This American melodrama, although obviously a perversion of Jefferson's idea of the "aristoi," capitalizes on the power derived from withdrawal to articulate the popular contempt for mass culture and a fear of drastic social change, cultural apprehensions that Thoreau would play upon in a very different way.

The fourth is decorated with illustrations by "P. Loomis." It is this fourth installment that describes Thoreau's voyage into the chaos and ancient night of nature, where he comes across a fresh footprint that makes him feel like Robinson Crusoe only to discover that the print was made by one of his own party. Loomis's engraving, meant to escort Thoreau's prose, actually contradicts his theme. His illustration is a pastoral engraving of hikers, looking like innocent shepherds, pausing to rest or to picnic. If placed in the first or the fifth installment—the setting out or "The Return Journey" sections—the drawing would have been appropriate, but placed in the passage describing nature's harsh, dangerous, and alien virility, it controls the wild temper of Thoreau's prose. The magazine tames the text much as Edward Hicks did in his nature painting *The Falls of Niagara* (1825) a generation before. Hicks controlled the stunning wildness of Niagara Falls with a balanced composition and a massive frame as well with a well-ordered verse that traverses all four sides of his painting:

With Uproar hideous first the *Falls* appear,
The stunning tumult thundering on the ear.

Above, below, where'er the astonished eye
Turns to behold, new opening wonders lie,

This great o'erwhelming work of awful Time
In all its dread magnificence sublime,

Rises on our view amid a crashing roar
That bids us kneel, and Time's great God adore.

Hicks employs all the artistic conventions of poetry and painting and picture framing to control the stunning tumult, the dread magnificence, and the hideous uproar of nature in order to soothe "the astonished eye" with conventional religious sentiments. And as one comes to the conclusion of Thoreau's last installment, one might choose to read the other "Contents—Entirely [so-called] Original" of the magazine: Kirkland's "Sightseeing in Europe," Lydia Sigourney's "Unspoken Language," or a poem by "A. W." called "The Art of Lying."

But before readers would encounter Thoreau's five-part essay, even before they would come to the table of contents, they would first be influenced by the magazine's title page. At the top, they would notice, called to their attention by that semiotician's dream of the nineteenth century, a collared hand, sporting a studded cuff, pointing at the warning that someone known as "N. Bailey" has been stealing subscriptions. The warning inadvertently draws attention to the omnipresence of "confidence men," a term that 1850s America would bestow upon the world.

The rest of the page contrasts strongly with this caveat against hucksters. Positioned directly below the warning bristles an angry American eagle triangulated by the twenty stars of the union, menacing arrows, and the peaceful olive branch. The eagle is bracketed by angels holding quill and stylus. Below this design sits the main illustration occupying the most space: an Indian, cradling a gun, bow, and arrows, gazes bemusedly from a rocky promontory across the bay. His vision passes over sailing ships and a newly built two-decker steam sidewheeler towards what looks geographically like Manhattan, except that the city is decorated with domes, spires, and minarets, resembling Byzantium more than contemporary New York. As Joseph Ellis has pointed out, the dream of an American Athens had faded by the early nineteenth century, and Kirkland's illustrator was using lapsing myths nostalgically to call to mind the former generation's dreams of a classical New York City and a contemplative (armed but impotent) Indian.[5]

Editor Caroline Kirkland's literary prominence, which resulted in her winning the editorship of *The Union Magazine,* ensued from the fact that she had been dragged by her husband out to the Michigan frontier and had written factual accounts about what she found there, most of it repugnant to a civilized New England settler, as suggested by the title of one of her books, *Our New Home: Who'll Follow?* The book's implication was that only the desperate would do so. When she published Thoreau's equivalent of going west to "see the elephant"—going north into the wilds of Maine—Kirkland handled her presentation neatly. She domesticated Thoreau's wildness with manifold representations of civilization—Loomis's illustration, essays on European sightseeing, poems with sobbing angels, and a title page that depicted what the age would call a savage, helplessly contemplating, despite his arms and his arts, the advance of a civilization proud of its spanking-new steamboats and aspiring to rival the many-domed splendors of ancient civilizations.

Kirkland and her staff had no ulterior motives. Quite the reverse. It is all the more revealing that *The Union Magazine*'s staff functioned spontaneously and automatically, simply sensing what would be "appropriate" for a particular issue. It is more telling that they were merely selecting whatever seemed (as editors still say) "suitable to our editorial needs." When presenting Thoreau's piece on alien nature, they unwittingly framed its wildness with a magazine cover filled with tame pictorial icons so familiar that they were trite. It was like printing an insult, but framing it as humor. Or, it was like J. P. Marquand's expensive, leather-bound, gilt-lettered copy of *Walden.* Probably they were not aware of the contradiction between the confidence-man warning and the pleasant portrait of civilization, and their readers probably separated the two in their own imaginations. Probably they chose the cover picture of the foregrounded Indian about to be supplanted by civilization with no more thought than it looked "nice" or "right" or "good." And yet, that picture's elements are emblems for many of their culture's aspirations, anxieties, and regrets. They probably did not intend to domesticate Thoreau's essay by inserting Loomis's engravings or by following it up with highly conventional pieces. They probably did not consciously seek to control the wildness and alienation of "Ktaadn." Probably they did not *mean* any of this, but that is what they did.

In extreme contrast to *The Union Magazine*'s domesticated presentation of Thoreau's essay lies the cultural phenomenon of Phineas T. Barnum. While *The Union Magazine* nominated John Quincy Adams as America's Representative Man, other reviewers chose Barnum. In 1850, one argued that, "Adopting Mr. Emerson's idea, I should say that Barnum is a representative man. He represents the enterprise and energy of his countrymen in the 19th century."[6] Thoreau's acquaintance with Barnum is firm. He visited Barnum's American Museum in New York City, and he was duped by Barnum's first elaborate public scam—the Hoboken Buffalo Hunt.[7] In *Walden*'s conclusion, Thoreau's images of buffalo and pygmies probably were based on the only ones he had seen, courtesy of P. T. Barnum. But I am not seeking specific sources, nor biographical links. I highlight Barnum precisely because this representative of popular culture seems to be a polar extreme from Thoreau. The differences between the two artists are obvious. The one aimed at spirituality, while the other was obsessed with money. Both kept their eye on what the slang of the day would call "the main chance," but one would define it as living fully while the other would see it as social and material success. Thoreau would show great concern about his governance over his readers, but Barnum delighted in audience manipulation and his power over the public. These essential differences must be remembered if the following argument is not to be distorted.

First, I should point out that the "Barnum" I mean is the antebellum impresario. The usual image of Barnum is one that developed after the Civil War. By the 1870s, Barnum had become a cultural icon, fondly referred to as Kris Kringle, his exhibitions described as "The Great Moral Show." By the 1880s, American popular culture had transformed him—as it had Emerson, who sometimes shared the lecture bill with Barnum—into a "yea-sayer," a public figure who proffered a positive, contented, and optimistic vision of existence in which difficulties existed only to be transcended, and life was an encounter that could be won.[8] However, the "Barnum" of the 1840s and 1850s was considered, like the early Transcendentalists, as a curious, even dangerous character. Known as a shrewd Yankee and another avatar of Sam Slick, renowned for his cunning, energy, and ingenuity, Barnum was also noted for his curious mixture of cynicism and idealism. He considered the ministerial profession to be a fraud, and he persistently assailed politics, even when running for Congress. He championed many social reforms, supported civil rights, abolition, temperance, and women's rights to some extent, and he opposed business monopolies as the enemy of the free-enterprise system. Like Thoreau, whose gathering of plant and animal specimens helped to establish Louis Agassiz's collection at Harvard, Barnum's zoological contributions were gratefully received by museum curators at the Smithsonian, Harvard, Tufts University, and elsewhere.

At one point in his career, Barnum retired, so he reports in his autobiography, "to a secluded spot on Long Island where the sea-wind lends its healthful influence." In that nature retreat, Barnum recorded that "I humbly hope and believe that I am being taught humility and reliance upon Providence, which will yet afford a thousand times more peace and true happiness than can be acquired in the din, strife and turmoil, excitements and struggles of this money-worshipping age. The man who coins his brain and blood into gold, who wastes all of his time and thought upon the almighty dollar, who looks no higher than blocks of houses, and tracts of land" misses the inspiration and rejuvenation Barnum claims to cherish.

As the above paragraph indicates, thematically Barnum and Thoreau are close. Reading samples of those two men's writings, a naive reader uninfluenced by historical interpretations could easily conclude that far more thematic similarity exists than difference. In fact, if one treated Barnum's American Museum as though it were a text, one would find it to read like Thoreau's. The American Museum's exhibits celebrating the bounty of nature would be linked, like *Walden*'s chapters, only by the loosest of organizational structures, and its individual exhibits, like selections of Thoreau's sentences, would vary the serious with the silly, the sublime with the ridiculous, the instructive with the playfully humorous, the sincere with the hoax and the practical joke. In one version of *Walden,* Thoreau portrayed himself as a modern-day Momus, Jupiter's trickster, jester, or fool, and James Russell Lowell, one of Thoreau's severest critics, characterized Thoreau as a gamester or confidence man.[9] Thus, it is not surprising that a reviewer for the *New York Knickerbocker* should note in 1855 that two remarkable books were published over the past year: Thoreau's *Walden: Or, Life in the Woods* and Barnum's *The Life of P. T. Barnum, Written by Himself.* The reviewer synthesized these antithetical books by citing their exaggeration, claiming that *Walden*'s "Rural Humbug" was balanced by the city humbug of Barnum's *Life.* A more recent scholar would also link both texts, taking them as forms of American autobiography that, like Whitman's and Franklin's, create idealized character types.[10]

These uncongenial authors who would become antithetical cultural icons shared one rhetorical experiment—the hyperbolic language of exaggeration. As the various manuscript revisions of *Walden* show, one of the passages that most troubled Thoreau was one in which he confronts the question of how to admit that he is bragging. Should he simply brag, acknowledging that the reader will see through his exaggeration? Should he claim that he brags for humanity as well as for himself? Should he boast, but then immediately warn his readers that he is boasting? Should he brag, but then confess that he could also tell stories about himself that would flow as filthily as the gutters? Should he crow lustily but control the crowing with a domesticated image of a hen-yard rooster whose crowing is to serve moral aims? Eventually, Thoreau would refine this problem into a valued rhetorical approach. He would come to praise the virtues of what he called *"Extra-vagance!"* and he would aver that he could not possibly, under any linguistic terms, "exaggerate enough."

While his rhetoric of exaggeration could be compared with other sources—Bushnell's language of liquidation, for example—it also parallels the language used to great success by the impresario who is Thoreau's cultural Other. Barnum invented no exhibit; he took available ones and presented them in more original form. In textual terms, he really had nothing new to say; his success lay in how he said it, in his language and style. Like Thoreau, Barnum bragged of his bragging, eventually claiming it as a supreme rhetoric. Barnum argued, "If my 'puffing' was more persistent, my posters more glaring, my pictures more exaggerated, my flags more patriotic and my transparencies more brilliant," it was the result of more energy and ingenuity, not fewer scruples. Neil Harris asserts, "So completely did he explore the possibilities exaggeration offered, and so shrewdly did he broadcast his own discoveries, that his technique deserves a more dignified label—"an aesthetic"—for it embodied a philosophy of taste."[11]

Barnum would welcome Harris's assertion, but Barnum might go a step farther (naturally) and claim that his exaggeration was not only an aesthetic but a rhetoric because of its effect upon the reading experience. A strong communication between exhibitor and viewer required a certain degree of exaggeration, even humbug. Much as Thoreau marveled why people chose to live such "mean, moiling existences," Barnum reasoned that Americans were more duped by believing too little than too much. "Many persons have such a horror of being taken in that they believe themselves to be a sham, and in this way are continually humbugging themselves."

In Thoreau's rhetoric, exaggeration often takes two extreme forms— puffing and deflation. He can present himself as the only one of his contemporaries who knows how to live life to the fullest, and he can parody, mock, and deprecate himself. He can paint his days at Walden as a glorious existence, and he can begin *A Yankee in Canada* by saying that what he got chiefly by going to Canada was a cold. Similarly, Barnum could describe his exhibit as the greatest show on earth, and he could expose his own humbugs and frauds. When attendance at one exhibit began to decline, he wrote an anonymous letter to the newspapers claiming that his exhibit of an ancient woman (Joice Heth) who had presumably been George Washington's nursemaid was in fact "a curiously constructed automaton," and attendance revived. Another time, he hired someone to prosecute him for fraud, to sue that Barnum's bearded lady was really a man. Either form of exaggeration—that his show was the greatest value on earth or a consummate fake—drew.

The important point about the rhetoric of exaggeration is its powerful effect on readers and viewers, at least so claimed the architects of that rhetoric. Over and over again in his autobiography, a recurring theme seems genuine: Barnum marvels at the effects of his exaggerated language. He seems awed by the sheer exhilaration of debate his advertisements and exhibits generated. They stimulated more intellectual curiosity than did a bare recital of literal truth or those "closed texts" of previous museums whose exhibits' authenticity was unquestioned. As Harris explains, Barnum did not fear the public's doubt; he invited it. He understood that the opportunity to debate genuineness was more exciting than the discovery of a fraud or a settled truth.[12] The stimulation of argument was more valuable than the resolution of a debate. In Thoreauvian terms, marching, not music, had meaning.

The rhetoric of doubt necessitated by exaggeration involved revolutionary implications. It suggested a kind of linguistic renewal of a democracy that was seen to be failing politically. Casting doubt upon an issue involved not only epistemological questions but also hierarchical and social reconsiderations. One astounding example was Barnum's Feejee Mermaid. Barnum's mermaid apparently was the body of a fish and the head and hands of a monkey that someone had stitched together so cunningly that even naturalists were at odds about whether the article was genuine. This was Barnum's crowning exhibit, as it caused consternation even among experts about the truth of the matter. In contrast to exhibits like Jumbo or Tom Thumb or Jenny Lind, which capitalized on other cultural interests (the American penchant for bigness, the dwarf strutting as a general, the commercialization of art), the Feejee Mermaid was more like the Constitution's "open language." The genuineness of the curiosity, the meaning of the thing was indeterminate, a fact Barnum was sure to exploit. Subjective opinion must be based on a controversial objective entity. In promoting the dubiety of the object, Barnum mocked authority, particularly those who represented the rising stature of the scientist. Barnum's mermaid could make scientists look as fallible as those authorities who debated the genuineness of the platypus three centuries before.

Moreover, Barnum instructed readers/viewers on how to receive his mermaid. In towns where the exhibit was generally thought genuine, he would write letters to the local newspapers, signing them with the authoritative letters of scientific expertise (D.D., M.S., Ph.D.), claiming the mermaid a fake. In towns where the mermaid was considered a fraud, Barnum's letters would appear insisting it was real. He kept the intellectual pot boiling. In towns where confusion reigned—the most interesting situation of all—he papered the community with posters that clamored,"When *doctors* disagree, / *Who* is to decide?" Barnum's rhetoric encouraged skepticism about any authority, even the authority of the advertisement's author, a self-acknowledged trickster.

It went further than that. His humbug was more revolutionary than even a Transcendental rhetoric. While the mermaid debunked authority, it did not elevate the individual. If one could not rely upon experts, nor could one "trust thyself." Barnum tapped into America's anxiety about the impossibility of any decision. Each self could form its own opinion, to be sure, but the issue itself could not be settled. One could not reason; one could only observe the passing spectacle and hope to be entertained. If it should be resolved, then the issue would no longer generate debate. It would cease to have life. Vitality would be drained; power would be lost. Ultimately, impotence or passive observation were the only choices. For Emerson, mankind was a "golden impossibility." With Barnum, thought and reading eventually became a gaudy show. However, Barnum claimed that his rhetoric encouraged doubt, sapped deference to authority, and enkindled thought, three aims that Thoreau would frequently laud. As Neil Harris argues, Barnum discovered early in his career that "an exhibitor did not have to guarantee truthfulness; all he had to do was possess probability and invite doubt. The public would be more excited by controversy than by conclusiveness."[13]

As a rhetoric that glorified doubt, exaggeration could more successfully fire the intellect than could an explicit recitation of what to think, what to do, and how do it. Barnum's rhetoric was drastically different from *The Union Magazine*'s domestication of Thoreau's "Ktaadn" by surrounding it with traditional images and stereotyped language. However, Barnum's hyperbole also risked committing the same rhetorical error as explicit language. Without promising to "guarantee truthfulness," it simply fed its readers and did not whet their hunger to taste meaning. In contrast, a Constitutional language, a Bushnellian language of liquidation, and Thoreau's wild rhetoric hoped to avoid passive consumption of the text and to promote creative reading by promising that truthfulness could be attained, or that at least the illusion could be entertained.

Barnum soon abandoned his wilder rhetoric. By the 1860s, he had ceased to expose the unreliability of authorities; he no longer poked fun at himself or glorified doubt. By the 1880s, he had abandoned his American Museums for the circus, and instead of encouraging reader/viewer participation, he enjoyed audience manipulation. He invented the three-ring circus for the reason that so much would be happening that audiences would sit stunned in their seats, overwhelmed by the swirl of spectacle. Apparently, the same phenomenon was occurring in popular culture at large. In prize fighting, for example, adoption of the Queensberry Rules (1867) confined and ordered what had been open and slipshod. In late nineteenth-century America, when the boxing ring was moved indoors, the collaborative crowd became the regulated audience.[14]

In fine, viewers had been transformed from creative readers, as they had been invited to be by the American Museum, into spectators, passive consumers of the text, Barnum's advertisements for the postwar circus illustrate the point. His posters bragged that "Contemporaries Shrink Away As [the circus] Approaches." Instead of promoting curiosity and controversy, his circus posters promised "A Satiety for the Public Appetite." The concluding lines of an 1881 circus advertisement demonstrate that Barnum had totally abandoned his flirtation with the language of desire: "To Behold This Repository of Sweeping Greatness Ends All Desire To See More, Since, of Its Genus, There Is Nothing Left to See." Barnum's Royal Nonesuch represented a language as closed as could be, a rhetoric far removed from Thoreau's wild rhetoric.

But even in the era from 1835 (when he first exhibited) to the Civil War, Barnum's language was often closed. In lectures like "The Art of Money-Getting" (first delivered 29 December 1858), didacticism prevails. His text reads like a string of platitudes, in contrast to the more open, original language of Thoreau's "Life Without Principle" and Barnum's own advertisements. His writings offer extensive quotations from famous Americans like Benjamin Franklin and Henry Ward Beecher, importing these icons without reservation or exaggeration. He frequently lapses into sentimentality and nostalgia, stock phrases and stereotypes, in propounding his clear, unmistakable moral messages. In other words, he is fond of using the other diction that, along with the language of desire, comprised the discourse of the day. His *Life* often reads like an adult version of those immensely popular "Rollo books" by John and Jacob Abbott—two hundred volumes of instructive stories for children beginning in 1832, twenty-eight in the Rollo series alone, with didactic titles like *The Way to Do Good: Or, the Christian Character Mature* and *Marco Paul's Adventures in Pursuit of Knowledge: Springfield Armory*. Edgar Allan Poe would not have bothered to complain of "The Heresy of the Didactic" if a hegemony of didacticism did not exist, not only among successful poets like Longfellow, Holmes, and Bryant but also in the culture's discourse at large. Although an adult autobiography instead of a children's story, and although written by a "humbug" instead of a Congregational clergyman like Abbott, Barnum's *Life* remains a conduct book, a specialized form of the how-to-do-it book, a genre as popular as the travel book, the journal, or any of the other favored genres of the day.

Conversely, even what seems an explicit how-to-do-it manual easily oozes into the realm of the conduct book. Orson S. Fowler, for example, developing one theme that would also emerge in *Walden,* instructed Americans on how to build *The Octagon House: A Home for All or a New, Cheap, Convenient, and Superior Mode of Building.* Fowler's book was so popular that, after initial publication in 1848, it was reprinted in 1849, 1850, and 1851; a revised edition appeared in 1853 and was reprinted at least four times thereafter. Although Fowler's purported theme was now to live cheaply, his actual focus centered on two cultural virtues—individualism and humanitarianism—while arguing for specific social reforms with respect to diet, dress, sex, and temperance.[15]

Parallels between Thoreau and the tradition Fowler represents are immediate. Both are individualistic and humanitarian, both wish us to live cheaply and to live well, both offer specific advice on how we should reform our lives—but the obvious difference, the crucial difference, is rhetorical. Fowler seeks to make his meaning sufficiently explicit and persuasive that readers will become converts and actually build his house and live their lives precisely as Fowler instructs. Thoreau, on the other hand, paints a glorious picture of his life at Walden but wards off imitators, telling his readers to go their own way and not follow his. The Walden experiment is portrayed as very tentative; it has to be made to seem temporary since, Thoreau argues, permanence is stagnation. In Thoreau's corrected proof of 119 sheets, he made only one significant last-minute change in the text's meaning: in the fourteenth paragraph of "Spring" he instructed the printer to change the phrase from "the life and joy of the pond" to the "pond full of glee and *youth*" (my emphasis), thereby rendering the experiment even more remote, an experience not merely eight or ten years in the past but an event from a different phase of existence.

As I will demonstrate more specifically in later chapters, Thoreau's art was essentially parodic. With the smallest language units, he would often pun and offer curious etymologies, freeing individual words from single, denotative meanings. On the broadest level, even the genres for his works are like puns on a larger scale. He would begin from the most established and popular genres and, through parody, produce more original works. He would tell readers how-to-do-it by building a cabin from boards purified by nature and then immediately advise them that the Indian teepee is superior to any house, hut, or cabin. He would reform burglary by telling readers not to lock their doors nor own anything worth stealing, but he would confess that he kept his own desk drawer locked. He would work on a travel book printed as *A Yankee in Canada,* but its opening lines would mockingly lament that what he got chiefly by going to Canada was only a cold. He would depict his trek into *The Maine Woods* as his odyssey into America's deepest wilderness, but he would choose to relate how frequently he encountered people and evidence of civilization, how cluttered even Maine's wilderness was. He will have "travelled much" in his most famous book, but only within a few miles of his cabin. Instead of Barnum's "The Art of Money-Getting," he would write "Life Without Principle," which is in fact a life full of principle, but without monetary principal. *Cape Cod* can seem an extended narrative whose main intention is to set readers up for a single concluding joke, that "A man may stand there and put all America behind him." But after readers finish laughing, they might wonder whether the joke means that Thoreau has turned his back on America or whether he has offered a parodic persona of America's Representative Man, an image more dynamic than the cultural icons of Barnum or Franklin, Webster or Clay. Among other effects, parody would be one rhetorical strategy by which he could guard against didacticism and prosyletization.

In this chapter, I have tried to put America behind Thoreau. In religion, the dynamism of his era's discourse ranges from sermons that specified clearly what Thou Shalt and Shalt Not do to Bushnell's language of liquidation; in politics, from explicit position statements about crucial social ills to the living language of the Constitution and the lampoons of Crockett's campaign. With popular discourse, *The Union Magazine* demonstrates one way his culture domesticated themes of wildness, whereas Barnum's rhetoric involves exaggeration and didacticism, open and closed language. Barnum's glorification of doubt could have been illustrated in other contexts. Folklore studies have done much work on the concept of the trickster; historical and literary studies have fully explored the phenomenon of the confidence-man. His wild rhetoric could also be compared to the western language of the hoax and the tall tale, as scholars like Constance Rourke, Kenneth Lynn, and Richard Chase have done. One could even cite Karl Marx's *Das Kapital,* a seemingly closed text if ever one existed, whose first words would be the epigraph: "Doubt Everything."[16] The fact that so many widely different approaches would arrive at similar results appears to reinforce this study of the discourse of Thoreau's age. Thoreau says in *Walden,* "This is the only way, we say; but there are as many ways as there can be drawn radii from one centre" (11).

Barnum would seem to fall at the farthest extreme from Thoreau, and yet they share many of the same rhetorical concerns of their times. Barnum is also intriguing for being an exhibitor, and *exhibit* is a fine word for discussing rhetoric. It implies that the presentation of the thing is as crucial as, perhaps even more significant than the thing itself. The word suggests that attention to readers' reception of and participation in the exhibit is as important as are authorial intentions. "Exhibit" suggests a communication in which meaning is a fusion of the text or the thing with its presentation, with the exhibitor's intentions, and with the viewers' or readers' responses. Having backgrounded the discourse of his age, we may now turn more specifically to Thoreau's textual "exhibits."

CHAPTER TWO

Thoreau in Form

I. TROPHIES OF THE SELF

The opening paragraph of *Walden*'s "Conclusion" endorses doctors who "wisely recommend a change of air and scenery" to the sick (*W,* 320). Thus, the Walden experiment concludes in new beginnings, and Thoreau's textual experiments suggest a change of venue for all writers, whether lively or ill. The second paragraph of *Walden*'s "Conclusion" parodies those who hunt nature's creatures, killing giraffes, snipes, and woodchucks to mount as trophies on their walls. He asks if it would not "be nobler game to shoot one's self." Taken together, these articulations of the artist's diverse roles imply that his personas of the self are greatly influenced by literary form. His ideas seem different as they are represented within generic models and against different literary scenery. His ideas owe as much to the way they are framed within genre as they were influenced by the language of his times.

Thoreau experimented much with literary forms, and he could write with equal facility in the genres of the conduct book, the jeremiad, the how-to book, the historical sketch, the natural history or popular science essay, the travelogue, the lecture, the letter, the poem, the book review, and the journal. In the "Solitude" chapter of *Walden,* Thoreau relates, "I only know myself as a human entity; the scene, so to speak, of thoughts and affections; and am sensible of a certain doubleness by which I can stand as remote from myself as from another." In *Walden* and other prose

pieces negotiated through public literary demands, the author was committed to specific narrative voices, but in his poetry, letters, and *Journal*
he could indulge in the infinity of thoughts and affections; his self could
be portrayed not only in its doubleness but in its perpetually shifting
shades, without privileging one voice, mood, or manner over any other.
The *Journal* would appear to be the form of writing freest of generic
convention, but, given Thoreau's tendency to inaugurate a literary form
only to subvert it, one wonders even there. The *Journal* seems to make
the fewest concessions to reader conventions and expository structures.
The writer seems to speak to himself; he seems to write for himself in any
diction he chooses. Thus, the *Journal* seems to lay bare "the hidden
Thoreau." So it would seem, although it is quite possible that this tactic
itself is a narrative ploy. What *seems* his freest genre may be his most
cunning artifice, carefully manipulating the impression of literary privacy.

Recent critics like Sharon Cameron and Lawrence Stapleton have
asked readers to view Thoreau's *Journal* as his supreme form because it
best reveals the hidden man or because it represents a form of writing
closest to nature itself.[1] But one's conversion to this view is stymied when
one stumbles across the abrupt statement early in his *Journal* career (18
June 1840) that he is "startled when I consider how little I am *actually*
concerned about the things I write in my journal" (*PJ1,* 131). One must
also acknowledge the fact that Thoreau felt as free to contradict himself
through literary forms as he felt obliged to represent his philosophy
differently within genres. Hence, in one genre he would proclaim that he
would never, not ever, write upon a particular subject, but then he would
weave that very issue into a text so skillfully that it would become one of
its most memorable episodes. A quick example is his *Journal* entry of
more than a thousand words for 3 October 1859. Framed as fiction, with
the narrator cast in third person, the crucial aesthetic question is whether
to stand in a hog pasture gazing across the valley at a farmhouse wreathed
in smoke or to attempt an "inside" look, thereby confronting the "haggard
poverty and harrassing debt," the "coarse haste and bustle," the "intem-
perance, moroseness, meanness" and the "vulgarity" of everyday life. For
a moment, that is, Thoreau contemplates whether to accept the Realist's
burden "to go into an actual farmer's family at evening, see the tired
laborers come in from their day's work thinking of their wages, the
sluttish help in the kitchen and sink-room, the indifferent stolidity and

patient misery which only the spirits of the youngest children rise above"
(12:367).

This *Journal* transcription elects to rise above such naturalistic incli-
nations. Thoreau will take the distanced, Transcendental view of matter.
The farm will be remembered only through remoteness, only by its
smoke curling from its chimney, its gray-slated roof. Thoreau will spare
himself the disillusion Melville records in "The Piazza" (1856), where he
feels compelled to ascend to disappointment and disenchantment. Thoreau keeps his narrator standing resolutely among the hogs, gazing across
the valley at the farmhouse, and he well understands the reason:

> When I look down on that roof I am not reminded of the mortgage which the
> village bank has on that property,—that that family long since sold itself to the
> devil and wrote the deed with their blood. I am not reminded that the old man I
> see in the yard is one who has lived beyond his calculated time, whom the young
> one is merely "carrying through" in fulfillment of his contract; that the man at the
> pump is watering the milk. I am not reminded of *the idiot that sits by the kitchen
> fire* (emphasis mine).

Such are the facts (Thoreau thrice reminds himself) of which he does not
want a realistic view to remind him. He wishes to "imagine a life in
harmony with the scenery and the hour." If it is an illusion, then he hopes
it is the kind with which "we thus forever delude ourselves" (12:366).

However (and there seems to be a perpetual "howeverness" in Thoreau),
his insistence upon a literary Transcendentalism is contradicted by his
practice. Although his *Journal* promised that he would never pen a
naturalistic view of life as represented by "the idiot by the fire," he did
exactly that in *Cape Cod*'s fifth chapter, called "The Wellfleet Oysterman."
The oysterman may be the "merriest man that we had ever seen, and one
of the best preserved" (even though considered "old and foolish" by those
who know him most intimately), but his son is "a fool" to Thoreau and is
mockingly called "the wizard" by his companion (*CC,* 104–5). Regardless of the label, and regardless whether the oysterman's son is depicted
as a scarecrow when standing in the fields or as an idiot when sitting by
the fire, the point has been made with regard to literary form. In the
Journal, Thoreau theorizes how an inside, realistic look is undesirable
and unaesthetic; yet in his practice he was preparing precisely the inside
look he had proscribed in the genre of the journal.

The day after Thoreau journalized on literary Transcendentalism, he addressed the topic of his own wild rhetoric. The smoke from the farmhouse chimney, which he said was as interesting and as fair as any cloud in nature, was followed by an explication of his own smoky language. Thoreau advises that if "you would fain perceive something," then "you must approach the object totally unprejudiced. You must be aware that *no thing* is what you have taken it to be." Reality is limned as what Thoreau called "ITness" in *Maine Woods,* an ultimate, undecodable, indecipherable wall. Reality finally is a hieroglyphic for which no rosetta stone exists. It is a blank slate upon which one can write almost any message that seems to make sense. A wise writer, so Thoreau says, is one whose "greatest success will be simply to perceive that such things are, and you will have no communication to make to the Royal Society," whether that Royal Society be the prestigious scientific body or the aristocratic circle of expert readers. Later, he writes:

> It is only when we forget all our learning that we begin to know. I do not get nearer by a hair's breadth to any natural object so long as I presume that I have an introduction to it from some learned man. To conceive of it with a total apprehension I must for the thousandth time approach it as something totally strange. (*J,* 12:366–69)

After "any natural object," one could interject "or any text." The value of a wild rhetoric, or so this *Journal* entry suggests, rests in rendering a text as estranged as nature, as inscrutable as reality, as free of authority as an authoritative elder *(Walden)* or a "learned man" here. After readers have learned and then forgotten all their learning, they *begin* to know. Accenting beginnings over an established plane of knowledge, Thoreau promises buddings, explorations, and starts. He promises awakenings, not full wakefulness. He promises much, but what he clearly admits is the ultimate strangeness and estrangement of reality, nature, and the text.

This "ITness," as *Maine Woods* calls it, is forcefully conveyed in Thoreau's ascent of Ktaadn as discussed in the previous chapter. Elemental reality and the text ultimately as *tabula rasa* are presented in that book sinisterly, even frighteningly, as Chaos and Old Night. This menacing mood also surfaces in his *Journal.* On 31 October 1850, for example, he gazes through a stately pine grove and sees the setting sun "falling in golden streams through its aisles," but he feels only alienation in the presence of such beauty. He asks, "But what was I to it?" (*J,* 2:76). Sometimes this mute reality looms in Thoreau's verse, as when he comments, "We see the *planet* fall, / And that is all" (*Poems,* 85), but reality's

ITness can also be presented in more friendly and pleasant fashion, as in the couplets "The chicadee / Hops near to me" and "The needles of the pine, / All to the west incline" (*Poems,* 187, 22). This form of language whereby the text is stripped of imposed meaning may be called "The Unsaid." Nature is sheerly there, an uncarved block not amenable to sculpting. The Unsaid concentrates on the IT of reality, on what another poet calls "the thingness of things," and the narrative "I" stands helpless before it except to observe and to record. The Unsaid conveys a sense that reality is opaque, that events defy interpretation and are invulnerable to penetration. In Unsaid writing, reality is left linguistically raw.

However, Thoreau employs two forms of language to respond to the Unsaid. One may be called "The Said," and the other the "Un-said." In the former, the "I" becomes active, confronts raw reality, and imposes its interpretive will upon it in order to achieve inspirational effects. A phenomenon is perceived, but the report of that phenomenon is in fact a record of one's own senses and desires. Consequently, Thoreau rewrites the first letter of the Puritan *Bay Psalm Primer* to read optimistically:

In Adam's fall
We sinned all.
In the new Adam's rise.
We shall all reach the skies.
    (*Poems,* 245)

More philosophically, his *Journal* for 19 August 1851 says, "I am not concerned to express that kind of truth which Nature has expressed. Who knows but I may suggest some things to her? . . . I deal with the truths that recommend themselves to me,—please me,—not those merely which any system has voted to accept" (12:403). In order to make these three forms of language clear as they metamorphose through literary forms, let us center on the single image of the mountain ascent, portrayed linguistically as the Unsaid of "Ktaadn," the Un-said in the *Journal,* and the Said in *A Week on the Rivers.*

Much controversy surrounds Thoreau's ecstatic vision atop Saddleback Mountain in *A Week.* In contrast to Ktaadn's blunt alienation, "There was not the substance of impurity, no spot nor stain" at Saddleback's summit. "It was a favor for which to be forever silent to be shown this vision" (*Week,* 188–89). Some complain that Thoreau is not silent, that he sullies the vision of purity with clichés and hackneyed allusions when making himself "a dweller in the dazzling halls of Aurora" and invoking Homer's formulaic "rosy fingers of the Dawn, in the very path of the Sun's chariot." William Bysshe Stein is even more severe, accusing Thoreau of phoniness. He feels that the vision is spoiled by its language and that the experience sounds false. Stein says, "Instead of responding spiritually to the sight, he affects an aesthetic enthusiasm, even as the trite verbal expression of his emotion implies. . . . The pedantry of a bookworm underscores the insincerity of the rapture."[2]

More damningly from a rhetorical point of view, John Carlos Rowe believes that the Saddleback description emphasized the ITness of reality; the dominant presence "is not the concealed divinity arising to view, but the central 'I' imposing its will on all that it sees."[3] These objections center on Thoreau's language of the Unsaid, where reality is mute, so alien that it cannot speak. Language users must speak for it, filling its silent gaps with words. Thoreau's first book was obviously Transcendental in texture; textually, it was a response to the raw reality he had earlier revealed in "Ktaadn." In *A Week,* he imposes upon the mountain what he wishes the mountain would say. He speaks meaning into nature's blank text. After all, he has posited the importance of *"fronting* IT'" (*Week,* 304), and his Saddleback description puts the best possible front on nature, paints his best face on matter, erects the most effective Transcendental facade.

In sharp contrast, the language of the Un-said presents reality as through an oracle. In Un-said language, a pine tree or mountain or other emblem of reality is characterized as though it could utter volumes of wisdom if only we could make it speak "naturally"—that is, without seeming to force meaning upon it. In the text of the Un-said, sentences are like the antihero who promises much, who suggests profound truths, but who does not deign to speak clearly. This Un-said language remains silent or only whispers. Its principal linguistic forms are riddles, parables, conundrums, absurdities, and contradictions, as in the terse poem, "Between the traveller and the setting sun, / Upon some drifting sand heap of the shore, / A hound stands o'er the carcass of a man" (*Poems,* 206).

In *A Week's* Saddleback account, Thoreau tried not to leave matter Unsaid. He spoke the experience into a mystic vision of the Transcendental sublime. His description is far different from the Ktaadn episode, where the IT of nature is left Unsaid, is sheerly there—alien, empty of meaning, valueless to the writer. Reality is poor material whether for the farmer or for the framer of words. But Thoreau's Un-said must be suggestive. It must entice thought, even as it offers pure description with minimal interpretation. A third mountain ascent is more true to the Unsaid than Saddleback or Ktaadn, an ascent made only in recurring dreams. No matter, Thoreau asserts in his *Journal* for 29 October 1857, for "dreams are real, as is the light of the stars and moon" (10:141). Like the imagination, persistent dreams are "a debatable ground between dreams and waking thoughts." They are like the "imaginary line which separates a hill, mere earth heaped up, from a mountain, into a superterranean grandeur and sublimity."

This *Journal* passage proffers an Un-said text. Thoreau climbs that imaginary line without rhetorically depicting the "mere earth heaped up" of Ktaadn nor the "superterranean grandeur" of Saddleback. In this dreamy ascent made "for the twentieth time at least," he scales "that summit above the earthy line" where the IT of reality is "unhandselled, awful, grand. It can never become familiar; you are lost the moment you set foot there. You know no path, but wander, thrilled, over the bare and pathless rock, as if it were solidified air and cloud. That rocky, misty summit, secreted in the clouds, was far more thrillingly awful and sublime than the crater of a volcano spouting fire" (10:143). This form of language differs as much from Saddleback's forced language and the "spouting fire" of Transcendental orthodoxy as from Edward Hicks's *The Falls of Niagara,* where the stunning tumult makes viewers adore "Time's great God" on bended knee. It is also radically unlike Ktaadn, which provokes barren, emotionless depiction. This dream passage prizes power, delights in being thrilled.

The sentence that summarizes the entry reads, "This is a business we can partly understand." That summary controls the language and prevents it from becoming too spiritually saccharine; the "thrillingly awful and sublime" are domesticated by the word "business," and the power of the dream, the thrill of the imagined experience, derive from the ontological presumption that this is a business that we *can* partly understand because we can never fully understand it. This vision of a "misty summit secreted in the clouds" cannot be made clear without losing rhetorical power. If made wholly manifest, its mists would vanish, and the summit (the idea, the experience, the emotion) would stand stark and—for Thoreau—less provocative. The mystic thrill would degenerate into "made words" of public discourse or the forced feeling of the Said. The rhetoric would then achieve only Hicks's resolution or the nihilism of Ktaadn.

Thoreau prefers a wilder rhetoric, and the description of his dreamed ascent results in a prose description that qualifies as one of Thoreau's most poetic lines, rounding out his *Journal* speculation, almost a pure haiku describing the mountain summit: "A hard-featured god reposing, whose breath hangs about his forehead."[4]

Thoreau's persistent theme is his desire to write in smoky words, to create a rhetoric bathed in mists. As he says in one poem, "We should not mind if on our ear there fell / Some less of cunning, more of oracle" (*Poems*, 84). Yet that misty rhetoric wherein power is always hidden behind clouds, is not without poetic agony—desire's necessary consort. The noblest thoughts and longings can be suggested through an Un-said language; still, the ideal, made powerful and thrilling through its remoteness, also makes it achingly indeterminate. An Un-said language might aim for a rhetoric that "freely breathes" like "unsung poetry," expressing "thoughts conversing with the sky," but the ideals it suggests exist, if anywhere, far off and remote in "a vale which none hath seen, / Where foot of man has never been" (*Poems*, 53). In another poem he explains that beyond words, as beyond the stubble of a harvested field, "There lurks a ripe fruit which the reapers have not gathered" (136). The Unsaid, as the language of Tantalus, promises delicious and refreshing fruit while placing it just beyond the grasp of language. "But man never severs the stalk / Which bears this palpable fruit"—"palpable" from *palpare*, evidently in the sense that it can be brushed by words but never plucked.

Thoreau's wild rhetoric forces linguistic agony. He creates texts that allow readers to "hear beyond the range of sound," to "see beyond the range of sight," to speak beyond the range of language, to point beyond the range of signs. In reaction to this idealistic aim, he laments the limits of language and blames its failings variously on himself or on reality: "The verse is weak and shallow as its source." He wearies of his constant gropings and eternal wariness. His poem "Inspiration" builds to the kind of soaring flight we are accustomed to expect at the climax of Emerson's essays. However, its promises of a "natal hour," the unfolding of "my prime of life," and the full flowering of "manhood's strength" culminate instead in: "'Tis peace's end and war's beginning strife" (*Poems*, 231).

His wild rhetoric is a linguistic agon, a rhetorical struggle, a war between language and meaning. Obviously, Thoreau thought it a battle well worth waging, and he pursued the contest most intensely in the more pliant genres of prose, especially that seemingly freest of all prose genres called the *Journal*. And there we shall pursue him, as he explores the problems of public and private writing, the potentially infinite expressions of the self, the possibilities of nature and experience, his study of language as perception of sense reception, and his almost erotic pleasure in the practice of his literary craft.

2. THE *JOURNAL*

Carl Bode has criticized what he calls "the mistaken belief" that Thoreau's poems were "mere fragments woven into the prose" (*Poems,* viii). Until recently, Thoreau's *Journal* has been treated similarly. Seen as a mine for more polished productions, it has been relegated to the secondary status of the preliminary sketch. Others, however, view the *Journal* as Thoreau's preeminent genre. Privileging the *Journal* over his published pieces, they feel it is closer to the bounty of nature that Thoreau perceived, truer to the protean nature of Thoreau's own thought, and more parallel as a writing experiment to the "sojourneying" quality of life he sought.[1] As one of the most controversial current debates about Thoreau's canon, this disagreement is a useful place to begin exploring the critical problem of the *Journal*. Several minor but interesting questions pertain. One could speculate endlessly on the care Thoreau expended in transcribing his *Journal* notebooks, transposing many of them into account ledgers of uniform size, placing many of those books into a chest he had crafted to fit the volumes exactly. Was this effort expended for himself alone, or does it indicate that he expected a future public to open the chest and discover an American classic in its two million words?

One could also conjecture why he chose accountant ledgers for his notebooks. He complained that they were the only type available, but a man who sent away for special shoestrings made from a South American jackass could surely send to Boston for a different type of notebook (*Life,* 290–91). Even the most fundamental matters, such as his choice of the kind of notebook, seem to mean something, but what? Was his choice meant to image the self as that shrewd, money-conscious Yankee reflected in *Walden*'s lists of expenses, or as the poet who redefines "cost" in terms of life spent?

A more sophisticated problem is the definition of writing itself. When Sharon Cameron asserts that the *Journal* is primary after nature itself, she suggests that the *Journal* is more like nature than are his other works.

Somehow one kind of writing can more closely resemble something outside the realm of writing than it does another kind of writing; somehow a literary genre can transcend the boundaries of literature. In like manner, it is a bold declaration indeed to say that a draft is "better" than its author's final copy, as Sherman Paul does when he daringly proclaims that the conclusion to *Walden*'s 1849 draft is more successful than its published version.[2] As some of Thoreau's most public works, *Walden* and "Resistance" are his most generous negotiations with reader expectations, cultural myths, and publishers' demands, but that fact does not make his less negotiated works "better" or "more successful," "truer" or "more representative." To make that claim would contradict the essential point of the *Journal,* which represents the self in such various dress. None of the ways one dresses—to deliver a formal lecture or to visit close friends or to lounge at home and read a book—is necessarily "more representative" of one's "truer self." Thoreau is still "Thoreau" regardless of whether one imagines him in slouch hat and corduroys or in the frock coat, starched shirt, and bow tie of E. S. Dunshee's 1861 ambrotype, which a close friend said was "one of the most successful likenesses we ever saw."[3]

Thoreau is still "Thoreau," and writing modes are still "Writing." That *Journal* entries, like his verses, have been so intricately interwoven into his books and essays argues the intimate interrelationship of the various types of writing that experts call genres. If some anthologists mislead by singling out a few published works and issuing them under titles like "The Best of Thoreau," they err no more than scholars who segregate his writing performance by calling the *Journal* "Thoreau's principal, if not his greatest work."[4] That a *Journal* passage can slide so smoothly into another text and back again, sometimes seeming the heart of a longer work and sometimes a rough draft, suggests a sense of manifold forms of expression as diverse as the perceptions of reality and the avatars of the self. *A Week on the Concord and Merrimack Rivers* may be wilder and less negotiated than *Walden,* and the *Journal* may seem even less domesticated than *A Week,* but they are all varieties of writing, different manifestations of the same activity. The *Journal* may seem closer to nature than to his other writings, but the difference is an illusion. The *Journal* is first cousin to his books, his essays, his poetry and letters; nature belongs to another family altogether.

Indeed, rendering the judgment that Thoreau's "truest self" appears in the natural, unstructured style of the *Journal* may be a case of cultural determinism. Since America has come to value an independent self expressed in a style that seems original, what seems to be the most private and spontaneous of Thoreau's genres may be his most subtle public achievement. In fact, that is what his manuscript revisions often indicate. In the dreamed mountain ascent discussed in the previous section, he interrupts his analysis just as he reaches its climax to say, "Now I think of it." Later, he would labor over the phrase to make it seem more spontaneous by interpolating, "It chances Now I think of it." And, in the margin, he would, upon reflection, make the passage seem even more impulsive: "Now *first think of it* in this stage of my description—which makes it the more singularly symbolical."

One of the most pleasurable reading experiences is to see identical words vary their brilliance because of their different generic and rhetorical frames. It is like seeing the same magnificent jewel ensconced in different settings, once in a ring, again in a necklace, once more in a box jumbled together with other gems. Such manifestations achieve the state of flux *Walden* prizes—a text that melts, thaws, and flows. It effects the impression of two or more states at once, much as *Walden* is simultaneously a withdrawal from and an attack upon society, much as its "life in the woods" coexists simultaneously with the town and the deep "backwoods" of nature.[5] The fact that certain sentences, even whole paragraphs coexist in different genres at the same time tends to collapse the conventional boundaries between literary genres, subsuming the various typologies into the single, all-encompassing rubric of "Writing." Just as some Transcendentalists concentrated on the spirituality behind any specific religion, Thoreau privileges the sheer activity of writing beyond any of its particular genres. He attempts the illusion of pure writing as opposed to "wrighting"—the manufacture of literary pieces for public consumption.

Thoreau's writings blur genre boundaries, exposing their contrived nature, baring their artificial markers. In the previous section, the central quotation was the haiku-like line from his *Journal:* "A hard-featured god reposing, whose breath hangs about his forehead." Here it is appropriate to mention that the quotation functions as a rhetorical gate. Set up as a single paragraph, it swings the text from a long prose description of his dreamed mountain ascent to an idealized poem about mountain climbing. The reader is compelled to make a rhetorical decision about genre. Should the line be considered prose, a part of the previous *Journal* entry, or a poem less idyllic and less structured than the one that follows? What difference in texture would the identical words have because of the way they are framed or, to use the image in *Walden,* the way they are "yarded"?

Thus, a *Journal* entry transcribed for 1842 (*PJ1,* 414) appears intact as the opening paragraphs of an early essay called "Dark Ages," published in *The Dial* (*EE,* 143). Serious readers face the task of deciding what to do with a book-length text like *Huckleberries.* Edited by Leo Stoller and printed by the prestigious New York Public Library, *Huckleberries* makes scholars feel like the spectator viewing Barnum's "the great whatzit." Should one take *Huckleberries* as a text Thoreau brought all but to completion, as Stoller claims, or should one defer instead to the jumbled notes of the *Journal* that are the basis of Stoller's edition? A similar problem attends Thoreau's "Night and Moonlight." Experts will confide that no reliable text of this fascinating essay exists, but there it stands in all its seeming integrity in the fifth volume of his *Writings.* A remarkable example of interweaving genres is the *Journal* entry after 15 December 1838 on the theme of sound and silence. Its main point is, "All sound is nearly akin to Silence—it is a bubble on her surface which straightway bursts—an emblem of the strength and prolifickness [sic] of the under-current" (*PJ1* 60–64). This five-page entry had to await eleven years and a two-week excursion before surfacing long after his brother's death as the conclusion to *A Week on the Rivers.* To frame a five-page idea adequately required an entire book. The identical sentiments that sound so private, oracular, even secret in the 1838 *Journal* reappear in 1849 to satisfy one of the most public of reading conventions: a concluding summation to round off a book.[6]

As genre seeps into genre, as private expression melds with public concession, so Thoreau's attention devolves onto the primary particles of language. Obviously, he condemns cliché-ridden expression stuffed with received ideas. In his *Journal* for 17 December 1851, he bristles at a too public, overly polite language, especially from those who should know better: "One of the best men I know offends me by uttering made words —the very best words, of course, or dinner speeches, most smooth and gracious and fluent" (3:141). Thoreau's strongest complaint is rhetorical, concerned with the effect of made words upon the audience: "It produces an appearance of phlegm and stupidity in me the auditor. I am suddenly the closest and most phlegmatic of mortals, and the conversation comes to naught." Disgusted by made words, he writes a forceful paean to a wilder rhetoric before the month ends:

> If there is not something mystical in your explanation, something unexplainable to the understanding, some elements of mystery, it is quite insufficient. If there is nothing in it which speaks to my imagination, what boots it? What sort of science is that which enriches the understanding, but robs the imagination? . . . If we knew all things thus mechanically merely, should we know anything really? (3:156)

Still, this mystical rhetoric must be intricately interwoven with established reader expectations. And so, where ellipses appear in the above quotation, Thoreau has inserted a sentence that sets limits to his wilder rhetoric: "Just as inadequate to a pure mechanic would be a poet's account of a steam-engine." In *Walden,* where the artist poetically transmutes the locomotive steam-engine, he also calls himself an employee of the railroad. Similarly, Thoreau produces public texts that might engage a mechanical, literal reader as well as a philosophical or cultural rebel. While seeming to speak urgently "only to you," its text also makes readers feel free to exclaim euphorically that *"Walden* has something for everyone."[7]

A more problematic investigation of language's fundamental elements occurs in his entry for 16 October 1859. Influenced by the Young America movement, which championed all things American and despised all imported manufactures, Thoreau deployed political/economic rhetoric to argue for a distinctively American language. Not content with Noah Webster's halfway measure of spelling "labour" without a "u," he wanted all words to be native born. He asks, "What if there were a tariff on words, on language, for the encouragement of home manufactures? Have we not the genius to coin our own?" It is well that he left these claims interrogatory, for his examples undermine his argument. After stating the noble sentiment that "a more intimate knowledge, a deeper experience, will surely originate a word," his exempla contradict his overt message: "When I really know that our river pursues a serpentine course to the Merrimack, shall I continue to describe it by referring to some other river no older than itself which is like it, and call it a *meander?* It is no more *meandering* than the Meander is *musketaquidding.*"

Still there are those question marks, safely placed, and wisely so. For, should Thoreau's tariff be enacted, he, as a practicing writer, would be left with precious few words, only two in the example he himself cites. Even granting the poet the obvious concessions, the problem still remains of what "native" name to call the river. Should "A Week on the Concord" be changed to "A Week on the Musketaquid"? Should some other name just as indigenous as Musketaquid be chosen? Five years earlier, *Walden* had highlighted the problem when Thoreau researched the etymology of the pond's name only to conclude that its original naming was perhaps whimsical, possibly divine, certainly obscure. Moreover, whether called the "Concord" or the "Musketaquid" or the "Meander" or any other name, the same river would flow, further scuttling his tariff proposal.

Beyond single words, language at large poses the same problems, or so Thoreau implies in entries like the one for 12 July 1840. He might argue a tariff on imported words, he might insist upon a private language that unmakes what he called "made words," but he would also assert that "a word is wiser than any man—than any series of words. In its present received sense it may be false, but in its inner sense by descent and analogy it approves itself. Language is the most perfect work of art in the world. The chisel of a thousand years retouches it." A wealth of rhetorical meaning is encoded in that concluding verb. "Retouches" implies an incidental tampering with the larger scheme of language; it also suggests that a wilder rhetoric can restore touch, can bring readers to a more intimate relationship with a fundamental linguistic experience called "language." A seemingly private rhetoric can return to the original sense of words within their public domain of shared language.

Yet another nuance of the problem: even Thoreau's most private genre of the *Journal* is not very "private," at least not by contemporary standards. Its language is not as private as Poe's poems "Ulalume" and "Eulalie" or his early sketches "Shadow" and "Silence." It is not at all original like the *sui generis* verse experiments of Emily Dickinson. Indeed, Thoreau scathed the idiosyncratic language of friend Ellery Channing's poetry as "sublimo-slipshod," and his criticism reflects his age's more general impatience with the Spasmodic School of writing, as exemplified by William Aytoun's *Firmilian, or the Student of Badajoz,* published the same year as *Walden.*

Despite contradictions, variances, and flashes of warring insight, the journals remain eminently readable. Even in manuscript with loose orthography and frequent abbreviations, his entries parse. If readers puzzle at the lack of controlling structures and the cacophony of ideas, Thoreau tells them how to cope. He carefully guides readers through what seems literary chaos. Thus, on 22 January 1852 he instructs readers that they should approach his entries as "nest eggs." Just as a farmer places an egg to encourage a hen to lay her own, *Journal* ideas are inserted into the textual nest in order to entice further thoughts. Each thought, then, is valuable not so much for itself, not for its own truth or falsehood, value or triviality, but for its pregnancy, its potential to give birth to other thoughts. These further thoughts, of course, lead to other entries. His famous language of a strutting rooster or a crowing chanticleer is most valuable when leading to fertility, when encouraging or announcing the potentiality and promise of intellectual life.

The potentiality of further thought mirrors Thoreau's concept of the self. His *Journal* presents the self as a mine supplying the raw material for an infinity of voices, personas that could be endlessly refined for more publicly negotiated exhibitions. Small wonder, then, that he would figure the narrowing of the infinity of voices into a single persona as a "scalping" or as being "caged in the woods." His *Journal* reveals a modern concept of the self as effervescent, as perpetually virtual, self-contradictory, and self-dissolving.[8] His *Journal* proposes a concept of the self that only a language of desire can approximate, at least for public consumption.

Not only is Thoreau's private language less private than that of contemporaries like Channing, Dickinson, and Poe, but his *Journal* is also traditional, or at least it follows much-respected models. His *Journal* more fully realizes the stylistic characteristics that Thoreau praises in his essays on Carlyle and Raleigh than does his more public prose. Actually, his *Journal* is more like an "essay" in its original sense as an experiment, an assay of ideas, a trying out of form and material. That explains why when reading Thoreau's *Journal* one recalls Emerson's comments on the archskeptic Montaigne, the writer who defined the essay by example. In *Representative Men* (1850), Emerson lauded Montaigne for his "game of thought," for demonstrating "how subtle and illusive the Proteus [of life] is." Montaigne had struck "the right ground of the sceptic,—this of consideration, of self-containing; not at all of unbelief; not at all of universal denying, nor of universal doubting,—doubting even that he doubts."[9]

The atypically fragmented syntax may imply anxiety within his praise for Montaigne's game of thought, a game also played out in Thoreau's *Journal*. Emerson's recourse is to aesthetic taste or, if one prefers, moral mood or religious faith:

A book or statement which goes to show that there is no line, but random and chaos, a calamity out of nothing, a prosperity and no account of it, a hero born from a fool, a fool from a hero,—dispirits us. . . . We love whatever affirms, connects, preserves; and dislike what scatters or pulls down. ("Montaigne," 96)

Emerson's praise and fear of Montaigne could equally apply to Thoreau's language experiment in the random and scattered play of the *Journal.* When Thoreau streamlines his moods in his public works, he will be more affirmative, heroic, and inspiriting along Emersonian lines, as in *Walden,* "Resistance," and "Life without Principle." But he will also streamline the *Journal*'s varieties of the self as less heroic personas. He will present himself as the novice and "army chaplain" of *Maine Woods.* In *Cape Cod,* he will appear almost as personification of the worst that Emerson fears in Montaigne.

When Emerson reveals what he most dreads in Montaigne, he could be anticipating the ultraskeptical mood Thoreau would strike in *Cape Cod:*

All moods may be safely tried, and their weight allowed to all objections; the moral sentiment as easily outweighs them all, as any one. This is the drop which balances the sea. I play with the miscellany of facts, and take those superficial views which we call scepticism; but I know that they will presently appear to me in that order which makes scepticism impossible. ("Montaigne," 96)

In his *Journal,* Thoreau offers no final sentiment that a moral sense or any one sense will outweigh another. His thoughts lead on to thoughts; his assertions beg their contradictions and denials. In *Cape Cod* the ocean drowns the drop. As much as *Walden* will affirm, *Cape Cod* will deny. *Walden* insists there is solid bottom everywhere; *Cape Cod* exposes how many ways one can be deceived. *Walden* promises truth, but *Cape Cod* insinuates that only mirage and illusion prevail.[10]

Thoreau poses serious interpretive problems, especially in his *Journal.* Cameron says that his *Journal* asks readers "to assume a scholar's role" when approaching this "great nineteenth-century American meditation on nature."[11] Right as Cameron is, it is also true that the *Journal* defies scholarly attention. A close reading of a text twice as long as all his other works combined would require at least twenty book-length studies. More importantly, framing the *Journal* thematically might violate its very nature. Attempting to apply a thesis in order to make the *Journal* more public, to domesticate it as a more tractable and coherent whole, risks being procrustean. Such efforts can abridge the *Journal*'s essential nature and its crucial claim that reality, the self, and their various possible expressions are infinite. The *Journal* is as full of thematic holes as it can be made to seem a whole. The circlet of straw around his bundle of two million words can metamorphose into airy wisps and, worse, can provoke readers to girt them with steel bands called theses.

Witness the entry for 19 July 1840 mentioning a two-day hiatus: "These two days that I have not written in my Journal . . . have been really an aeon in which a Syrian empire might rise and fall—How many Persias have been lost and won in the interim—Night is spangled with fresh stars." Was his absence "good," since it makes the night seem "spangled with fresh stars," or "bad," since so much space has been lost to the telling expression of profound thoughts, inimitable insights, and unique perceptions? Regardless of how a reader may decide this question of value, the significance of these words is to say how much remains unsaid. A two-day hiatus from writing can miss an entire aeon, and the obverse is that only a miniscule portion of an aeon can ever be snared by the web of words. This passage and the absent entries it draws attention to signal the ephemeral quality of the enterprise. Even blank pages could speak volumes. Conversely, two million words would also fall short of the mark, would still fail to capture the wealth of life that writing hopes to convey.

How does one discuss the *Journal* in a controlled, orderly, and readable way and still remain true to its ever-fluctuating nature, a wild style of writing that reflects his mercurial, multitudinous selves? One possibility is to highlight ideas that are less starkly encoded in his more famous works, to accent thoughts in the *Journal* that seem contrary to his more famous images. One could then emphasize such "contrarities," trusting Thoreau's icon to correct any overemphasis and to challenge arguments when they appear to be resolved. One can highlight surprising aspects of Thoreau, relying upon more established and more conventional views to disagree; the points then will be in the seams and gaps of this disagreement. As with Thoreau's wild rhetoric, meaning will lie in the differences, the gap between antitheses, the opposition of contrary views. Three such contrarieties are his exploitation of nature, the incidental quality of existence, and the presentation of rhetoric as an erotic gesture that subsumes both nature and experience. In his notes on Raleigh, Thoreau cited Raleigh's three essentials: nature, nurture, and use. In his rhetoric, nature and nurture would be subsumed by the use of literacy.

In his biography, Robert D. Richardson frequently cites Thoreau's statement in the "Bean-Field" chapter of *Walden* that he worked in the field "only for the sake of tropes and expression, to serve a parable-maker one day" (*Life,* 152). It was not only the bean-field that was exploited, but all of nature; all of reality eventually became raw material for his prose, a transformation that not only translated but obliterated the original sources for his creative works. One remarkable passage is the *Journal* entry for 30 April 1839. The previous night he had seen a painting that represented "the plain of Babylon, with only a heap of brick dust in the centre, and an uninterrupted horizon bounding the desert" (*PJ1,* 72). Much as he admired the picture, Thoreau wished the artist would be more daring and take his art one step further: "I would see painted a boundless expanse of desert, prairie, or sea—without other object than the horizon." Thoreau seems to be anticipating J. M. W. Turner's later experiments like "Boats at Sea," anticipating John Ruskin's defense of Turner in *Modern Painters* (1843), even foreshadowing modern conceptions of minimalist art.[12] However, the important point is the articulation of an aesthetic ideal as spoken by an author who would become famous for his love of nature and whose prose would become renowned for its vivid painting of the concrete and the particular. When he describes a sparrow alighting on his shoulder, readers feel that they can almost see it there. But the sharpness of this image, and the sense of harmony between man and nature it symbolizes, is at odds with aesthetic aims as put forth in this passage.

In fact, many *Journal* passages make nature secondary not only to the artist's vision but also to the creation of prose that dissolves both subject and object, leaving the reader to read meaning on the wrinkles of mists and misty words. The sharpest image and the clearest message would be consumed by a smoky rhetoric. Richardson says, "We may well suspect a sense of fun that revels in the mischievous when he says, 'the soldier is the practical idealist—he has no sympathy with matter, he revels in the annihilation of it' " (*Life,* 70). I say that we may well suspect also that Thoreau is quite serious. Ultimately his love for reality, that joy of living in the nick of time, results in total abolition, a rhetoric that transcends both optimism and nihilism, culminating in a sheer state of being thrilled. This rather mystical point is illustrated by Thoreau's descriptions of a tanager. When surprised by one at Loring's Woods, he records how he was transported and how Concord woods seemed transformed into a magical place: "That contrast of a *red* bird with the green pines and the blue sky! Even when I have heard his note and look for him and find the bloody fellow, sitting on a dead twig of pine, I am always startled. . . . That incredible red, with the green and the blue, as if these were the trinity we wanted" (*J* [23 May 1853], 5:187). To call bird, pines, and sky a "trinity" seems strong praise indeed, even if the trinity of nature is abstracted into colors, not living objects. The joy Thoreau felt is clearly conveyed, even though he includes those disruptive, qualifying details about the dead twig and the murderous or profane characterization of the bird as "the bloody fellow." Still, the expression of joy is explicit; Thoreau's love for concrete particulars is surely relayed.

However, the pure expression does not last through the paragraph. The qualifier that red, green, and blue are *"as if"* a trinity is quickly pursued. The red-bird is reduced to a subsidiary function; he is made servant to another rhetorical effect. Natural objects merely enhance a wilder rhetorical aim: "How he enhances the wildness and wealth of the woods! This and the emperor moth make the tropical phenomena of our zone. There is warmth in the pewee's strain, but this bird's colors and his note tell of Brazil." Thoreau may delight in pewees, loons, chipping-squirrels, and sparrows, but he privileges the tanager and emperor moth over them, and above them he privileges notes telling of Brazil, a land he never saw, would never see. And beyond Brazil? Only a wild rhetoric can tell. Thus, Thoreau returns to his red bird exactly a year later, saying,

> The red-bird which I saw on my companion's string on election days I thought but the outmost sentinel of the wild, immortal camp,—of the wild and dazzling infantry of the wilderness,—that the deeper woods abounded with redder birds still; but, now that I have threaded all our woods and waded the swamps, I have never yet met with his compeer, still less his wilder kindred.

Thoreau reinforces the point forcefully: "We soon get through with Nature. She excites an expectation which she cannot satisfy. The merest child which has rambled into a copsewood dreams of a wilderness so wild and strange and inexhaustible as Nature can never show him" (*J* [23 May 1854], 6:293–94).

Perhaps a wild rhetoric also excites an expectation that it cannot satisfy, but Thoreau believed that writing stood a better chance, possibly the only chance, of accomplishing his supreme aim. His outburst against nature was precipitated by a trip to the White Mountains, which turned out to be "smooth molehills to my expectation. We *condescend* to climb the crags of earth. It is our weary legs alone that praise them." When we choose experience over writing, when we prefer life to the expression of life, we condescend. Perhaps these sentiments result from postpartum depression following *Walden*'s birth. That is a clean way to dispose of the entry, but if true, then a more severe depression came more than five years after *Walden* was published. In his *Journal* for 26 August 1859, Thoreau wrote,

> The boy does not camp in his father's yard. That would not be adventurous enough, there are too many sights and sounds to disturb the illusion; so he marches off twenty or thirty miles and there pitches his tent, where stranger inhabitants are tamely sleeping in their beds just like his father at home, and camps in *their* yard perchance. But then he dreams uninterruptedly that he is anywhere but where he is.

Even Thoreau's arch-critics would not demean the Walden experiment so severely nor point out that Walden cabin was less than a mile from Concord, much less twenty or thirty miles. Not even Lowell would cavil that Thoreau camped out in his literary father's back lot.

Considering such expressed condescension towards nature, one can understand John Burroughs's puzzlement that Thoreau should be bruited as a naturalist. During the period of his iconization in the 1890s (which was also the era when America was establishing what Thoreau would enjoy as a supreme American oxymoron, the posted national park or "designated natural wilderness area"), Burroughs was baffled why Thoreau should be idolized as a close observer of nature when he sees "what all, even a schoolboy sees."[13] Burroughs could not fathom why Thoreau would be esteemed as a nature lover over William Bartram, Thomas Jefferson, or Benjamin Franklin. Finally, Burroughs concluded that it must be because Thoreau was that peculiar thing called an American writer, and his layman's criticism strikes to the heart of the rhetorical matter; Burroughs cites the fact that Thoreau's *Journal* descriptions force feeling instead of being led by it: "He makes such a determined set at things, he turns them and wrenches and squeezes them, and tries to kindle his fancy by them and will not let them go till they have yielded him a drop or two of the precious elixir, he so thirsted for, but they do not always yield it." Burroughs means this criticism as complaint, but he has unwittingly touched upon Thoreau's rhetorical essence. He has caught the sense of "thirst"; he has intuited the language of desire. Harrison Blake prized the rhetorical effect that Thoreau's letters seem perpetually "in the mail," while Burroughs thought it was a stylistic fault, but he has sensed the same rhetorical force that Blake appreciated.

Burroughs, the lover of an objective nature, might well marvel at a Thoreau whose words seemed to supplant and to subsume nature. In an apposite *Journal* passage of 2 September 1851, Thoreau says: "A writer, a man writing, is the scribe of all nature; he is the corn and the grass and the atmosphere writing. It is always essential that we love to do what we are doing, do it with a heart." What he was doing more than anything else was writing. At its most satisfying, writing was not a mirror of society in the realistic tradition of Stendahl and Balzac, nor was it a mirror of the self. In the 1950s, it was fashionable to publish books with titles like "The Heart of Thoreau's Journals," and Thoreau would approve the pun. Writing was done with a heart, not a mirror. It was an act of love, and the words it produced were, like one's offspring, at once related to yet separate from their parent, having a life of their own, many lives of their own.

The Princeton Edition shows no commas in "A writer, a man writing," suggesting a departure from Emerson, who distinguished between the farmer and the man on the farm, the thinker and Man Thinking. This idea is reinforced when the writer, at first depicted as merely a scribe, rises to become the very corn and grass writing. Indeed, the writer expands to become even "the atmosphere writing," a rhetorical depiction much more abstract than that referring to specifics such as corn and grass. Readers are made to wonder whether the more operative word is "atmosphere" or "writing," the author as circumambiant air or the even more indeterminate process of writing. One wonders if the individual is writing for the public, or if public language is writing through the individual.

One of *Walden*'s most troublesome sentences says that "Nature is hard to overcome, but she must be overcome." The statement is particularly disconcerting since it follows such loving depictions of relationships with nature, relationships all the more welcome since nature's antithesis, society, has been discarded as foul, contaminating, and impure. But Thoreau's hope was that his wild rhetoric transcended nature by replicating its style. Thus readers encounter frequent passages wherein nature is lauded only to be overcome by language. In one example, Thoreau says he thrills to nature because of its unending, multitextual possibilities. Thus, he marvels at the seeds of the rhexia on 28 March 1859; like his wild language, they promise effuse succession and entice "the wild goose and countless wild ducks," possible emblems for wilder readers, who have "floated and dived above them."

In brief, he figures nature's style as a wild text given to many interpretations: "So Nature condenses her matter. She is a thousand thick. So many crops the same surface bears" (*J*, 12:98–99). Similarly, when Thoreau describes that epochal moment in his life when he chose to dedicate himself to prose, he employs parallel imagery, saying that "it is harder to write great prose than to write verse" because, as he told Emerson, "In writing conversation should be folded many times thick," requiring at least three readings before the beauty of its prose could be approached, three readings before the meaning of its characters could begin to be suggested (*Corr*, 125). Of course, the rhetorical question is that if a line of text must be read at least three times before meaning begins to emerge, then what is the source of that meaning—the author, the text, or the reader? Thoreau's references to this multifolded style occur most frequently in his *Journal* for 1851 during that two-year respite he took from *Walden*'s revisions. Apparently, he was working through his rhetorical theory and clarifying his smoky, misty language before returning to the last four drafts of his *Walden* project.

In his review "Thomas Carlyle and His Works," Thoreau reiterated his commitment to a many-folded rhetoric, claiming that Carlyle's multitextual prose was superior to explicit and coherent language. He compares Carlyle's style to "the froth of wine, which can only be tasted once and hastily. On a review [a rereading] we can never find the pages we had read. The first impression is the truest and the deepest, and there is no reprint, no *double entendre,* so to speak for the alert reader. Yet they are in some degree true natural products in this respect. All things are but once, and never repeated" (*EE,* 241). In his *Journal* for 20 May 1851, Thoreau worries that most minds are like parasitic plants that feed off other organisms. "There are minds which so have their roots in other minds as in the womb of nature,—if, indeed, most are not such?!" But he also believes that in order to grow, a mind must develop "from the first in two opposite directions" (*J*, 2:205, 203). To encourage that growth, writers should produce multifolded texts wherein "there are two sides to every sentence." As he said at the outset of his career in 1841, "When I utter a thought I launch a vessel which never sails in my haven more, but goes sheer off into the deep" (*PJ1,* 220).

In the well-known anecdote about his night in jail, Emerson is made to ask, "What are you doing in there, Henry?" Thoreau purportedly replies, "What are you doing out there, Waldo?" That the anecdote is apocryphal is all the better, for it demonstrates the interpretive quality of his prose. Readers may argue about whether his "history of 'My Prisons' " in "Resistance" is a noble deed or a paltry gesture, and some have felt free to create an anecdote out of thin air. Reading Thoreau is essentially metaphorical. Apocryphally, Thoreau gazes out at Emerson; metaphorically, readers gaze in toward Thoreau. One can take the prison anecdote even further metaphorically. Thoreau stands in the prison-house of the self, gazing through a window out at reality, wondering what it is doing out there. Reality is framed by the spectator's view through the window, and its glass shows a distant, external reality, upon which is superimposed the reflected vision of the observer's self. On the surface of the glass can be seen both the writer's and his readers' reflected images. The more scholarship we read, the more readerly images are imposed on the glass. We see Thoreau in the prison-house of language; we say what he says.

Thoreau's awareness of the prison-house came early. By 7 December 1838, he was writing, "We may believe it, but never do we live a quite free life, such as Adam's, but are enveloped in an invisible network of speculations—Our progress is only from one such speculation to another, and only at rare intervals do we perceive that it is no progress" (*PJ1*, 58). The choice is between, on one hand, silent wonder, or, on the other, a nexus of inference and reference, interpretation and translation. Twenty years later, on 31 March 1859, Thoreau made another remarkable statement about apperception. Stoking a fire in the kitchen stove one morning, he thought he saw a piece of

red or scarlet flannel on a chink near a bolt-head on the stove, and I tried to pick it out,—while I was a little surprised that I did not smell it burning. It was merely the reflection of the flame of the fire through a chink, on the dark stove. This showed me what the true color of the flame was, but when I knew what this was, it was not very easy to perceive it again.

Remarkable as this anecdote is for psychological and philosophical reasons, the next sentence is virtually stunning: "I think that my senses made the truest report the first time" (*J*, 12:102). As he put the matter succinctly on 5 August 1851, "The question is not what you look at, but what you see" (*J*, 2:373).

All reality (nature, people, manufactured things, the various socialized selves) is subsumed into perception, and the only perception of perception is through language. Thus, in a paean to nature, Thoreau's greatest praise is that walking through the woods and over the fields fills us with such "expansion of being" that we are made eager to return to books again. In his exaltation of humble huckleberries, he confides that a good book on the berry "should be the ultimate fruit of the huckleberry field."[14] In his *Journal,* he contends that "the fruit of a tree is neither in the seed nor the timber,—the full-grown tree,—but it is simply the highest use to which it can be put," and that highest use appears to be literacy, a reading experience that "only the genius of the poet can pluck." Punning like Whitman, Thoreau writes, "The ripeness of a leaf, being perfected, leaves the tree at that point and never returns to it" (*J,* 12:24). The page, when perfected, becomes the public domain of readers.

As with nature, so with people and personal experience. When young, he wrote the couplet, "My life has been the poem I would have writ, / But I could not both live and utter it." But after he had lived more life and had developed a greater commitment to utterance, he composed a different couplet, at one point intending it as *Walden*'s epigraph: "Where I have been / There was none seen."[15] The couplet may be considered as criticism of how social relationships interfere with true communication between individuals, but it also suggests that communication succeeds only in language, never in experience. Where he has been, he saw no one really, and none saw him. In a *Journal* entry written about the same time as the couplet, it appears that someone had berated him for being antisocial and that Thoreau felt guilty about the accusation. He defends himself by claiming that he might sometimes prefer human contact to language, but the latter proves to be far less disappointing. Accused of being more committed to writing than to friendship and of being cold toward others (even though at the time he was helping to clothe Concord's poor), Thoreau responded: "It is not words that I wish to hear or to utter, but relations that I seek to stand in; and it oftener happens, methinks, that I go away unmet, unrecognized, ungreeted in my offered relation, than that you are disappointed of words. . . . I am disappointed of relations, you of words" (*J* [21 December 1851], 3:148–49).

Through language, Thoreau hoped he could effect those relations with friends, nature, and life. Through writing, nature could be imagined as a personal relationship, a human connection, a rapport, not sheerly an IT. As he says on 30 June 1852:

Nature must be viewed humanly to be viewed at all; that is, her scenes must be associated with humane affections, such as are associated with one's native place, for instance. She is most significant to a lover. A lover of Nature is pre-eminently a lover of man. If I have no friend, what is Nature to me? She ceases to be morally significant. (*J,* 4:163)

But Thoreau's keenest friendship was imagined in the activity of writing / reading. In *A Week,* he had said that it takes two to speak the truth, but ten years later he put the matter more concretely—and more erotically. Exploiting the locution that interfused writing, speaking, and reading— that called both a lecturer and his text "a reader"—Thoreau proclaimed on 3 March 1859:

> Talk about reading!—a good reader! It depends on how he is heard. There may be elocution and pronunciation (recitation, say) to satiety, but there can be no good reading unless there is good hearing also. It takes two at least for this game, as for love, and they must co-operate. (*J,* 12:9)

In both passages, one casting nature as a human relationship and the other discussing relations between individuals in the reading process, emphasis is put on love and on being a lover. On occasion, this emphasis would be cast so erotically as to characterize writing as a sexual activity. In the *Journal* for 4 August 1841, for example, Thoreau confides, "My pen is a lever which in proportion as the near end stirs me further within —the further end reaches to a greater depth in the reader" (*PJ1,* 315).

Throughout Thoreau's *Journal* he reminds readers of the erotic engagement of writing. Even a casual reader notices how frequently he offers up his body as a metaphor for his prose, much like Jesus telling his disciples to eat of His bread and to drink of His wine for they are also His body, His flesh, and His blood. Thoreau can thrill over the sheer act of writing, regardless of what he has written, as when he is ecstatic over the autoerotic pleasure of writing in moonlight, one elbow cocked upon a fencepost, his other hand moving his pen through the "creamy, mystic medium" of the blank, soft-white page bathed in the luminosity of the moon's reflected glow (*J,* 5:278). Whether such eroticism is hermaphroditic, as Cameron says, or essentially narcissistic, as Miller claims, I leave to others to decide.[16] With my orientation to language, discourse, and rhetoric, these passages reveal the tribute Thoreau paid to words, equating the enciphering of a single word with sexual excitement. The body of a text is as precious as one's own body; in fact, more precious considering the fate of one's physical body, which is to cause one more depression in the earth like those hollows marking the existence of Walden's previous residents in "Former Inhabitants; and Winter Visitors." And so, one frequently hears Thoreau exclaiming how the writer sends "a tap-root to the centre of things," and how he "penetrates yet deeper by his roots into the womb of things." And so, one hears Thoreau insisting that thinking and writing are "wombed and rooted in darkness, a moist and fertile darkness,—its roots in Hades like the tree of life" (*J,* 2:204).

Such erotic effusions make one doubt whether his representations of frustration are really such. They may actually be the seed bed for euphoria or nest eggs of ideas he would later develop. I refer to the period of late 1850 when he was entering sentiments such as, "I would write of the things I love." A well-known entry says, "I feel ripe for something, yet do nothing, can't discover what that thing is. I feel fertile merely" (*J,* 2:101; 16 November 1850). Again, on 31 October 1850, he would say, "What is this beauty in the landscape but a certain fertility in me? . . . I see somewhat fairer than I enjoy or possess" (*J,* 2:77). By the next year, Thoreau came to believe that fertility was sufficient. He imagined writing to be full compensation for those disappointing relations in life—whether in society or in nature. He could not "discover what that thing is," but he could polish a closer approximation in his language, a linguistic approximation that was paradoxically truer than what a Henry James character calls "the real thing" itself. By 1851, he would present language as an urgent if not desperate enterprise. Like a minister cajoling sinners on their deathbeds to repent, he would urge: "Improve every opportunity to express yourself in writing, as if it were your last" (*J,* 3:140).

In 1843, he had told Richard Fuller that the most he had learned in college was how to express himself, but shortly after graduation he had determined that expression was more valuable than the self. In 1840, he had written in the privacy of his *Journal* that "a word is wiser than any man" and that "language is the most perfect work of art in the world" (*PJ1,* 160). In 1853 he went on public record, reiterating much the same point, asserting in *A Yankee in Canada* that "I want nothing better than a good word. The name of a thing may easily be more than the thing itself to me" (*Writings,* 5:20). By All Soul's Day, 1857, he had refined his definition of "a good word," saying, "A higher truth, though only hinted at, thrills us more than a lower expressed" (*J,* 10:153). Considering his theories about the power of a wild rhetoric, he might also have written,

"A higher truth, *because* only hinted at, thrills us more than one explicitly expressed."

Of the two million words of Thoreau's *Journal,* the following quotation offers a clear representation of his manifold utterances on language as distilled through his various selves. On 12 February 1851, when about to plunge into the last series of *Walden*'s drafts, Thoreau wrote:

> We have a waterfall which corresponds even to Niagara somewhere within us. It is astonishing what a rush and tumult a slight inclination will produce in a swollen brook. How it proclaims its glee, its boisterousness, rushing headlong in its prodigal course as if it would exhaust itself in half an hour! How it spends itself!

A Freudian might be more interested in the quotation's libidinal suggestions, and a cultural historian may be more intrigued by Thoreau's Whitman-like insistence on letting nature flow freely, but a rhetorician is most fascinated by how the author converts the external reality of nature as symbolized by Niagara Falls into the human network of language.

Unlike Edward Hicks, who rapidly transformed "the stunning tumult of Niagara" into orthodox worship through many massive framings, and unlike Whitman, who advises that we tear the doors from their jambs and the jambs from their hinges, Thoreau dovetails the stunning outpour of natural and spiritual drives into language. As soon as Thoreau imagines a miraculous natural phenomenon, he finds a "correspondence" in our human nature. As soon as he posits an exemplum of natural freedom verging on chaos, he converts it not only into discourse, but into the most controlled and public forms of discourse, as in oratory and poetry. The rest of his quotation reads: "I would say to the orator and poet, Flow freely and *lavishly* as a brook that is full,—without stint." Then he muses in delight, "Perchance I have stumbled upon the origin of the word 'lavish' " (*J,* 2:155–56). In this passage, the student of rhetoric would be most fascinated not by its sexuality and certainly not by its apparent resolution of a complex phenomenon. Its most intriguing dimension is the complexity of the problem it presents, made even more complex because of its apparent resolution.

Thoreau instantly transforms an observation about nature into an inquiry about language, even to the extent that—more than reality, more than nature, more than the self—Thoreau, as a student of rhetoric, has approximated, has come "next to," has come close to, has caught a hint of the original meaning of a single word. More than most, more than language perhaps allows, Thoreau has penetrated to the core of rhetoric's primary thrill, its penultimate "meaning," an experience made all the more intense because of language's ultimate limitations, its final walls, its insurmountable barriers to communication. In a career that produced over three million published words (only a hundredth of the words he wrote, Thoreau said), in a life that sought to be free and independent and to "travel much" wherever he might be, in an ecstasy of spiritual and libidinal impulses as powerful as Niagara Falls, the supreme thrill was the contemplation of a single word. So Thoreau confides, though prefacing his proclamation with "Perchance."

In his *Journal,* Thoreau could freely experiment with such rhetorical notions, governed by no other rule than that someday others would read them. The diversity of selves, thoughts, moods, and opinions that the *Journal* could italicize instantly becomes more regulated in the correspondence Thoreau exchanged with many individuals over more than twenty years. To go from the *Journal* to his correspondence is to enter a completely different rhetorical situation. Because of the specificity of his audience, the writer is less free to experiment with any idea or expression that happens to strike his fancy. Not an abstract future reader, nor a broad New England audience, nor an adversarial lecture audience, nor an anonymous book buyer, the explicit "co-respondent" forces Thoreau to dress (and to address) his thoughts accordingly. The self of Thoreau as tailored to suit these discrete others appears as particularly as any public performance can demand. Once brought from the privacy of his *Journal,* the most private of his language experiments, and lit by the glare of his letters, myriad exposures of Thoreau's self appear.

3. CORRESPONDENCE

On 11 November 1851, Thoreau said, " 'Says I to myself' should be the motto of my journal."[1] He also said that one of the principal advantages of journal writing was that "to-day you may write a chapter on the advantages of travelling, and to-morrow you may write another chapter on the advantages of not travelling." Not only "may" but "ought." To give the impression that the *Journal* is the most private of genres, its author should seem to be talking to himself, and its topics should have as many aspects as radii can be drawn from one center. When letters are exchanged, however, the communication model changes. The "I" speaks to an identifiable other, and topics are comparatively unified and coherent. Thoreau's letters are more a literary performance, like his formal pieces, and they seek to establish a true "correspondence." Each letter, as correspondence with a specified individual, negotiates Thoreau's private thoughts and personal expression with the recipient's interests, sympathies, and sensitivities. He valued this "correspondence": "An echo makes me enunciate distinctly—So the sympathy of a friend gives plainness and point to my speech. This is the advantage of letter writing" (*PJ1, 211*).

As he expressed the idea more poetically to Harrison Blake, "It is so long since I have seen you, that as you will perceive, I have to speak as it were *in vacuum,* as if I were sounding hollowly for an echo, and it did not make much odds what kind of a sound I made." He assures Blake that "we learn from the echo; and I know that the nature toward which I launch these sounds is so rich that it will modulate anew and wonderfully improve my rudest strain."[2] Thus, his voice is made to correspond with a specific other, unlike the *Journal*'s spontaneous "says I to myself" quality and also unlike the anonymous "others" who might peruse his essays.

Thoreau's correspondence can be studied for this modulated voice, a study that would prove useful in examining the negotiated voices in his published prose, or his letters can be scanned for information interesting in itself. Although I emphasize the former method, the latter can produce a wealth of interesting material. One can discover how he complained that he was forced into "serving Mammon" at the same time that he was lecturing on the evil of serving Mammon in "Life Without Principle." He would admit that frittering one's life away with detail was a fate he could not always escape (357, 559). Conversely, one admires his persistent rebuff of Horace Greeley's requests for essays on Emerson, Hawthorne, Alcott, and others, even after Greeley had doubled his offer to a guaranteed fifty dollars per article—a resistance made all the more remarkable by the fact that Thoreau was still in debt from his first book and that *Walden* netted only $51.60 in its first year (174, 229, 279, 360). One can also trace his evolution into an established writer. Rufus Griswold had rejected his poetry for *The Poets and Poetry of America* in 1841 (54), and Margaret Fuller had said that she could "not read [his "The Service"] through without *pain*" (42). He had told his mother in 1843 that he could not interest publishers, that "my bait will not tempt the rats; they are too well fed" (141). But by 1848, he had gained the respect of a small following. Six years before *Walden*'s publication, his letters about the

Walden experiment were invoked as "the magnificent weapon" against intellectual loafing (224, 228). Horace Greeley was printing extracts of his letters in the *New York Tribune* and quoting him in his lectures (324, 328, 336). Louis Agassiz was intrigued by *Walden* when it was still in draft form (244). Charles Scribner wanted his biographical sketch for his *Cyclopaedia of American Literature* (327), and aspiring young writers were asking his advice on literary themes and stylistics.[3]

One can find the usual "Thoreau" in his letters, the writer besotted with puns who whimsically wondered whether a person fond of buds qualified as a Buddhist, who could shamelessly wrench "onion" to pun on "union," "desert" on "dessert" (9, 83, 139, 299). The poet of haiku-like verse could in a letter admirably capture the personality of a close friend in a one-sentence prose paragraph: "Channing dropped in on us the other day, but soon dropped out again" (431). The oxymoronic "Thoreau" also appears, a writer who could be warm, kind, and encouraging in one letter, in another so severe that he would make a correspondent feel humiliated for having written (415). Likewise, one friend might berate Thoreau for being overly social, while another would strongly advise him that he desperately needed to socialize more (537). His letters can also set dates for his development in other genres, can clarify that by 15 February 1843 he had "given off writing poetry" and that by 21 May 1848 he had made up his mind that "lecturing is of little consequence" (88, 227).

Unfamiliar views of "Thoreau" also appear, the kind of revelations that a more conventional reader would describe as "uncharacteristic of Thoreau." The man noted for praising the flute as his favorite musical instrument participated in his era's craze for mechanical music boxes; evidently, entrusting a music box with a friend, as Thoreau did with Hawthorne, was a special sign of friendship (76). The ethnographer famed for his sympathetic studies of Indians never lost the tendency to group them all as "Indians," even when he encountered distinctly different tribes in Minnesota (621).[4] One of the most remarkable of these unusual views was his reaction to the fate of the man who had bought his Walden cabin. Hugh Whelan, Emerson's gardener, was a drunk who habitually quarreled with his wife, possibly over his philandering, and who, Emerson reported, had simply run off one day. Rather than reviling this shiftless heir to his cabin as a ne'er-do-well and a wastrel, Thoreau instead responded with profound sympathy. Whelan's problem he told Emerson, was that life was too dull: "Life is not tragic enough for him, and he must try to cook up a more highly seasoned dish for himself." Empathizing with all such "soldiers" who find life too humdrum and boring, Thoreau thinks it would be a service if towns, along with maintaining gun rooms, barrooms, reading rooms, and other rooms to alleviate life's monotony, should keep "a steep precipice whereoff impatient soldiers may jump" (203–5). Jumping off cliffs may not be as desirable as marching to ethereal music, but Thoreau treats this pathetic figure much more sympathetically than he handles, say, John Field more publicly in *Walden*.

However, my approach to Thoreau's correspondence centers on his modulated voices: the crucial elements of the self, writing, and reading that configure his rhetoric. The previous section on the *Journal* discussed how nature became subsumed by Thoreau's fascination with language; a parallel event is articulated in his letters on the self. He writes to Calvin Greene, a correspondent from what were then the wilds of Ann Arbor, Michigan:

> You may rely on it that you have the best of m in my books, and that I am not worth seeing personally—the stuttering, blundering, clod-hopper that I am. Even poetry, you know, is in one sense an infinite brag and exaggeration. Not that I do not stand on all that I have written—but what am I to the truth I feebly utter? (407)

The self is inferior to its expression, and "an infinite brag and exaggeration" is a prerequisite of any approximately true expression of a disappointing natural/cultural self. And so Thoreau later tells Greene that he is impatient with their exchange of letters and urges him to try a truer medium of self-expression. "Can't you tell the world of *your* life also? Then I shall know you, at least as well as you me" (485).

This reverence for literary expression was an early conviction. The point of the Walden experiment was, he says in one letter, to allow him "more leisure for literary pursuits than any contemporary" (224). As early as January 1840, in a letter to his sister Helen written in Latin and signed "H. D. Thoreaus," perhaps already generating the idea of the various forms his selfhood could take, Thoreau insisted bluntly that "an honest book's the noblest work of Man. ... It will do the world no good, hereafter, if you merely exist, and pass life smoothly or roughly; but to have thoughts, and write them down, that helps greatly" (38). Fifteen years later, after he was already an established writer, Thoreau would exclaim his pleasure over receiving new books, saying without an ounce of irony that to get new books made him as joyful "as I might [be at] the birth of a child" (397).

Thoreau best appreciated a certain kind of book that exhibited a wild rhetoric, one that encouraged its readers to interpolate, to interpret, and to translate as much as to study and to decode. He preferred the kind of writing that replicated the spaces and silences of nature while reflecting the multitudinous variety of its author's various selves. I believe that one reason Thoreau rebuffed the friendship urged by Daniel Ricketson was because he missed the essential wildness of *Walden*'s rhetoric. Ricketson tried to solidify the language of liquidation, to clarify thoughts that Thoreau believed must be left obscure, and to typecast *Walden*'s author. He called Thoreau a "feelosopher" (302), as though he belonged to the "spasmodic school of poetry" or wrote "sublimo-slipshod" verse like Ellery Channing's. Ricketson made his rhetoric seem easy to decode and spontaneous in composition. But it was not a poetic wildness and spontaneity that Thoreau privileged, nor a rule-bound set of compositional strictures, nor an emphasis on a strictly private language, nor a kow-towing to demands of the literary market place. Rather, in *Walden* it was the wrestling match between extremes that he valued: a rhetoric always on the verge of running wild, a wildness perpetually threatened with domestication.

And so this aspiration influenced Thoreau long before he gained sufficient mastery over language to articulate his desire. Even in the early phase of his career, when he was fond of calling himself a poet, conjuring myriad expectations of what the productions of a poet should be like, he proffers himself as a "creedless poet" (53). After he had become established as a noteworthy writer in his own right, he advised younger writers to strive for an equal oxymoron of wildness and rule. He critiqued a young writer named Wilson Flagg as being "a serious person" but qualifies,

He is not alert enough [to be a fine writer]. He wants stirring up with a pole. He should practice turning a series of somersets rapidly, or jump up and see how many times he can strike his feet together before coming down. Let him make the earth turn round now the other way—and whet his wits on it, whichever way it goes, as on a grindstone;—in short, see how many ideas he can entertain at once. (489)

Yet, one should not run too hastily to claim Thoreau as a postmodernist critic. His advice about stylistic acrobatics, jumps, and turnings is still anchored to his image of the grindstone, emphasizing the impression of hard work, not pleasure and play. Most of all, his recommendation of a stylistic acrobatics is predicated on the fundamental qualification that the writer seems "a serious person." Still very much part of the discourse of his age, he presumes that a person who wishes to become a great author will be serious, earnest, and sincere. Responding to aspiring writers, he might issue invitations to a dance or to a somersault contest, but he expects them to come dressed as ministers, reformers, or truth-seekers.

The root of this paradoxical rhetoric lay in what I referred to earlier as "likeness" in the political and religious language of Thoreau's times. Certainly "likeness" is an oft-recurring theme in many of Thoreau's most personal letters. When Lucy Brown (for whom Thoreau wrote "Sic Vita") innocently inquired whether he might feel the natural longing to see his deceased brother again, he brusquely replied, "I do not wish to see John ever again—I mean him who is dead—but that other whom only he would have wished to see, or to be, of whom he was the imperfect representative. For we are not what we are, nor do we treat or esteem each other for such, but for what we are capable of doing" (62). The troubled syntax of Thoreau's quotation speaks as provocatively as do the words, and it can be studied in various ways. Thoreau's brief response is further evidence of his belief that meaning could be "folded many times thick." Language is used to dissolve its own explicit meaning; the stumbling rhythms betray an intense grief that belies the acceptance of death that the surface meaning of the words seems to intend. Language also functions as an act of vampirish love, as a "more perfect representative" than the real. Even the death of the one person Thoreau evidently loved most can be turned into a literary performance. Even a query that invites Thoreau to assuage his grief through a ritualistic, formulaic response is taken as an opportunity to demonstrate his originality of thought and expression.

Language also establishes a trauma that will be worked out therapeutically in words, resulting in frequent descriptions of death and decay, a mucking about in the mud and mold of earth as though it were a thawing grave. John's death would further become an encoded image of Thoreau's pleasure with failure, his rejoicing that idealistic communes like Brook Farm and Fruitlands collapse, that ninety-six out of every hundred businesses fail (497), that America itself, emblem writ large of his beloved and admired elder brother, had proved unable to fulfill its promise. Language can also be a mask. The shocking response that he prefers not to see John again may be a blind behind which crouch intense sorrow, disappointment, and guilt. Perhaps it is this nexus of emotions that lurks behind the curious interruption in *Walden*'s second chapter, which asks, after imploring the half-dead of desperate men to waken, "I have never yet met a man who was quite awake. How could I have looked him in the face?"

His language in the letter to Lucy Brown can also be seen as developing a rhetoric of desire, a rhetoric that depends on "likeness" and remoteness of meaning, a language that is essentially metaphorical. He will not supply Lucy Brown with an explicit response, for to do so would be to produce "made words"; the meaning, because settled, would be dead as a corpse. He must fashion a reply whose words are as distant from conveying a single, settled emotion as John's real self was from his promise. In being distanced from explicit meaning, those words are, ironically, closer to a true meaning. Or so he wished to believe. By imaging an abstract loss in opaque symbols of desire such as his hound, bay-horse, and turtle-dove, he could achieve the rhetorical effect of enticing readers into being as desirous to recover them "as though they had lost them themselves." Thoreau did not answer Lucy Brown's inquiry in his letter; a true treatment of the problem she unwittingly posed required an entire book. Thus, in what he considered his most original published work, he would interweave an intricate pattern of elegiac descriptions of his brother. The elegiac pattern would seem so distanced from the book's obvious, explicit story of the excursion he and his brother made on the Concord and Merrimack Rivers that it would take more than a century for a reader to detect the pattern and expose its code.[5]

It is not quite accurate to say that "John" is encoded in *A Week on the Rivers*. Rather, it is Thoreau's remembrance of John that even an entire book can represent only partially. In fact, one wonders how much Thoreau was describing John's death in his letter to Lucy Brown, and how much he was describing his own, eternally remote selfhood. This possibility is particularly convincing considering that a little more than a year after the letter to Lucy, he wrote to Emerson's wife in almost identical words without the syntactical struggle: "I, perhaps, am more willing to deceive by appearances than you say you are; it would not be worth the while to tell how willing. . . . My actual life is unspeakably mean, compared with what I know and see that it might be" (120). He further informs Lidian that the ground from which he makes these observations on the self "ranges from heaven to earth and is all things in an hour." All things in an hour, and every hour something else.

He had told Richard Fuller that what he "was learning in college was chiefly, I think, to express myself" (95). More than nature, more than reform, more than any explicit topic, Thoreau's main aesthetic concern was self-expression. And yet that self constantly eluded expression. When after long, hard effort, a "crystal of Self"—as Thoreau named it (422)—was successfully portrayed, it immediately shifted into another avatar. Personally, Thoreau might be joyed one day at this excess of selves, and frustrated by it the next. He might exult one time that the self, like nature, was an unlimited bounty as endless and ever-changing as the sea, and the next time he might be discouraged that the self is never settled, that it always remains "a bundle of vain strivings." He might posit the self as transcendent of time and the world, but he would also admit he was well aware that "I am the world I condemn" (299). He might tell one correspondent that he had "the best of me in my books," but he would reveal to another aspiring writer that he had published only a hundredth of the words he had written (572). In the *Walden* chapter ironically called "Solitude," he would simplify the matter of various selves by streamlining it to two, while still capturing that sense of infinite remoteness. He was often alert, he admitted, to a certain doubleness of selfhood, of one self standing apart and gazing upon another. He used the image of a spectator at a play, and asked where was the "true self" in that image? Which was more "real," the self performing on the stage of the written page or the self speculating on the self? Of course, the spectator in the audience is also a performing self. Once noted and framed in the role of "spectator," that self plays a performance. And so, an even more remote spectator must be creating the literary role of "spectator." The final conclusion—or "inconclusion"—must be that all writing is "wrighting." All writing is manufactured for readers, all writing poses the self for an audience.

Even if one resists pursuing this image to that extreme, the conclusion is inescapable that Thoreau casts the spectator as the "truer self," totally hidden in the darkness and the obscurity of the audience except for the narrow beam of the writer/usher's muffled flashlight. Every writer (or so I assume) is conscious of a "writing self" that attempts to express personal thoughts in an original way, and a "reading self" conscious always of how the words he or she pens might be received by others. As Gertrude Stein so aptly put it, she wrote only for herself—and for strangers. She sought private expression of the self while remaining powerfully attentive to how her expression might be received and interpreted, not only by her contemporary and future readers, but also by those readers (known mostly because they were writers) long since dead. In Thoreau's passage, the reading self is privileged over the performing self. The rhetorical response and the rhetorical effect are more crucial than the private self expressed. Expressed outside of language, the self, Thoreau said in a letter of 28 May 1850, is contemptible: "We who walk the streets and hold time together, are but the refuse of ourselves, and that life is for the shells of us —of our body and our mind—for our scurf—a thoroughly *scurvy* life" (259; the pun on his name may be intentional). Such thoughts lead him to demean his own obsession with literacy, saying, perhaps as a self-criticism of his rhetorical emphasis on silence, that "not writing is the most like writing in my case of anything I know." But such thoughts lead Thoreau back to considerations of how his works will be received.

As I have defined rhetoric, the reader is most essential, more central than theme, technique, aesthetics, or other literary concerns that are subsidiary to the question of reception. And so, although the apparent point of this letter for 28 May 1850 seems to be the rather prosaic and businesslike matter of accepting a hesitant invitation to "lecture to a small audience in Worcester," the thrust of the letter devolves upon reader response. Thoreau would be glad to lecture, if "only the parlor be large enough for an echo, and the audience will embarrass themselves with hearing as much as the lecturer [the performing Thoreauvian self] would otherwise embarrass himself with reading" (260). Paradoxically, that love for writing that Thoreau so often portrays as autoerotic or narcissistic as frequently expresses the passionate need for a readerly Echo, the nymph whose love Narcissus could not return.

This depiction of a self-embarrassed lecturer presenting a mere "crystal of his self" and his equally embarrassed reader is not to be taken lightly. In fact, the characterization strikes to the core of Thoreau's wild rhetoric. As a professional writer, he wanted a "concordant audience" (260), but that concordance was predicated upon opposition as much as concurrence. One should not receive a single word Thoreau had to say without arguing with him. Therein lay life, as Darwinian nature seemed to define it. But this argumentative, adversarial, and irreconcilable natural style also desired communication, even communion—the sharing of an original, stimulating, and provocative idea. When not arguing with Thoreau, a "concordant audience" negotiates with the text, gropes for a meaning that ultimately springs from the reader but has been inspired by the text's words. Thus in *Walden*'s "Solitude," after revealing "a certain double-ness" of the self and after presenting life as "a kind of fiction," Thoreau concludes his paragraph with the sentence, "This doubleness may easily make us poor neighbors and friends sometimes." Seemingly a proverb, the wild rhetoric of this sentence creates a multifolded text, enticing its readers to attempt various, conflicting interpretations of what the sentence might mean.

Although at first glance its meaning seems explicit, readers soon note the use of "sometimes," "may," and "us," which prevent the sentence from being a pure maxim. Though seeming to be a proverb, its wisdom applies only occasionally, and the adage is cast conditionally. Readers are not sure whether the "us" derives from the editorial "we" and is in fact a self-confession pertaining only to the author, or whether it includes readers who also are alert to this "certain doubleness" in themselves, or whether it is a statement upon the human condition at large. Even the meaning of a single word like "us" could include anywhere from only one or two persons to all of humanity. Moreover, when pushed, the main verb gives. Does an awareness of doubleness cause us to be poor neighbors and friends, or does it reveal that our friends are poor? Finally, is this relationship good or bad? A good proverb should have a moral, but this statement's meaning is indeterminate. Initially, it seems to lament that the writer is unable to have good neighbors or friends, but earlier Thoreau had said that *Walden*'s pages are addressed to "poor students." Remembering that address, readers may infer that having poor neighbors or being unable to imagine good ones is a desirable situation.

In 1856, Benjamin B. Wiley, a banker, stockbroker, and would-be Transcendentalist, wrote to Thoreau asking that he domesticate his wild rhetoric and clearly answer significant, thorny questions more explicitly. On 12 December, Thoreau replied that he could not, that any terse and explicit answer would have to be superficial. He responded instead as a "poor friend" and supplied Wiley with further oracular statements, concluding his letter: "Crack away at these nuts however as long as you can —The very exercise will ennoble you,—and you may get something better than the answer you expect—" (447). As in the more personal letter to Lucy Brown, Thoreau has responded in a language whose meaning cannot be decoded. Meaning must be elusive to be desirable; language must, like Echo, simultaneously encourage and baffle her auditors. In his wily letter to Wiley, Thoreau would like to think that this reading exercise is also ennobling.

In a letter to Harrison Blake on 8 August 1854, Thoreau wrote three paragraphs, using a different form of language in each of the three paragraphs. The last paragraph is explicit, offering practical advice and observation, instructing Blake not to drink too much sweetened water in the sun, asking him how his crops are growing, inquiring whether he planted any "Giant Regrets" last spring (331). The first paragraph is full of maxims and noble statements. It offers definite assertions, such as, "A man about *his business* would be the cynosure of all eyes." The paragraph clarifies "his business" to mean "fulfilling the end of his being." But the intervening paragraph is written in a language quite different from the epigrammatic and explicit styles of the others. It is stocked with "nuts" like those he sent to Wiley and to Brown. What seems at first a simple boat trip, for example, transforms into a zen experience. In a the middle of a lake, "Vast hollow chambers of silence stretched away on every side, and my being expanded in proportion, and filled them. Then first could I appreciate sound, and find it musical."

It would be presumptuous to "explain" what Thoreau means by those words. In humble honesty, one can only explain the various meanings he might intend, some of which are irreconcilable, or one can explain how the text can allow readers to translate the words in different ways. In a letter to Harrison Blake for 26 September 1855, Thoreau makes clear that he champions the latter approach. In a rare admission, he settles for the indefinite, clearly prefers the inscrutable. He asks, "To what end do I lead a simple life at all, pray?" He answers his own question: it definitely is not "so all our lives be *simplified* merely, like an algebraic formula" (384). He warns Blake against writing explicitly, against providing answers, rules, and maxims: "Don't spend your time in drilling soldiers, who may turn out hirelings after all." Thoreau even goes so far as to define meaning, significance, or "import" in terms of a wild rhetoric. He tells Blake that he has no desire to be a literary drill-master, a didactic preacher, or a rhetorical arithmetician: "I would fain lay the most stress forever on that which is the most important—imports the most to me,— though it were only (what it is likely to be) a vibration in the air."

Next to Blake, Thoreau corresponded most with Daniel Ricketson, but he was impatient with the kind of reading Ricketson represented. Upon *Walden*'s publication, Ricketson wrote a long letter on 12 August 1854, generally praising the book. Although he noted that "to many, and to most, it will appear to be the wild musings of an eccentric and strange mind," it did not seem so to Ricketson. To him, *Walden* "appears to evince a mind most thoroughly self possessed, highly cultivated with a strong vein of common sense. The whole book is a prose poem (pardon the solecism) and at the same time as simple as a running brook" (332). Thoreau chose to let Ricketson stand for the kind of anonymous, "sympathetic" other who was reading his works only for their practical observation and coherent truths and not for their wild rhetoric. This kind of reader, Thoreau tells Blake on 26 September 1855, "sympathizes with much in my books, but much in them is naught to him,—'namby-pamby,'—'stuff,'—'mystical.' Why will not I, having common sense, write in plain English always; *teach* men in detail how to live a simpler life, etc.; not go off into———?" (384). Thoreau confides that he has "no designs on men at all," and thus has "no scheme" to his philosophy or to his books. Any scheming must be plotted tentatively by readers. His best readers will not, even in praise, ask pardon for typological or generic "solecisms."

Thoreau prized Blake as a reader; their exchange of letters constitutes a true correspondence among a "concordant audience." As correspondents, the meanings of their letters never "agree." Thoreau and Blake

will stand on solid foundations to one another,—I a column planted on this shore, you on that. . . . We will not mutually fall over that we may meet, but will grandly and eternally guard the straits. Methinks I see an inscription on you, which the architect made, the stucco being worn off to it. The name of that worldly king is crumbling away. I see it toward sunset in favorable lights. *Each must read for the other,* as might a sailer-by. Be sure you are star-y-pointing still. How is it on your side? (385; italics mine)

Reading another's letters, as described in this passage, is the process of tendering meaning upon obscured, hieroglyhic writing. Not only is the act of reading privileged, but its meaning is based upon dimly lit verbal guides. "Each must read for the other," and meaning resides only in reading. The watery straits might post two sentries on the alert, but it is their alert reading that produces significance. Or, as Thoreau represented the idea by an illustration, asking, "How will this do for a symbol of sympathy?" (420),

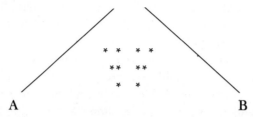

Representing the same idea more verbally, Thoreau assured Blake, "If you look at another star I will try to supply my side of the triangle" (300).

Thoreau hoped his communication triangle was "hypaethral," a word he liked. Its apex was open to the skies, and closure would not seal his letters. Thus, he warns, "I trust that you realize what an exaggerater I am,—that I lay myself out to exaggerate whenever I have an opportunity, —pile Pelion upon Ossa, to reach heaven so. Expect no trivial truth from me, unless I am on the witness-stand. . . . If it isn't thus and so with me, it is with something. I am not particular whether I get the shells or meat, in view of the latter's worth" (304). This letter's imagery is significant for another reason. The blithe dismissal of "shells or meat" echoes the problem about writing that Thoreau recorded in his *Journal* early in his career. On 4 March 1838, he complained:

> But what does all this scribbling amount to?—What is now scribbled in the heat of the moment one can contemplate with somewhat of satisfaction, but alas! to-morrow—aye to-night—it is stale, flat—and unprofitable—in fine, is not, only its shell remains—like some red parboiled lobster-shell—which kicked aside never so often still stares at you in the path. (*PJ1*, 33–34)

By 1853, Thoreau had kicked aside the problem. Dismissing the worry whether meaty thoughts were captured, he cared only that expression was effective, its language sufficiently remote, its meaning left to the reader to gnaw.

As he says in another letter, punning once again on "translation" of an author through reader interpretation, he hoped his words were "elevating as a ladder, the means by which we are translated" (311). He returns to shellfish imagery, recalling his parboiled lobster and denying the easy moral of Oliver Wendell Holmes's chambered nautilus: "Let not the shell-fish think to build his house of that [the beautifully tinted inner lining] alone; and pray, what are its tints to him? Is it not his smooth, close-fitting shirt merely, whose tints *are not* to him, being in the dark, but only when he is gone or dead, and his shell is heaved up to light, a wreck upon the beach, do they appear." He admits to the great amount of "drudgery," of "humdrum and prosaic labor [that] goes into any work of the least value," but the meaning of the work produced through such Herculean labor is left to the reader to discover, like a wanderer contemplating the beauty, truth, and value of a shell found on the shore.

The imagery of the shellfish's shirt leads in another letter to coat imagery: "Change the coat—put the judge in the criminal box and the criminal on the bench, and you might think that you had changed the men" (320). Thoreau might as appropriately have added that the self seems to change depending on how it is garbed or how it is boxed or framed. Punning on didactic as well as legal language, equating judicial decisions (*"sententia"*) with "criminal *sentences,"* he asks, "How much juster is one or the other? Men are continually sentencing each other, but whether we be judges or criminals, the sentence is ineffectual unless we condemn ourselves." No matter how we dress our selves, the result is deception, unless the dresser alert the reader to the flaws in his fabric. "No doubt the thinnest of all cloaks is conscious deception or lies it is sleazy and frays out, it is not close woven like cloth—but its meshes are a coarse net-work. A man can afford to lie only at the intersection of the threads, but truth puts in the filling and makes a consistent stuff."

Only a rhetoric whose seams and stitches are exposed, whose loosely woven pattern is left to readers to fill with meaning, can faithfully reflect that sense of his many selves, selves that remain ultimately hidden despite the most heroic efforts at self-expression and biographical search. So, in his letter to Blake of 10 April 1853, Thoreau marvels: "It is wonderful that I can be here, and you there, and that we can correspond, and do many other things, when, in fact, there is so little of us, either or both, anywhere" (302). The self constantly fluctuates, sometimes looming large, at other times almost vanishing. "Suddenly I can come forward into the utmost apparent distinctness, and speak with a sort of emphasis to you; and the next moment I am so faint an entity, and make so slight an impression, that nobody can find the traces of me." Most remarkably, Thoreau recognizes the paradox that in the act of describing his most hidden self he calls attention to that secreted self and makes the secret noisy; his most private self becomes broadly public: "If you hear a noise,

—'t aint I,—'t aint I,—as the dog says with a tin-kettle tied to his tail" (303).

A lesson Thoreau shared with Hawthorne's art was that the performing self can shout more loudly when seeming to whisper. It is now time to see how those selves sound when spoken from more public stages, to study how those selves are dressed when they go abroad in Thoreau's lectures and published works.

CHAPTER THREE

Before Walden

I. EARLY WRITINGS

Although Thoreau proclaimed on 17 September 1849 that *"I have chosen letters for my profession,"* he had made the decision much earlier (*Corr,* 249). By 1843 he was already determined to become a professional writer as he made the rounds of New York publishers to see how he might break into the literary marketplace. He retained lofty conceptions of literature, yet he was not above characterizing his writings as "bait to tempt the rats" (*Corr,* 141). Solid research has elucidated the economics of American publishing and the demands of the literary marketplace, but many fundamental questions remain.[1] One is the clear definition of magazine readership, a crucial issue when discussing intended rhetorical effects. Determining the character of different magazine audiences is less clear in America than in other countries. In England, for example, conservative reviewers commended Byron's *Don Juan* for its wit and verve when it was published in an expensive quarto edition limited to fifteen hundred copies, but they denounced the poem as blasphemous, immoral, and seditious when it appeared in the inexpensive duodecimo edition of tens of thousands. The "meaning" of the poem had changed with the shift in format and the change in audience. The same poem, praised when recommended to that elite audience Byron called "the twice two thousand," was deemed licentious when the audience was thought broader and of lower station.[2]

Still, one pattern seems to emerge from Thoreau's career. He had a habit of baiting with lettuce to tempt rats and with moose meat to tempt rabbits. Generally speaking, the more "wild" an essay, the more genteel the magazine that published it. With some exceptions, the more pleasant an essay's sentiments, the more likely its publishing outlet was radical. As a case in point, one of his wildest essays, "Walking, or The Wild," was eventually published in the *Atlantic Monthly*.[3] Its civilized subscribers would hear Thoreau advise them to be "absolutely free from all worldly engagements," and they could not forget the essay's famous motto: "In Wildness is the preservation of the World." The *Atlantic* was probably not as conservative as the *North American Review* nor as urbane as the *Knickerbocker Magazine,* but it was certainly less radical than the Transcendentalist enterprise called *The Dial,* where Thoreau published a much tamer companion piece to "Walking, or The Wild."

"A Winter Walk" (*The Dial,* October 1843) contains lines that rival the domestic coziness of Whittier's "Snowbound" (1866) or one of Longfellow's "Fireside" poems (1849). The *Atlantic*'s more conservative readers would hear Thoreau say that had he to choose between living near "the most beautiful garden that ever human art contrived, or else [by] a Dismal Swamp, I should certainly decide for the swamp." In contrast, *The Dial*'s presumably more radical readers would hear him luxuriate in more civilized pleasures:

Our hearts are warm and cheery, like cottages under drifts, whose windows and doors are half concealed, but from whose chimneys the smoke cheerfully ascends. The imprisoning drifts increase the sense of comfort which the house affords, and in the coldest days we are content to sit over the hearth and see the sky through the chimney-top, enjoying the quiet and serene life that may be had in a warm corner by the chimney-side, or feeling our pulse by listening to the low of cattle in the street, or the sound of the flail in distant barns all the long afternoon.

If Thoreau stayed true to form, he probably would have hoped for his wildest essay, his unfinished "Night and Moonlight," to appear in a magazine with the most conservative readership in the trade.

An important exception to this pattern is Thoreau's "The Landlord," a neglected essay that is his most generous negotiation with the literary marketplace. Calling "The Landlord" his most liberal concession to reader expectations is a kindness. Some have complained that the essay is "one of the few pieces that Thoreau consciously wrote to sell." Others have blasted it as too "commercial," a failure because "aimed at the market."[4] Published in the *Democratic Review* for October 1843, the essay's Chaucerian mellowness has struck readers as somehow un-Thoreavian, but its liberality is quite appropriate to the Young America predilection of the magazine that published it. The essay smiles upon America's archetypal innkeepers, more bourgeois than Longfellow's village blacksmith. The landlord is "the lord of the land" and his knowledge of human nature is superior, Thoreau says, to his beloved Homer and Shakespeare. He is something more than a good man; he is a "good fellow." Because of his benign curiosity about humanity, he is perhaps "the farthest traveled of all" who stop at his inn. Most of all, he is a good host. In contrast to the combative tone Thoreau is famous for, here he says that the landlord "is wiser than to contradict his guest in any case; he lets him go on; he lets him travel." His public house is the best of all the structures that can be grouped under the rubric "house": the schoolhouse, the almshouse, the jailhouse, and the dwellinghouse. The landlord's inn, Thoreau says without a trace of irony, is superior even to the ancient Parthenon and St. Paul's cathedral.[5]

"The Landlord" is crucial to Thoreau's canon precisely because it seems so untypical of the icon we recognize as "Thoreau." It poses what Thoreau had called a problematic nut to gnaw. It makes one puzzle why Thoreau wrote it or submitted it under his name. It resembles Melville's "Paradise of Bachelors" without the distaff "Tartarus of Maids." One rereads Thoreau's essay, trying in vain to detect markers that signal parody, burlesque, exaggeration, or at least a cavalier experiment in style. One toys with the idea of simply dismissing the piece as an early work, a youthful mistake. But then, one would have to come to grips with those other fine pieces from the same phase of his career, respected essays like "Natural History of Massachusetts," "A Walk to Wachusett," and "A Winter Walk," which no one would reject as youthful indiscretions or immature work.

"The Landlord" is significant precisely because it shows how important he considered audience. The essay defines one extreme to his rhetorical horizon. In *A Week,* he might want to write sentences "which no intelligence can understand," but sentiments in "The Landlord" are familiarly American. As much as Thoreau thrilled to the sheer pleasure of writing, he had an equal commitment to rhetoric and its presumption of reader participation and effect. As much as he enjoyed perfecting the array of words upon a page, he delighted in devising various strategies by which readers would be enticed into the text to become coconspirators in the creation of meaning. These strategies ranged from entertaining readers as pleasantly as the landlord to attacking readers for their mean, moiling lives.

His testing of different audience situations, his experiments with signalling readers on how to receive his texts, his complicated use of pronouns and the sense of collusion they suggest, are all strategies he tested to refine his concerns with reader response. In the compositions before *Walden,* we can see an artist at work, trying out various colorations and techniques, experimenting with sundry devices that would be interwoven more sophisticatedly in later works. These youthful experiments, handled bluntly in early lectures and essays, became subtle strategies in works like "Resistance to Civil Government" and *A Week on the Concord and Merrimack Rivers,* as well as *Walden* and later works. In the first decade of his professional writing career, he felt the need to define clearly the reader's role, to specify precisely how he meant his audience to receive his texts. Later he would trust more to the power to his prose—and to the intelligence of his readers—and make the signals more muted.

To clarify his thoughts on language, one can begin with two different essays on two different topics in two different magazines: "Natural History of Massachusetts" and "Thomas Carlyle and His Works." As editor of *The Dial,* Emerson had asked Thoreau for a simple review of a recent publication by the state fisheries department. Thoreau responded with an elaborate exegesis on natural history, writing, reading, remembering, vision, and belief called "Natural History of Massachusetts" (*Dial,* July 1842). Five years later, Horace Greeley persuaded *Graham's Magazine* to publish Thoreau's review of a controversial author, entitled "Thomas Carlyle and His Works" (March and April, 1847). The editorial policies of *Graham's* and the *Dial* were as different as were Greeley and Emerson. Separated by five years, the essays address completely different topics and were intended for very different audiences. But they demonstrate quite similar rhetorical issues and techniques. By clarifying these two seemingly antithetical essays, a triangulation of Thoreau's thoughts upon language, style, and rhetoric can be established.

2. "NATURAL HISTORY"

According to Emerson's concept of a "bi-polar unity," antitheses merge into a spiritual synthesis through the power of reason. In the privacy of his journals he sometimes worried that though preaching the gospel of one, he frequently perceived the fact of two, but in public he stayed loyal to an ultimate oneness that was true, beautiful, and good. Quite understandably, then, he criticized Thoreau's oxymorons. Even though they frequently merged opposites into a pleasurable oneness, their synthesis did not always mean progress or idealism. Thoreau's oxymorons presented concepts like "a savage spirituality," for example, but neither spirituality nor savagery was privileged over the other. His oxymorons would often reveal excitement about the process of merging rather than the achievement of synthesis. They lauded confusion as often as coherence.

Thus, in "Night and Moonlight" he creates a passage in which civilization and nature, the past and the present, thought and contemplation, and other forces of the universe are spun together in a whirl of indecipherable oneness:

> The village street is then as wild as the forest. New and old are confounded. I know not whether I am sitting on the ruins of a wall, or on the material which is to compose a new one. Nature is an instructed and impartial teacher, spreading no crude opinions and flattering none; she will be neither radical nor conservative. Consider the moonlight, so civil, yet so savage! (*Writings,* 5:332)

All walls to thought, all walls created by thought, are dissolved in nature's mute, impartial oneness. Nature is a teacher, but more like the serenely silent statue of Buddha than like a hortatory preacher or orating politician, or even a "Yankee Transcendentalist." "She" can be instructive, but she never instructs.

Rather than balance antitheses, Thoreau's oxymorons move beyond merging to a melting. They accent concepts that are littoral—that, like the shore, lack distinct boundaries and feature overlapping elements. In "Natural History of Massachusetts," favored words are "elasticity," "flexibleness," "flux," "decay," and "overflowing." Even rocks, age-old symbols of stability, are melting. He sees ice crystals "lying upon granite rocks, directly over crystals of quartz, the frostwork of a longer night, crystals of a longer period, but, to some eye unprejudiced by the short term of human life, melting as fast as the former." Further, even the fundamental categories by which we begin to arrange scientific knowledge—such as divisions of animal, vegetable, and mineral—are artificial: "Vegetation is but a kind of crystallization" (*Writings,* 5:129). Even the term "Natural History" is oxymoronic. It means man's record of nature, codified, synthesized, categorized, and it means nature's story, ever evolving, ever changing, never complete. Neither nature nor history can be captured in a story; they are too vast to be accurately framed. Narrative can capture only a small part of their full stories; only a few details can be selected to fit a plot or point of view. As he says in "Walking," "Nature is a personality so vast and universal that we have never seen one of her features." We perceive features only when the eye is prejudiced by a frame.

In like manner, he approves Carlyle's belief that a true history, a full story, the whole truth cannot be told: "The writer fitted to compose history, is hitherto an unknown man. The experience itself would require all knowledge to record it." Since that is impossible, one can aim "only at some picture of the things acted, which picture itself, will at best be a poor approximation, leav[ing] the inscrutable purport of them an acknowledged secret" (*EE,* 266). Even a small part of the whole story is so ambiguous as to be inscrutable. Thoreau notes that Carlyle and Emerson, both admirers of Goethe, paint two very different pictures of who Goethe is. To describe objectively even one man in all of history or one fact in all of nature is as forbidding as fullfilling what Thoreau calls an "impossible precept, '*know thyself*' " (*EE,* 251, 254).

Given these heuristic problems, Thoreau uses "Natural History" to describe how nature's story can be told and read. In other words, he delineates the narrative possibilities by which nature can be transformed into a story or a history. From the outset, he expresses admiration for two narrative features—that nature speaks in myriad tones, from a vast choir of voices, and that nature, in contrast to a decaying civilization, plodding lives, and despondent philosophies, is luxuriant and revels in "purling play." Nature is a multivocal, sporting game. Its voices are virtually infinite; the cheering sounds of the cricket, the wise and wily serpent, the minnow swimming boldly against the current, the wild laughter of the solitary loon, the jingle of the song sparrow, the plaintive notes of the lark, the jarring screech of the fish hawk are all voices Thoreau hears in nature. They are the multiple voices that will resound in his own works.[1]

Sometimes these voices are duets, their contrasting sounds complementing each other and suggesting the rich possibility of yet other voices. Thus the vireo's pleasant clarion and the "brazen trump of the impatient jay" both strive "to lift our thoughts above the street," much as the crow's haunting melancholy suggests a bravery that floats the bird "up above the clouds, over desponding human crowds." Even when in conflict, voices create a chorus, "The nuthatch and chickadee flitting in company through the dells of the wood, the one harshly scolding at the intruder, the other with a faint lisping note enticing him on." These coupled, contrary voices will lead to further voices, such as that of the partridge, the robin, the shrike, and the lark. And they will lead to Thoreau's own echoing voices in the essay, sometimes scolding intruding readers, sometimes enticing them on with lisping notes. Like the jay, shrike, and fish hawk, Thoreau will issue maxims that are explicit in their meaning, shrill in their urgency. He will shriek, "Society is always diseased, and the best is the most so." He will whisper, "In society you will not find health, but in nature." He will promise that "the practical faith of all men belies the preacher's consolation." He will insist that the universe is "perfect in all its details. Nature will bear the closest inspection; she invites us to lay our eye level with the smallest leaf, and take an insect view of its plain."

He will also contradict his own maxims, will dissolve their single-noted voice. His advice to take "an insect view" will be vitiated by the proverb, "Wisdom does not inspect, but behold." Undermining any settled systems and confident proverbs, even those he himself has just uttered, he concludes the essay insisting that "we cannot know truth by contrivance and method; the Baconian is as false as any other." To seem truthful, the writer must appear to escape methods and structured narrative. Consequently he pays special attention to those voices and images that are polyphonic or constantly in flux. Some say nothing definite or utter different ideas at once—what he calls the "unanimities of nature." He loves "the silent influence which flowers exert," for his "most delicate experience is typified there." He enjoys the river overflowing its banks, the spring wind "laden with a strong scent of musk, [that] by its freshness advertises me of an unexplored wildness." He also mentions that oft-invoked Romantic image, "the nonchalance of the butterfly carrying accident and change painted in a thousand hues upon its wings."

In contrast to cheering crickets or shrieking jays, these images emphasize wildness, flux, indefiniteness. In their multivocality, they elude Aesopian equations, refusing to establish a correspondence between an object and its referent—refusing to associate a hare with speed, a tortoise with persistence. In their multiplicity and confusion of voice, Thoreau's images accent his assertion that "Nature is mythical and mystical always." "She has her luxurious and florid style" as well as a careful, more Spartan-like technique. In addition to a variety of styles, she also works "with the license and extravagance of genius." Of course, what nature speaks is really what Thoreau hears. His description of nature's voices is actually his report on how he reads, and what he reads in nature is how he means to write. "Her" genius is his, and his readers can safely substitute "Thoreau" whenever Thoreau writes "nature."

Using a fine pun—puns, by nature, speak in at least two voices at once —Thoreau marvels at what he calls a "woodland quire," suggesting a choir of voices and the quire of pages that contain his manuscript. "In May and June the woodland quire is in full tune, and given the immense spaces of hollow air, and this curious human ear, one does not see how the void could be better filled." Thus, Thoreau returns to his fascination with the void's role in creating meaning and his respect for "this curious human ear" as essential elements of his rhetoric. Ultimately, nature is an empty mold that physical manifestations strive to fill; it is like a text enticing readers to fill its void. Just as he had collapsed the naturalist's boundaries of animal, vegetable, and mineral, so he suggests the artificiality of literary genres and literal reading: "As, indeed, all rhymes imply an eternal melody, independent of any particular sense."

Nature, in fine, says nothing. It speaks in many voices, but its statements are oracular. It is reading that claims what nature's voices say. "Natural History" is not so much a review of books or nature or nature books; rather, it depicts Thoreau as a reader. His review describes how he reads and re-views, whether his text is nature or books. Near the end of "Natural History," he admits that he is in fact writing "the natural history of man himself," or of one man reading. He allows that the volumes cited at the outset of his essay have been selected "with as much license as the preacher selects his text." And Thoreau has turned over the leaves of nature and has tuned its many voices as freely, necessarily, as he reads any book. Nature is a better text than these particular nature books. It disports in a greater variety of style and voice, but it remains a text to be read, a hollow mold that awaits readers to fill it with meanings that seem to fit.

Rather than a review of books of nature, his essay is about literacy, a description of how books and nature are read. After he refers to the "woodland quire," he portrays his readers as solitary ramblers ransacking nature for objective correlatives, seeking "a response and expression for every mood in the depths of the wood." He had begun the essay by capitalizing upon readers' discontent with civilization, by reminding them how they feel "degraded when considered as the members of a political organization." In contrast to society's decay, nature is healthy. In contrast to the "din of religion, literature, and philosophy," nature's voices are fresher, more melodious, more beautiful. Nature's voices are healthy and restorative; they can, like books on nature, "restore the tone of the system." Nature is a better text than civilization, or so Thoreau begins his essay. But its "betterness" must be determined by readers. Reversing John Locke's famous image, Thoreau converts reality into a *tabula rasa* awaiting inscription by readers. The nature of nature, the essence of reality, the meaning of a text, all depend on how it is read. The reader is made responsible for nature's significance, and the voices nature speaks are only those that are heard. Its sounds have meaning according to the narrative frame placed upon them. Nothing nature "says" can resist the interpretative power of readers, and so, "To the sick, indeed, nature is sick, but to the well, a fountain of health." Readers who attend to "the spirit in which [nature] requires to be contemplated" are true heroes; Thoreau admires readers like Thales and Linnaeus more than history's Napoleons, though they commonly err in their interpretations.[2]

Admirable readers are imaged in the nocturnal spear fishing Thoreau describes at some length in "Natural History." The ostensible purpose of the expedition is inferior to the activity itself. Spearing fish and forking them into the "boat, as potatoes out of a pot," is less vital than "the real object of his pursuit," the "beauty and never-ending novelty of his position," the perpetual shifting of positions while reading and studying a word on a page or a star in the sky.

> And much speculation does this wandering star afford to the musing night-walker, leading him on and on, jack-o'-lantern-like, over the meadows; or, if he is wiser, he amuses himself with imagining what of human life, far in the silent night, is flitting moth-like round its candle.

Wise readers value texts that enkindle their own musings; still wiser readers value the amusement they enjoy when using nature and language to contemplate the wider realm of human activity. Humanity's flitting around the candle is more intriguing than the cottager's candle or the heavenly stars, just as the process of reading and meaning-making is more fascinating than the message of a particular line or paragraph.

Thoreau reads Carlyle as a "natural" writer, an author whose rhetoric echoes the voices of nature he hears in "Natural History." He bestows much praise on Carlyle, but his strongest admiration is for Carlyle's lively and lifelike style, which frees the reader to muse and to be amused. His thoughts are not new—"No man's thoughts are new," Thoreau says of Carlyle and himself—but stylistic expression can create the impression of newness. The illusion of "freedom and naturalness" can be achieved by folding language many times thick, and by humor. Humor accepts and excepts nothing. It is an "indispensable pledge of sanity, without some leaven of which the abstruse thinker may justly be suspected of mysticism, fanaticism, or insanity." More crucially, its greatest rhetorical value "consists in the mutual play and interchange of a genial and healthy humor, which excepts nothing, not even themselves, in its lawless range." Humor and seriousness, urgency and nonchalance, sublimity and silliness corruscate like the wings of Thoreau's butterfly to produce the impression of a natural style: "Such a style—so diversified and variegated!"

The crowning achievement of a "natural" style is the way it frees readers to translate. Stylistic variety, indeterminacy of meaning, and the "absence of cant and dogma" conspire to make readers roam among Carlyle's words as though rambling thorough nature's woods, attempting to wrest meaning from the many voices heard.

> He removes many cart-loads of rubbish, and leaves open a broad high-way. His writings are all unfenced on the side of the future and the possible. He does not place himself across the passage out of his books, so that none may go freely out, but rather by the entrance, inviting all to come in and go through. No gins, no net-work, no pickets here, to restrain the free thinking reader.

Carlyle's readers are forced to be free thinkers. His unfenced texts demand interpretation and translation. He "lets us" (and makes us) "wander broadly underneath [the open heavens], and shows them to us reflected in innumerable pools and lakes. We have from him, occasionally, some hints of a possible science of astronomy even, and revelation of heavenly arcana, but nothing definite hitherto" (*EE,* 252–53).

That is what Carlyle's rhetoric does—or rather, that is what Thoreau's reading of texts called "Carlyle" discovers. In the same essay, Thoreau has said that Carlyle's Goethe and Emerson's Goethe are two different

"Goethes," and Thoreau's "Carlyle" is the "natural history" of his reviewing of words labeled "Carlyle." More accurately, Thoreau's "Carlyle" (whether "Carlyle" means Thoreau's essay, Carlyle, or his text) mirrors his own rhetorical aims. He had written the essay during his stay at Walden while striving to express his reflections in the ever-changing features of the pond. He had delivered it as a lecture on 4 February 1846 before publishing it in *Graham's Magazine* in March and April 1847. In one sense, it was a review of England's famous writer, but it was also a summation of his own literary aspirations. An exegesis of Carlyle, "Carlyle" also explains what he was attempting to do in his literary experiments. "Carlyle" was also a reminder to himself of an alternate possibility, a rhetorical option to the strategies he found successful in his earlier essays and addresses.

Before composing "Carlyle" in 1846, Thoreau had gained some attention with lectures and with his four published essays of 1842–1843: "The Landlord" in the *Democratic Review*, "A Walk to Wachusett" in the *Boston Miscellany*, and "A Winter Walk" and "Natural History" in the *Dial*. As different as they are, these four essays are united in their persistent concern with readers. Unlike his poetry and *Journal*, where readers can often stand apart from his text, readers are put to work in his other performances. They are asked to participate in the textual exhibit, to help shape, color, and contour the text. His lectures and essays demand an involved reader, not a distanced spectator. Whether imaged as friend or adversary, readers are drawn into Thoreau's writings. They are requested and commanded to become coconspirators in the creation of meaning. In "Resistance to Civil Government" and the two books he saw through to publication, his rhetorical tactics with respect to audience response are interwoven throughout the texts quite complexly. In earlier works where he experimented more broadly, his conceptualization of readers' roles is more transparent, particularly with respect to the reader as an "adversarial Other" and as an empathetic comrade.

Thoreau's frequent invocation of an adversarial other poses a special problem for the student of rhetoric. This strategy creates a rhetorical situation in which "true meaning" lies not in the text, nor in what the speaker says, nor in what readers suppose from what they hear. Readers are asked to be consciously antagonistic to what he is about to utter, to oppose what he will say. Truth falls somewhere between an exaggerated statement and its resisted reception. Its approximation results from the conflict of assertion and denial. The rhetorical situation is similar to the relationship Thoreau had with Harrison Blake, his most intimate correspondent, in which they were "flint and steel." Truth is never quite articulated; rather, it is suggested by the sparks struck when flint strikes steel, when an antagonistic reader conflicts with the protagonist of author or text. When this antithetical situation exists, readers are told to dig in their heels and oppose whatever Thoreau proposes. Indeed, readers must be antagonistic in order to enable the author to state his case more extremely. The first paragraph of "Walking, or The Wild" is a typical case. Thoreau instructs his readers:

> I wish to speak a word for Nature, for absolute freedom and wildness, as contrasted with a freedom and culture merely civil. . . . I wish to make an extreme statement, if so I may make an emphatic one, for there are enough champions of civilization: the minister and the school-committee, and every one of you will take care of that.

This rhetorical frame allows some readers to feel wise when they concur with Thoreau's thoughts, but its presentation is predicated on all readers being "champions of civilization"; not only clergymen and academics but also, he generalizes "every one of you" will rebut Thoreau's ideas. The presumption is that he speaks wildly and can only do so if he presupposes that all his readers, "every one of you," will disagree, thus allowing him to make rhetorical flights of fancy. He can air these inklings only because he presumes they will be censored.

Thoreau experimented with this technique until quite late in life. In 1859, when he lectured on "A Plea for Captain Brown," he still used this narrative strategy, only substituting newspapers for the clergy and school-committees:

> I do not wish to force my thoughts upon you, but I feel forced to correct the tone and the statements of the newspapers, and of my countrymen generally, respecting his character and actions.

The demanded reader as adversarial other has been softened from "every one of you" to "my countrymen generally," but the rhetorical effect remains the same. He imagines that his readers, their thoughts forced by the papers, will now attend to Thoreau's forced thoughts, allowing one to "correct" the other. The truth about Brown lies not in the papers, nor in "A Plea," but in the correction of the discursive extremes. If we agree with Thoreau, we are failing as his conceived readers. If we wish to agree with his remarks, we must, to be the kind of readers he demands, attend not only to his words but also to our understanding of their cultural opposition. To be good readers in this rhetorical situation, we must be like Harrison Blake, instructed to be flint to his steel, praised for a triangulation of meaning where the writer says one thing and his reader hears another, and where an approximation of truth arises from the never-converging apex of that communication triangle that Thoreau once drew in a letter to Blake.

A somewhat more complex conception of the reader's adversarial function is at work in the lecture Thoreau composed in 1851–1852, about midway between "Walking" and "Plea for Brown." "Life Without Principle" was also his most frequently offered address. At the outset, he tells his readers that he is not about to present a balanced textual argument: "As the time is short, I will leave out all the flattery, and retain all the criticism." He will not speak the complete truth, only one exaggerated side of it. Moreover, he makes readers responsible for this technique. Earlier, some representative of "every one of you" had "asked me what *I thought*," Thoreau exclaims, having been thrown into mock confusion. Moreover, that reader even went so far as to have "attended to my answer." Thoreau allows readers two rhetorical possibilities: they can stand in an inferior relation and imagine the author like a medical authority who brings balm for their maladies, or they can take a superior attitude and treat Thoreau as their tool. Consequently, Thoreau plays two rhetorical roles. He is the doctor administering to the sick: "I will give them a strong dose of myself." Conversely, he is merely an instrument: "It is such a rare use he would make of me, as if he were acquainted with the tool." The speaker as tool useful to the reader as workman and the speaker as doctor to his sick audience are roles presented at the outset, but the latter comes to predominate in the lecture. Its last sentence, for example, repeats Thoreau's hope that he and his purged reader can "meet healthy" some day "to congratulate each other on the ever glorious morning."

The reader's otherly role is meant to be more empathetic in early writings like "A Walk to Wachusett" (*Boston Miscellany*, 1843). The essay begins with a near haiku: "The needles of the pine / All to the west incline." Following this poetic delineation of a pleasant natural phenomenon, the first paragraph intimates that what is called "grandeur" in nature does not arise from the phenomenon but from our interpretation. Thoreau advises that our reading of nature can be enriched through familiarity with the literary tradition of nature writing as found in writers like Homer, Virgil, and Shakespeare. The use of "our" and "we" and "tradition" is deliberate. In this essay, Thoreau uses what might be called the democratic "we," asking in almost a Whitmanian sense that his readers see themselves as fellow travelers in the composition. Unlike "Natural History," which begins with an eccentric "I" and. a "you" representing corrupt civilization and then merges the adversarial pronouns into a more sympathetic "we" to conclude the essay, "A Walk to Wachusett" is all "we."

The explicit topic is the trip of the title, but its true subject is the act of reading. The silent villagers of an isolated hamlet seem to say, "Come and study us and learn men and manners." Wachusett seems to study the growth of towns as "new annals in the history of man." Thoreau reads the landscape "like a map." Even an adventure story like the tale of Robin Hood has its place—to be recited as the speaker plods homeward along the dusty road. The speaker is dismayed when the landlord hands him a Boston newspaper to kill time, for he would rather read what is near at hand, and he is pleased when he reaches the mountain top to find that there is enough light to read by even at night. The emphasis is all on the cooperative and reciprocal act of reading, whether reading men and manners or nature, landscape or history, stars or books, Robin Hood or Homer.

The narrative point of view mirrors the cooperative reading process. It is all "we"—an "I" and his nameless companion, who serves two purposes. He is an emblem for the friendly reader Thoreau expects, and his presence makes the narrative feel companionable. It also prevents the "we" from becoming the independent, abrasive, and oppositional "I" of the lectures. When they part at the end of the trip, the sense of "we" is preserved by keeping the narrator's identity indistinguishable from his companion's; one went to "Groton, the other took his separate and solitary way" to Concord. Interestingly, when the "we" is parted geographically, the speaker is narrated as a "he," not an "I." The first-person plural, when split, becomes third-person singular. Moreover, the speaker as "he" shares a simple communion meal with ordinary folk as his final adventure before returning home. The sketch's last event rejuvenates the narrator through "the brave hospitality of a farmer and his wife, who generously entertained him at their board" (*Writings,* 5:152). The "poor wayfarer" "silently accept[s] the kindness of the other." He can then push "forward with new vigor."

The audience of this essay remains an "other," but the "kindness of the other" is worlds apart from the passive, idealized reader of the poems and the other-self of the journals, as well as the adversarial "other" in some lectures. The "other" of the essay is empathetic, whether presented as the nameless companion's mute presence or the anonymous farmer's hospitality, and Thoreau repays their imagined generosity in kind. His "silent acceptance" of the farmer's communion meal is not silent; they have given him food and drink, and he in return offers this narrative to other wayfarers. His companionable text will generously entertain us at his board, allowing us to push "forward with new vigor." The audience situation of many of the lectures is like the one pictured in *Walden*'s "Visitors," where the guest and the narrator back up against opposite walls of the cabin so as to obtain "sufficient distance" and "considerable neutral ground" in order to "utter big thoughts in big words," where the ideas are menacingly metaphored as bullets plowing through the listener's head. But the audience of these excursion essays is more like that "welcome visitor" in *Walden*'s "Winter Visitors," with whom Thoreau "waded so gently and reverently, or we pulled together so smoothly, that the fishes of thought were not scared from the stream, nor feared any angler on the bank" (*W,* 269).

Similar patterns and rhetorical techniques function in *The Dial* pieces from this early period, "Natural History of Massachusetts" (July 1842) and "A Winter Walk" (October 1843). In the former, a friendly and companionable "I" gradually evaporates and is supplanted by what is grammatically called the royal "we," but its tone is more accurately that of a democratic "us" in the last dozen paragraphs, and the shift in pronoun tone occurs precisely when the text becomes more friendly and generous. In a similarly congenial mode, and in contrast to the Romantics' typically nightmarish depictions of mad scientists, Thoreau assures his reader that a true scientist "will still be the healthiest and friendliest man." He classifies his essay with other natural histories as "the most cheerful winter reading," and he spends several pages praising different approaches to nature, scientific and otherwise, approaches as varied and fertile as nature's own style. Indeed, in those pages Thoreau comes closest to echoing the most magnanimous passage in all his work—the journal record for 17 March 1842. The month before publishing "Natural History," the first of these four essays, he had visited an old schoolmate, an engineer building the Welland Canal around Niagara Falls, a man who held no truck with Thoreau's "motives and modes of living," a thorough-going materialist who cared only for "Creature Comforts." After their visit, Thoreau went home to write in his *Journal,* and his former classmate

> forsooth to mature his schemes to ends as good maybe but different.
>   So are we two made while the same stars shine quietly over us. If I or he be wrong—nature yet consents placidly—She bites her lip and *smiles* to see how her children will agree.
>   So does the Welland [*sic;* pun?] canal get built—and other conveniences while I live. Well and [pun?] good I must confess. (*PJ1,* 379)

Thus Thoreau defines nature's "luxurious and florid style" not in the sense of "purple prose" so much as in terms of its teeming diversity in which the individuated "I" and "you," "he" and "they" merge into a language if not a landscape of "we." In "A Winter Walk," a sketch so similar to *Walden* that it is almost an early draft, nature again is presented as integral in its diversity.[3] Appropriately, the narrative point of view is all "we," observers in tune with nature's cooperative spirit and the intended relationship between reader and speaker. As in "Natural History," the sketch ends with a farmer as everyman. Instead of rejuvenating only the narrator, this one, pleasantly snowbound, extends his generosity further and is "charitable and liberal to all creatures."

In "The Landlord," Thoreau travels as far as possible from his conception of the adversarial reader and calls for a most Whitmanian, collusive other. The landlord depicted in this sketch, described almost entirely as "he," deliberately blends the "I" with the "you." The good host may be seen as the reader congenially attending to the traveler's narrations or as the speaker defining his intended relationship with his audience, a relationship that comes closer to, though is gentler than, that of author as "useful tool," as suggested in "Life Without Principle." Most importantly, "The Landlord" establishes the reciprocal relationship between speaker and audience, writer and reader that Thoreau hoped to establish in these essays. The relationship is so symbiotic that it can be imagined in a single figure, the good host of the public house. These essays are "entertainments" in the double sense of the verb, in which a performer can "entertain" his audience, and an audience can "entertain" the thoughts of a speaker. Author and reader are mutual hosts; each "entertains" the other as its guest.

In his "Biographical Sketch," Emerson emphasized Thoreau's antagonistic, even "military" streak. Rarely "tender, as if he did not feel himself except in opposition," Thoreau found it much easier to say no than yes. However, Emerson also relates the time when a young girl asked Thoreau if his lecture would be "a nice interesting story" or one of "those old philosophical things," and Thoreau seriously responded. He thought hard, "trying to believe that he had matter that might fit her and her brother."[4] Moreover, one day, "talking of a public discourse," Thoreau commented "that whatever succeeded with the audience was bad" and "vaunted the better lectures which reached only a few persons," and Emerson replied, "Who would not like to write something which all can read, like 'Robinson Crusoe'?" Emerson does not record Thoreau's response in his "Biographical Sketch," but Thoreau's position on a companionable narrative tone and the involvement of the audience as the speaker's companion is presented in his more extended narratives.

Before moving on to that demonstration in "Resistance to Civil Government" and his first published book, a final comment on "A Winter Walk" is in order. That essay makes many rhetorical assertions, such as that truth lies somewhere "twixt Venus and Mars" or between love and war (or between voice and countervoice), and that nature's fantastic forms are most useful when they become models for art. However, one sentence is particularly astonishing. Thoreau writes that when winter's blasts (and the blasts of outward reality) drive all within (whether to shelter or into language), then, "All things beside seem to be called in for shelter, and what stays out must be part of the original frame of the universe, and of such valor as God himself." In rhetorical terms, whatever escapes the games and frames of language, so fastidiously and arduously constructed, must be "true." When a multifolded rhetoric speaks in polyphonic voices suggesting many possible meanings, then one has gone the farthest one can go in creating a style that appears to suggest something true, but that truth remains outside the text, beyond the sheltering grasp of author and reader.

3. "RESISTANCE" AND *A WEEK*

Sometimes Thoreau's audience is instructed to be adversarial; at others, it is invited to be companionable. Quite different audience expectations are put forth in an essay like "Resistance to Civil Government."[1] When the adversarial audience sets the rhetorical tone, as in "Walking, or The Wild," it is also made separate from the text. "Walking" could even be published (as in fact it has been) without its opening paragraph. Although there would be no loss in substance, the rhetorical signals would be lost. A completely different persona would be speaking, and the extreme, exaggerated voice could be missed.

With "Resistance," however, the audience enters directly into the text, and its presence shapes the argument and governs the rhetorical directions. The first fourteen of the essay's forty-five paragraphs (nearly a third of "Resistance") are given over to a determination of audience. There is no need to inspire the few heroes, patriots, and martyrs who already serve the state with their consciences, and it is futile to address the mass of men who unthinkingly serve the state with their bodies like machines or with their heads like politicians. The principal audience that Thoreau carefully describes are those who are already "well-disposed" to lead a just and moral life (paragraph 4) but "are daily made the agents of injustice," those "patrons of virtue" who could become in fact virtuous (10), those "most conscientious supporters" (14) who comply with the state even though they disapprove of its "character and measure." Without this presumed audience, "Resistance" makes no sense. Without the belief that a sufficient number of potential converts exists to make a difference, there would be no reason to compose the document. Without the hope that the audience of patrons could be converted into virtuous individualists, the argument would fall flat.

Thoreau has meticulously defined this audience after backing it into a corner. Those who had desired justice through government by minority rule are told they cannot have it, as shown by the Mexican War; those who had hoped for justice through majority rule are denied their desire, as proven by the support of slavery and the fate of the Indian. Since all existing states must involve rule by majority or minority, government by conscience, Thoreau argues, is the only hope for justice. In "Walking," the audience can stand apart as an opposed other; the speaker's "extreme statement" may then be justified as rhetorical opposition to adamant conservatism. However, the audience of "Resistance" participates in the framing of the text. It accounts for its genesis and its argument. Without it, the exercise is otiose.

Having inveigled the audience into the text and defined its character, the argument proceeds, first with a plan for resistance as "action from principle" (15–24), then as a "history of 'My Prisons' " (25–35), and concluding with statements of idealistic inspiration like "the lawyer's truth is not Truth" (42) and the expression of desire for a "still more perfect and glorious state" (45). The first section offers a plan in case patrons remain patrons through ignorance; they simply know not what to do. The last section is meant to inspire those who know but suffer cowardice. The audience, having been established in the first fourteen paragraphs, becomes a reader through these next sections, passively observing the speaker as he unfolds his plan, history, and inspiration. But in paragraph 39, the reader becomes an active participant in the text once again through a clever rhetorical manipulation of pronouns. The paragraph opens by representing the enemies of justice as "it" and "they"— the state, brute force, the masses of millions, the status quo, his neighbors, and "things as they are." The "I" has been a militant idealist in forceful opposition to the power of the third-person, but suddenly this division shifts:

Again, I sometimes say to myself, When many millions of men, without heat, without ill will, without personal feeling of any kind, demand of you a few shillings only, without the possibility, such is their constitution, of retracting or altering their present demand, and without the possibility, on your side, of appeal to any other millions, why expose yourself to this overwhelming brute force? You do not resist cold and hunger, the winds and the waves, thus obstinately; you quietly submit to a thousand similar necessities. You do not put your head into the fire.

Note the rhetorical reversals. The virtuous "I" has abruptly shifted to become momentarily the patron of virtue, the principal audience of the essay's first third. The "you," the second-person address heretofore reserved for the audience of potential converts to idealism, has come to represent the idealist. The characters of the "I" and the fallen "you" have been blurred.

This splitting/blurring device does not stop there. Immediately after the passage just quoted, Thoreau goes on to reason that it is not futile to resist the government and the state because they are "not wholly a brute force, but partly a human force." Therefore, appeal is possible "from them to the Maker of the them" and "from them to themselves." The first-, the second-, and the third-person pronouns have all been fractured, and for a time they all merge into a "we." Those clearly defined pronoun divisions at the essay's outset have blended. The typology that had divided humanity as idealist versus realist, politician versus reformer, patron of virtue versus virtuous person has collapsed, resulting in a new definition of humanity wherein the supposedly different types and various audiences reside within each individual. Rhetorically, the audience, the speaker, and the better part of the opposed other of "them" meet.

This fusion of types can cause audience confusion. "Resistance" had initially seemed an obvious lecture in the mode of "I say unto you." But by the thirty-ninth paragraph, it has intruded into the genre of the *Journal* with its motto, "Says I to myself." Readers who had resisted Thoreau's opening persona and felt themselves chastised as among the "they" at the beginning of the essay may be perplexed to find themselves among "us" before the essay closes. Readers who had identified with the essay's initial "I" and who had felt they occupied a higher moral ground than the "they" might be more than perplexed. They could be dismayed to hear that their "I" shared the same practical doubts as the "you," and that the "I," "you," and "they" were all nuances of "we."

In Thoreau's first book, the situation becomes even more complex, and audience roles are more elaborately developed. With respect to the interweaving of a narrative "I" with an adversarial "you" and an empathetic "we," *A Week on the Rivers* has three essential sections. In the first section alone, several permutations of the writer-reader relationship occur. The introductory chapter, called "Concord River," defines its audience as an initial reading "you," it effects the evolution of a passive speaker into an active "I," and it clarifies the writer's relationship with the reader. In "Sunday," *A Week*'s first chapter, the text blends together the narrator and reader. The "I" and "you" merge into a mystic "we" representing a common humanity. But, in contrast to "Resistance," where such fusion topples categories, this fusion of "I" and "you" into "we" concurrently creates a "they," a group antithetical to the solidarity and idealism of "we," an enemy not only of the speaker-audience but of the best instincts of humanity. But by the time the book moves to its final chapter, this antithesis is dissolved. In fact, all divisions, distinctions, and separations, including words—words as the divisive elements of a general language

—are absorbed by silence. By "Friday," the book's final chapter, the speaker is made one with his audience, personality and philosophy evaporate into silence, and the act of reading, wherein a book's value lies principally in its translation, in its never-ending "sequel" of perpetual interpretation, is elevated into literature's supreme—perhaps its only—activity.

A Week opens with a quiet "I." Passive verb construction and weak predicates are dominant ("it begins," "the shore is," "the meadows acquire"), and the "I" appears only when it is being acted upon by others—quoting the "historian of Concord," being told about floods by farmers, reading an almanac or Edward Johnson's book, or begging the reader's pardon in comparing Concord River with classical Helicon.[2] Suddenly a more active "I" breaks forth in the introduction's last paragraph, and its appearance keeps pace with the transformation of the river from a mere geographical entity into "an emblem of all progress" and a microcosm of universal laws. But in the next paragraph, this forceful "I," the persona that will dominate in *Walden,* is here immediately merged into a "we"— "we two, brothers and natives of Concord." The independent, acting "I" is again anchored by a "we" just as the reader is reminded that the independent and individualistic speaker of the text is also bound by his familial and societal relationships. Moreover, that familiar Thoreauvian "I" emerges only after "Concord River" has established the reader as the true voyager of the text.

In paragraph 2, passive construction has given way to "you," an imagined reader floating past the towns along the Concord and perhaps running aground on Cranberry Island, where one can freeze as icily as anywhere on the northwest coast. Then Thoreau introduces his first pun in the middle of the paragraph: "I never voyaged so far in all my life." That is, factually he never went so far geographically, yet going as far as Cranberry Island is microcosmically executing a voyage never to be exceeded, just as freezing to death is a final experience whether in Concord or Alaska. After this pun, the audience of "you" is clearly defined. The reader is not a "they," not those "who sit in parlors" and merely dream, experiencing neither firsthand nor vicariously through books. Thoreau's audience uses Thoreau's text as though it were borrowing his dory; it voyages through the words exactly as Thoreau once oared along the rivers, seeing "men you never heard of before, whose names you don't know" and experiencing sights denied the nonaudience of parlor dreamers.

There are two "theys" in this second paragraph. The first remains in their parlors declining the opportunity to read. The second consists of those men the reader-voyager shall see, men portrayed as objectified "others." Although their names may become known, they remain strangers, in contrast to the subjectival "we" of narrative "I" and reading "you." This "they" of "rude and sturdy, experienced and wise men, keeping their castles" sounds suspiciously like a pluralized version of Thoreau's Landlord. Like the Landlord, they are limned as "fuller of talk and rare adventure ... than a chestnut is of meat" and as "greater men than Homer, or Chaucer, or Shakespeare." These are men of action who, unlike "Thoreau and his reader and like the parlor dreamers, do not participate in the literary process. Their deeds are "written on the face of the earth," and as they continue to work they continually are "erasing what they have already written for want of parchment." This "they" is idealized but remains as alien to the literary experience as the "they" of parlor dreamers.

This division of two "theys" separate from the "we" of narrator and reader becomes more intensified in the mock sermon of the "Sunday" chapter. "Sunday" opens with the travelers in harmony with Nature; their campfire smoke "curled up like a still subtiler mist" through nature's "dense fog," which enveloped both river and land. But "before we had rowed many rods," the sun rose and dispersed the mists. As the fog fades, exposing distinctions between water and woods, the text presents ontological distinctions between sin and innocence, memory and experience, nature and art.[3] After geographical and philosophical distinctions appear through the dispersing fog, the text presents distinctions of several "theys" in opposition to the reader-narrator's "we." A poem by Channing is quoted only to be dismissed as "too serious for our page" or as too personally concerned, addressed only to an ideal other-self reader and not to the fellow traveler in the boat or in the book. "Two men in a skiff" are passed "floating buoyantly amid the reflections of the trees," a mirror reflection of the two brothers or of the reader and writer. However, they are alien to the text and are separate as "others" from the reading experience, remaining "they two" as distinct from *A Week*'s "we two."

The most remote "they" are those early "Yengeese," men of action like those ideally portrayed in "Concord River." But in this chapter, they are presented as white men "pale as the dawn" who soberly displace the native inhabitants even as they supplant Indian placenames with "a list of ancient Saxon, Norman, and Celtic names." These are the ancestors of present Yankees, a New England audience, the adversarial one Thoreau presumed in his lectures, who may receive the New Testament outwardly and defend it with "bigotry," but to whom its truth is "truly strange, and heretical, and unpopular." This is an audience that may have attended "barrels of sermons" but never truly heard them: "They never *were* read, they never *were* heard. Let but one of these sentences be rightly read, from any pulpit in the land, and there would not be left one stone of that meetinghouse upon another" (41). Expecting that his fellow traveler can "rightly read," Thoreau has posited these opposed "theys" in order to suggest a more intensified "we." When rightly reading, "we" experience a "higher poetical truth" than history or science provides. "We seem to hear the music of a thought, and care not if the understanding be not gratified." Through right reading, time and distance and cultural distinctions can be transcended, as witnessed by the universal enjoyment of ancient fables. The "universal language" available to right reading, Thoreau asserts, "is the most impressive proof of a common humanity," and "all nations love the same jests and tales." As evidence, Thoreau (perhaps recalling the same chat Emerson would later insert into his "Biographical Sketch") refers to Moslems reading an Arabic translation of *Robinson Crusoe* and exclaiming, "Oh, that Robinson Crusoe must have been a great prophet!" (20).

Ironically, when humanity is split into oppositional "theys," a cosmic "we" emerges, transcending the companionable "we" of author and reader. In parallel fashion, the human activity of making books is discussed generously and companionably only to be divided into several types, few of which are commendable, and then is elevated to a cosmic plane. In other words, Thoreau's discussion of books parallels his definition of genre as dependent upon his conception of audience function—from companionable essay to adversarial lecture to ideal reader of poems and journals. "Everything that is printed and bound in a book contains some echo at least of the best that is in literature," Thoreau says at one point (70), only to insist later that "all that are printed and bound are not books" (83) and to chastise books for being decadent, timid, mere "pencraft" and able writing, learned, flowery, labored or idle.

Indeed, he rejects all books except those that are bibles, and his definition of "bible" hinges on two elements. One, often discussed with little consensus, is that spiritual cliché: a divine truth. The other element involves a transcendence of text over personality. Just as Thoreau believes that the best religion is one that transcends "the personality of God" (39, 49), the best book is one that escapes the personality of a writer or a reader. Like those Moslems who revered Robinson Crusoe as his book's creator, a good book directs attention away from the author toward the independence of the text. The act of reading becomes elevated over a particular writer or a specific reader. Another name than "bibles" that Thoreau gives to this best of books is "mythology." "So far from being false or fabulous in the common sense, it contains only enduring and essential truth, *the I and you, the here and there, and now and then, being omitted*. Either time or rare wisdom writes it" (21; my italics). The writer has been absorbed into the text; the reader or, more accurately, the act of reading has become supreme.

That is the concluding message of *A Week*'s final pages, the last seven paragraphs of "Friday." The message opens with the natural activity of star-gazing, beginning with the "we" of Thoreau and John looking up "in silence to those distant lights" and ending with "you," the reader, earnestly extending your eyes upward to the "distant and unobtrusive" stars. This natural action sparks a mystic paean to the supremacy of Silence, that "sequel to all dull discourses and all foolish acts" as well as that natural conclusion to "the most excellent speech," wherein "no personality [can] disturb us" and that is compared to the mutely telling background of a painting regardless "however awkward a figure we have made in the foreground." All of creation is merely silence's "visible framework and foil," and "all sounds are her servants," only "bubbles on her surface, which straightway burst," only "heighteners and intensifiers of the Silence."

What Thoreau is doing is clear. Through common natural activity and philosophical speculation, he is building to a conclusion that demotes "his volume" to a mere "mole whereon the waves of Silence may break" and that elevates the reading experience, an activity that Thoreau expects to continue to grow long after the final page is turned, above the reading matter that provoked it. The text is made subservient to the reader's translation, and,

> A good book is the plectrum with which our else silent lyres are struck. We not unfrequently refer the interest which belongs to our own unwritten sequel, to the written and comparatively lifeless body of the work. Of all books this sequel is the most indispensable part.

To achieve this effect, Thoreau hopes that he as writer and character has become a figment of the reader's consciousness, that in this text he does not seem like the lecturer or opposed other, but has merged into the reading experience, much like his orator who "puts off his individuality, and is then most eloquent when most silent. He listens while he speaks, and is a hearer along with his audience."

The narrative "I" has been blended into a reading "we" of many readers reading diversely, conceiving different images of that speaking "I." Thoreau felt this to be necessary because of the impossibility of telling the whole truth as he pictured it, offering hints and suggestions instead, trusting to the reading experience to expand them. In a telling metaphor near *A Week*'s end, the text has moved from a narrative "I" peering at the stars to an idealized "he" or successful writer represented as a deep sea diver: "for when he at length dives into her, so vast is the disproportion of the told to the untold that the former will seem but the bubble on the surface where he disappeared." The speaking "I" through his disappearance draws attention to his text, a bubble of "the told" that in turn draws attention to the oceanic vastness of the untold, the infinite margins of the text that can be appreciated only by the perpetual process of reading. The actual two-weeks' experience that Thoreau compressed into a seven-days' narration offers only the illusion of completion or closure. The conclusion of his text depends on inconclusion, continual translation, the "most indispensable" sequel of eternal reading. To cease reading, or to become content with a final reading, is to parallel the negative imagery describing the journey's end in *A Week*'s last paragraph, where the boat is "grating against the bulrushes," and the vegetation is mashed like "flattened flags," and the wild apple tree is chafed by its chain. The text, however, tethered to its readers, does not end; it only awaits the next reading, its sounds "ever sounding and resounding in the ears of men."

4. A "CUMULATIVE TREASURE"

Oceans may be the final destination of the Concord and Merrimack, but many rivers conflate to sustain their levels. Silence may be rhetoric's ultimate goal, but many words, cunningly placed, are required to say so. Voyaging out from Concord may have been the impetus for the journey, but Thoreau and his other—his otherly companion, whether literal, fictional, or readerly—arrive finally not at a wild Tahiti but at yet another

"Concord," this one in New Hampshire, sometimes called "New Concord" because settled presumably by earlier voyagers from Thoreau's home town. After arriving at New Concord, where Thoreau and his other are "hospitably entertained," they then depart back to old Concord, the locus whence the narrative "we two" began (303). This voyaging circularity is conflicted by the narrative's quest. Channeled only by the two rivers' meandering courses, the voyage aimed at liberation. It entertained illusions of freedom from social rules, like the injunction against traveling on the Sabbath, as well as of the intellectual freedom to think as wildly as one might wish, a meditative and contemplative freedom reflected by the loose structures of *A Week*'s representation. In *Walden,* Thoreau spent two hundred pages preparing readers for his philosophy of melt, thaw, and flow. In *A Week,* dissolves occur on nearly every page. Even its genre melts. It invites and then defies categorization.

The text seems to offer itself as a guide to boating, but Thoreau waits until page 213 to disabuse us of that notion: the locks are fast closing, and boating will cease altogether on these rivers within a few years. If one seeks to reenact a similar voyage on different rivers, Thoreau informs such adventurous souls that it is not necessary to stroke oar at all; one need not travel to confront the IT of reality, he tells us, for the IT is everywhere, even in one's own backyard, even in one's own study, even in one's own mind (304). And, if readers believe they can voyage vicariously through travelogues, Thoreau reminds them that even his seeming journal is faulty in that regard. Although he and his bosom companion have sworn to record each and every noteworthy event, much has escaped record, particularly the most substantial moments (332). When caught up in an especially intense meditation or adventure, Thoreau has let the pen slip, so he tells us; therefore only inferior thoughts and events have been set down in this book.

Considering all these admissions, how then are we meant to receive *A Week?* Thoreau tells us it is not a travelogue. Nor is it a guide book. It is not an accurate record of experience, nor a diary. So then what is it? What genre does it fit? It does not even presume to be an ode upon nature, as his famous *Walden* will be taken to be, nor quite the seemingly revolutionary document "Resistance to Civil Government." How then should we receive this text that Thoreau has dumped onto our laps as a travelogue, as its title would indicate, and as a philosophical apology or aesthetic credo, as its context would suggest?

Linck C. Johnson has explained that *A Week* is Thoreau's complex working out of his relationship with his deceased brother, and *A Week* is an even more complex working out of Thoreau's difficulties in expressing any and all facts; that is, *A Week*'s main focus is language itself. At one and the same time, it articulates what he most aspires to do with rhetoric and confesses language's limitations. At one and the same time, it is a boast and a lament of precisely what he could and could not do with language. Just as *A Week* seems attracted to but shies away from fulfilling a particular genre, Thoreau's rhetoric desires to express it all, fears it has said nothing. It exalts silence as a supreme rhetorical aim but worries that his supreme rhetoric may be a humbug. His rhetorical goals are clear, but his confidence in achieving them is less sure. At its most successful, the rhetoric he aims at should dissolve all artificial divisions and categorizations. Hence, on even the most fundamental level, he often obfuscates just who is acting, the narrator or his companion. One might sleep peacefully while the other is wracked by nightmare. One might tether the boat while the other goes abroad. One might eat a melon while the other speaks with a farm girl. Whoever the "one" is, or whatever the point being developed, personality is insignificant. All are equally involved (dissolved) in the voyage, whether the literal voyage upon the two rivers or the more abstract voyage of literacy between a narrator and his others, who might easily believe they have occupied one end of the textual boat.[1]

On a more sophisticated level, Thoreau's hopes for rhetorical dissolves are all the more emphatic. In fact, the entire text of *A Week* seems directed to this end. It carefully argues the oxymoronic essence of nature and human activity. He goes to extreme ends to conflate seeming opposites. Hints of night are found in day, even in day's penultimate nooning (320). Summer's maturity is discovered in autumn's onset (334). Wildness felt in the rustle of wind in the leaves is blended with the rush of water over rocks (334). These rather simplistic paradoxes are echoed in humanity's efforts. Any biography is really autobiography, a reader's translation of another life (156). Any history is really a presentation of the historian's prejudices and his era's taste (155).

Thoreau's dissolves do not stop at that level. He extends the metaphor to encompass all matter and all means of knowing. An idea does not simply suggest its opposite; it merges with its other, just as *A Week*'s narrative "I" often becomes "one or the other." Even truth and falsehood are no longer distinct nor antithetical. As he says in one of his most stunning statements, "Falsehood never attains to the dignity of entire falseness, but is only an inferior sort of truth; if it were thoroughly false, it would incur danger of becoming true" (311). In truth, or in the expression of truth, the categorical true and false are trivial. Any idea settled as true or false is inferior to the attempt at a great dissolve. Settled ideas are like the feeling Thoreau has in a library that houses "all the recorded wit of the world, but none of the recording, a mere accumulated, and not *truly cumulative treasure* ..." (341; emphasis mine). Thoreau wants a rhetoric that floats ideas and impressions, not one that resolves them. Literacy should be an ever-evolving "cumulative treasure" of constant reading, not a static accumulation. He prefers what he variously calls a "universal language," a "mythology," or a "poetical truth," in which significance always remains elusive, in which "a variety of truths" are suggested but never promulgated. In his wild rhetoric, "the music of a thought" is heard even if "the understanding be not gratified." In that musical representation, "the I and you, the here and there, the now and then" are dissolved (58–61).

In the midst of his deployment of beautiful words and precise descriptions, he never loses sight of his goal of a transcendent rhetoric wherein words point beyond their statements, names suggest the unnamed, and meaning implies a more meaningful silence: "Buoyancy, freedom, flexibility, variety, possibility" are the essential rhetorical "qualities of the Unnamed" that Thoreau hopes the gaps and contradictions in his sentences will create (136). This rhetoric of "the Unnamed," Thoreau believes, is closer to life, more like the way he reads nature and perceives his own experiences. He attempts to perfect an "imperfect" style more natural than that taught in textbooks. Rejecting Aristotelian aesthetics, he records how "the Scene-shifter saw fit here to close the drama of this day, without regard to any unities which we mortals prize. Whether it might have proved tragedy, or comedy, or tragi-comedy, or pastoral, we cannot tell" (114). Nor would his readers be able to classify *A Week* as a particular literary genre. His text would resist any efforts to find structural unities. Even a vague, oxymoronic category like "tragi-comedy" is insufficiently loose to tether his text to a genre.

This description of the disunities of life mirrored in his literary expression follows hard upon more specific dissolves. He has noted the "innocent indifference of Nature," an indifference his most intense empathy cannot pierce nor sway. He seems almost to anticipate Melville by parodying a whale hunt as though prewriting *Moby-Dick* as a mock-epic. He and his companion hunt a "dark and monstrous" fish. The "bow-gunner" delivered his charge, while the stern-man held his ground," but they succeeded only in harpooning "a huge imprisoned spar, placed there as a buoy." Embarrassed, the merged "we" retreat: "So, each casting some blame upon the other, we withdrew quickly to safer waters" (113–14). Later, a passerby inquires whether they had any luck fishing, and one of them answers no, but they "had shot a buoy." They leave the puzzled bystander scratching his head. Readers would not be confused by the homophone; a readerly passerby might miss the pun of "boy" upon "buoy" because the words look so different in print. In fact, the pun was not intended. The speaker realized it was a possible pun only when he uttered it, realized it only because of his listener's reaction as the real-life passerby scratched his head.

Readers would not be misled by this particular word, but what other words had caused consternation and confusion? What other words had the author spoken whose different meanings he had missed, having no audience reaction to signal him as to other possible interpretations? Moreover, what deliberate damage to the credibility of the speaker and his text has been rendered by this self-parody? What authority has been diminished? What confidence can readers safely have when their author presents his profoundest beliefs in the context of misreading? He has deliberately revealed that he can easily make glaring mistakes like confusing a man-made buoy with a fish of nature. He has pointed out one homophonic mistake, leaving readers to suspect other linguistic errors. This is a technique Thoreau deployed in his other published works; he was fond of questioning his narrative authority, usually as he was about to pontificate upon an authoritative truth. He casts doubt upon his reliability just as he is about to land a huge philosophical fish.

Note where the self-parody is placed. Just as he is about to articulate his aesthetic ideal of trespassing generic boundaries and of creating an artistic style closest to life itself, he chooses to tell his readers that they are foolish if they place much faith in the authority of their author, in the reliability of his relation. What is the intended rhetorical effect of this deflation of authority? A text that elsewhere will champion the quest for ideals, the value of dreams, and the excitement of heroic living, here punctures an ideal as illusion. It is as though Ahab finally captures the great white whale only to discover it is Queequeg's coffin or an overturned whaleboat. It is worse than the supposed monster in Poe's "The Sphinx" that turns out to be only a bug. And, if Thoreau's biggest fish of all was writing itself, then what implications does this self-parody entail with respect to his obsession with a supreme rhetoric?

To address these complex questions fairly, I would like to curl back a bit and sneak up on them from the flank. The five essential qualities of his wild rhetoric of "the Unnamed"—"buoyancy, freedom, flexibility, variety, possibility"—are not as simple as they seem. After all, Thoreau has told us he has already mistaken a buoy for a fish, and his "buoyancy" may as readily be mistaken for a stagnant, because elucidated, concept. When the text has been studied and interpretation commences, the communicative voyaging may end up, like the boat at *A Week*'s conclusion, tethered to the shore. The safest waters we can retreat to, like Thoreau's "we" after their failed whaling expedition, is the bay in which Thoreau specifies what his writing is not. Hoping that a regrouping can launch a more successful attack, we can reform around his rhetoric's other, keeping in mind that one main aim of his wild rhetoric is to collapse boundaries, to dissolve antithesis, to merge all antitheses into oxymorons, paradoxes, and the "flexibility" of language. In short, we retreat to the "agonies" of his rhetoric, the agons, the struggles, the contests, the unresolved problems of his language.

Despite the disunities of *A Week,* it is clear what kind of language Thoreau opposes. He is against didacticism, rules, creeds, settled morals, pellucid style, explicit language, proverbial truisms. Once readers are *"sentenced"*—are made to receive an author's clear meaning without being provoked into thought by arguing with or puzzling through his words— they cease to be "freemen of the universe" (148). He laments that the stars themselves, if colonized, would cease to be symbols of imaginative stimulation and would become the loci of political debates on whether they should be free or slave states, meaning that a "free state" is as much enslaved, because committed, as any settled position (387). He scoffs at the usual kind of essay writing that has a thesis to prove, characterizing such as "one-idea'd, like a school-boy's theme, such as youths write and afterward [should] burn" (185). In *A Week*'s "Sunday" chapter, he gently satirizes rote reading, comparing didacticism to flies that annoy cows: "At a third of a mile over the water we heard distinctly some children repeating their catechism in a cottage near the shore, while in the broad shallows between, a herd of cows stood lashing their sides, and waging war with the flies" (80). The kind of language he opposes is clear, but not the kind of language he favors, especially since the kind he favors must dissolve all distinction and precision, including its own assertions and preferences. Thoreau lies in safe waters as long as he is discussing the kind of language he opposes, such as the "one-idea'd" instructions of the antithetical authorities of the priest and the physician, whose professions (i.e., that which they profess) is always "a satire on the other's, and either's success would be the other's failure" (257).

But he roils in troubled waters when he attempts to advance more positive statements. When he says, "We are double-edged blades, and every time we whet our virtue the return stroke straps our vice," his readers wonder whether their author can then utter any statement without immediately erasing it while remaining true to his rhetorical ideal (224). Likewise, in collapsing boundaries and in merging all distinction, has he not reinvented chaos, the chaos upon the waters before the invention of words and the Word? As long as simplistic proverbs and rote reading are the target, one can agree that "there are sure to be two prescriptions diametrically opposite" (256). But if antitheses are blurred, and if one humanistically presumes that "all things are good," then are we not left in a morass of meaninglessness, a swamp not of communication but of incommunication, in which "men fail at last to distinguish which is the bane, and which the antidote" (256)? Apparently, all one can do is offer various herbs or words and hear some call them toxic and others, beneficial. Thoreau might insist that he is "always agreeably disappointed" at such labeling, but the truth is that his phrases, like "the mystery" of language, are also labels (256). He fears that his supreme rhetoric of wildness, although exposing the limitations and inaccuracies of pellucid writing, does not offer a better resolution, in large part because the resolution he seeks seems to betray the rhetoric he privileges.

As a way to hedge this dread, he is fond of a teasing, taunting narrative strategy. In *A Week*'s most impassioned pages (the paragraphs on love and friendship that he presented to Harrison Blake in a slightly different form on Blake's wedding day), he graphically demonstrates the impossibility of having any significant effect on real-life friends and philosophical lovers, leaving the reader to infer that through writing, a more meaningful union can occur. When he says that "it is impossible to say all that we think, even to our truest Friend," he elevates his readers and makes them presume that they can fulfill a union with their author more substantial than can be achieved even by his "truest Friend."

Anonymous readers can know him more truly through words. Readers can know him "better" than those who knew him personally, intimately. "I could tame a hyena more easily than my Friend," Thoreau insists, continuing to capitalize the relationship, and his capitalization admits impotency—his lack of authority, his lack of author-ity in real-life relationships. He capitalizes, italicizes, underscores, bold-letters, highlights, and emphasizes his readers' greater contact, privileging their greater familiarity, their touch, their relationship with him. In this narrative strategy, he is powerless, or so he tells his readers (thereby gaining in authority with readers), to carve even "the smallest chip out of the character of my Friend, either to beautify or deform it." Thereby, he hopes to make his readers feel more valued than even his closest Friend. We are made to feel more intimate and empathetic, only to find that ultimately our superior relationship to Thoreau's Friend, against whom the author is powerless, makes us submissive to Thoreau's intentions, makes us less powerful than the author who is powerless before his Friends. At once, we readers are made the most puissant powers in Thoreau's universe and the most malleable to his words.

He would like his words to point to the Unnamed, to imply the unworldly, to suggest a universal language beyond language's web of signs. But he is aware that his aims may be quixotic; he recognizes that windmills suggesting giants must begin with windmills. The Unnamed, no matter how he capitalizes it, must start with names. Language must begin with words, and its meaning might also stop there. No matter how misty and smoky he wants his words to be, no matter how often he implores readers to seek his meanings beyond the words that suggest them, he is aware of the finality of language. He might desire to articulate "the naked and absolute beauty" of truth, but he knows that articulation demands communication, and communication entails negotiation with readers' demands and literary conventions. He might wish to articulate abstract conceptions, but he knows that "most men prefer to have some of the wood along with the principle; they demand that the truth be clothed in flesh and blood and the warm colors of life" (361). A new thought depends on the old, a new expression feeds upon established conceptions of literacy.

Locked within his own literate conceptions as surely as his boat is channeled along the rivers by their banks, he acknowledges that literacy is traditionary, that communication must depend upon translation and appropriation of meaning. Although he might want *A Week* to transcend literary categories of tragedy or comedy or even tragicomedy, he has no qualms about characterizing one death as a categorical tragedy. Commenting on the common experience that dead birds are seldom seen, he says that sparrows may seem "always *chipper,*" yet there "is a tragedy at the end of each one of their lives. They must perish miserably." Thoreau can afford to sound categorical, because the author's authority has been transferred. A sparrow's death is tragic, he can proclaim, not because Thoreau says so, and not so much because it is a raw fact of life, but because "not one of them is translated" (224). The true tragedy of the sparrow's death is that it has not been seen. Since it is not read, no epitaph can be written to be read by others; its death is a "tragedy" because it has no readers. Ultimately, writers write to say hello, to introduce themselves to the world. But the god-like role of marking each writer's rise or fall is reserved for those transcendent friends called readers.

Life, whether the life of a simple sparrow or the life of a complex text, matters only in the act of translation. Or so Thoreau believed. No life arises in the memorization of catechisms any more than in the swatting of flies. To ensure the translation of his words, the author then must guarantee that the reader is forced to interpret. To avoid stagnation of meaning, the writer must create texts that defy explicit decoding. One technique that insures forced translation is to insist on the perpetual remoteness of meaning and the persistent likeness of images. Another is to contradict a statement as soon as it is uttered. Not content to let matters lie even at that level, the author undercuts his own contradiction, effecting contradiction. One of the most blatant examples of this technique is when he offers two short poems, separated by only ten pages, that contradict each other even though each independently sounds wise. Thus, at one point, he incorporates his oft-quoted couplet: "My life has been the poem I would have writ, / But I could not both live and utter it." Elevating living over writing, privileging the art of life over the life of art, the couplet may seem ironic or contradictory, coming as it does after three hundred fine pages of prose in a text that took ten years to write. Be that as it may, the maxim is further vitiated ten pages later when Thoreau writes about the pointlessness of a life unexpressed in language: "And what's a life? The flourishing array / Of the proud summer meadow, which to-day / Wears her green plush, and is to-morrow hay" (353).

Another obvious technique that achieves contra-diction occurs when Thoreau spends pages revitalizing a stereotyped word, giving new mean-- ing to what Emerson called "rotten diction" only to dissolve the distinctions he has made. In *Walden,* he praises the Indian wisdom of living in teepees against civilization's slavery to houses, and yet he builds a cabin, a structure more like city-built homes than teepees. *Walden* also seems to valorize an Indian's tangible basket over a lawyer's argument woven of words, yet *Walden* and *A Week,* the basket "of delicate texture" that Thoreau did not deign to sell, resemble more closely the lawyer's word-weavings than the Indian's basket. Similarly, in *A Week* he constructs an elaborate network of words to define his radical concept of friendship. Yet in the midst of his disquisition he interrupts his argument to comment— to contradict his diction, to vaporize the various truths and countertruths he has proffered—to say, "But all that can be said of Friendship, is like botany to flowers" (285). A similar interruption occurs in the *Journal* after he has led readers up the Merrimack until it becomes the Pemmig-gewasset, and he suddenly wonders, "Why should we take the reader . . . through this rude tract?" (*PJ2,* 280).

Sometimes this technique is handled at long length. One example covers over sixty pages, beginning with an exchange of what Michel Foucault would call "the gaze of power" between the traveling narrator and his landbound lockskeeper at (appropriately) the Middlesex Locks, just at the point where he embarks upon the more lively currents of the Merrimack in contrast to the comparatively dead waters of the Concord River (79). The livelier waters encourage wilder thoughts, or so Thoreau signals. The transfer provokes commentaries on the scene-shifter and the disunities of experience, the ur-*Moby-Dick* self-parody, the criticism of rote learning, and the essential qualities of the Unnamed.

Thoreau also offers yet another example of eroticism in writing, this time using the image of casting one's seeds (125), and he proposes a thorny conundrum to his readers: "Read only great poems (ironically, poems greater than the text you now read), but truly great poems have not yet been written, not even by Homer or Shakespeare. Nevertheless, read only what you take or have been instructed to take as "great poems." They will fail to live up to your expectations, and that is good, for when they fail to be great, then you will answer by writing more (95).

Throughout these sixty-odd pages, Thoreau wanders from the sublime to the ridiculous and back again. He offers minute description and philosophical revery. He seems at one time completely serious, and at another intent on playing the fool. Often it is difficult to tell which mask he is wearing, to determine precisely when he is playing Gog or Magog or both. He seems all things in an hour, much like nature, much like his own self-characterization to friends in his correspondence.

The main point is that after this cornucopia of assertion and contradiction, seriousness and silliness, poetic description and prosaic quotation of second-rate historians, Thoreau pulls the rhetorical rug out from under any reader's feet. Whether his interpreter is studying him for his science or for his poetry, for his seriousness or for his comedy, for his politics or for his whimsy, any and all readings of the last sixty pages are sabotaged. Any ship constructed around any thematic keelson is scuttled. Thoreau concludes—or, one should say, he inconcludes—this section of *A Week* by claiming, "But how can I communicate with the gods who am a pencil-maker on the earth, and not be insane?" (140). Thoreau has supplied much yarn (and many yarns) in these pages, but as soon as a reader begins to weave a pattern from them, Thoreau unweaves the pattern just woven. He is naught but a pencil-maker and a pencil-mover. Any meaning from the lines his pencil has drawn is the responsibility of his readers—their pride, blame, perchance their shame, mayhap their honor.

Admittedly, it is difficult to follow this erasure over such an extended space, but Thoreau has provided more compact examples. One takes only six dense pages. Starting on page 152, he articulates many provocative points: writers are considered great because their readers offer such diverse commentaries upon their mentor's words; hence, writers are deemed "great" because of the shadow they cast among interpreters. Thoreau also argues that texts on reality are more significant than the reality they seek to capture. Reality is always the same, he opines; only the modes and degrees of seeing vary. He also reasons that remoteness is the quintessence of literary effectiveness, for a remote rhetoric provides a glimpse of reality "increate." Other abstruse ideas abound, more than this book can frame. But the chief idea is the freedom Thoreau believed lay in his blanked canvas, his un-written white page—his page, first covered with letters and then un-lettered, erased, un-written, re-blanked. Therefore, this section finishes with no ringing dictum or hortatory maxim. Instead, by way of erasure, an interruptive ellipsis to profound thought, it merely concludes succinctly and prosaically, "However we do not know much about it" (158). Six pages of dense, closely reasoned argument, only to dissolve in this disclaimer. It is like the reading experience in the "Matmaker" chapter of *Moby-Dick* wherein the most complex questions of fate, free will, and necessity are investigated, only to be interrupted by a call to action. Thoreau's meditation is interrupted by no shout of "Thar she blows!" His "waking dream" was disturbed merely when "suddenly, a boatman's horn was heard, echoing from shore to shore," echoing from thought against thought (158).

Having struggled through pages of careful textual interpretation, readers are told that their evidence was flimsy. It is like those codas Melville supplies to his short stories that seem meant to elucidate but only obfuscate. Willing readers give themselves up to Thoreau's words in an effort to understand his dictions, even as they involve contradictions, only to discover that he is fond of contra-dictions. Any intelligent reader might rightly balk. After all, readers are "intelligent" because of their wide reading, because of their membership in the community of literacy that Stanley Fish, Harold Bloom, E. D. Hirsh, and others have debated. But here is an author who seems to take away with one hand what his other has given, sometimes retracting his gift immediately, sometimes waiting more than sixty pages to deny.

But the last rhetorical straw has not yet been laid upon the reader's back. Thoreau has another rhetorical complexity to add. In addition to diction, contradiction, and contra-diction, he imposes his rhetoric of eternal remotion. Gratified though we readers may think ourselves to be, feeling that we finally understand what our author says, we are deluded, Thoreau informs us. If he has achieved his rhetorical ideal, we can never rest content. Our sense of having pierced through his various rhetorical levels to arrive at a truthful understanding is false. As Thoreau "makes clear," "For the most part we think that the highest is but little higher than that which we now behold; but we are always deceived. Sublimer visions appear, and the former pale and fade away" (291). Even the great writers of his generation fail in this respect. Goethe is inadequate, Thoreau says, for his thoughts and emotions are expressed too distinctly. He fails because his language is too well bred and too explicit. His writing lacks the language of desire. His words are not "moulded into forms which are incomprehensible, [do not] surround us with a grandeur which we find above our reach" (328).

If a writer writes rightly, and if a reader reads well, then readers (including the writer reading his own works, readers reading, and writers hearing what their readers have read) are conscious that words are quivering signals; words and reality are "these things [that] imply, perchance, that we live on the verge of another and purer realm, from which these odors and sounds [and squiggles] wafted over to us" (381). "Right reading" perpetually hovers on inadequate communication. Hence, "a fine communication from age to age, of the noblest thoughts" that are never quite "communicated by speech, is music! It is the flower of language, thought colored and curved, fluent and flexible." The "remotest" language is associated with "the divinest" and makes "a dream of our only real experience" (174–75). All attempts at literacy, at communication, are thus rhetorically given over to readers' whims, to whatever "aerial and mysterious charm" they decide exists in the text.

As writer, Thoreau knows of no better rhetoric than these oracular inkblots. But he erects one wall at least against communicative chaos with his concept of the reader as the echo that guards against narcissistic self-indulgence and sheer whimsy. At one point in *A Week* he suspects that writing is all a game: "It is almost the only game which the trees play at, this tit-for-tat, now this side in the sun, now that, the drama of the day" (320). But Thoreau also trusts to the night, to the shadow of readers reading, demanding that their midrash or commentary eclipse his scriptures. It is only through a wild rhetoric—that is, through a trust in his text being translated, and his anticipations of possible readings—that he can write what he wants. He can leave *A Week* hypaethral, disunified, disorderly, and rough-hewn because he believes that rough-hewn works best stand the test of time. Indeed, because rough-hewn, they demand time. Thousands of readings over centuries attempt to smooth the hardest edges of a rough-hewn work (377).

In his other published works, many concessions were made to literary expectations, but in *A Week,* as in his *Journal* (which he did not try to publish, to make public, to make publicly consumable), he strove to make his work less "confined by historical, even geological periods." He wanted *A Week,* like nature's pines, to "spire without end higher and higher, and make a graceful fringe to the earth," despite the falsity of even that fringe.

He wanted the "finer cobwebs" of *A Week*'s structures to resemble the leaves, tree tops, and horizons that are beyond human counting, beyond narrative frames. They should be "more various than the alphabets of all languages put together; of the oaks alone there are hardly two alike, and each expresses its own character" (160).

"There was but the sun and the eye from the first," Thoreau claims on page 158. From the beginning to now, there is naught but the sun and the eye, the IT and what an "I" does with it. All the rest is language. All the rest is an attempt to fill the gap between the sun and the eye with words. The most that a supreme rhetoric can do is fill the intervening space with an impression of what Thoreau calls "the increate." Still, he believes that rhetoric is humanistically beneficial. If a writer uses a wild rhetoric effectively, then a good reader can restore the world's (and its words') vitality. "Before the earnest gaze of the reader," Thoreau claims on page 370, "the rust and moss of time gradually drop off, and the original green life is revealed."

Thoreau bestows upon readers the power formerly granted to mythological vegetation gods. This power is consonant with Thoreau's own confessed function as a reader. When he reads Alexander Henry's accounts of his treks to the northland, Thoreau reading is both a global conquerer like Alexander the Great and simply a "Henry," as on his tombstone. The most important part of Alexander Henry's narration, so Thoreau instructs readers in his account, is the sequel, the imaginative carrying through of ideas and possibilities that the text has sparked (219). As he says with respect to his own writings, "If you would not stop to look at me, but look whither I am looking and further, then my education could not dispense with your company" (280). A good reader in Thoreau's terms does not tarry to interpret precisely what he means, but translates beyond his words' pronouncements. A good reader is indispensible to "Thoreau," not the autobiographical author who is, of course, dead, but to the meaning of that nexus of belief, opinion, commercial appropriations, economic considerations, marketplace factualities, ideas, collegiate influences, feelings, and stylistic expressions that some cataloguer will, for matters of convenience, file under a rubric titled "Thoreau."

The rubric "Thoreau" subsumes all readings, from the most fastidiously scholarly book to my automobile mechanic leaning against a wall of his garage reading *Walden* on his lunchbreak. It includes the stylish images of Thoreau as "inspirer" in Robert Pirsig's *Zen and the Art of Motorcycle Maintenance* and Stewart Brand's *Whole Earth Catalog,* as well as Zonker's Walden Puddle in Gary Trudeau's "Doonesbury" cartoons, not to mention classroom readings and collegial quips. The nation's most powerful corporations have coopted "Thoreau" in advertisements; simultaneously, America's most radical musical composers (Charles Ives, John Cage) accent his wildness in the compositions inspired by "him." Still others are more attracted to nostalgia and his idealistic conservatism in a world that seems to be disintegrating as rapidly as Thoreau's was in his own era.

But Thoreau is not yet done with his readers and will not let them off easily. Having elevated them to a magnificent height, he expects more from his intimate readers. As he explains at the midpoint of *A Week,* his friends, neighbors, and even his enemies have missed his intentions, but he expects and demands that his literary others do more, see more, hear more, interpret more (206). He expects a divine relationship with readers. He demands an erotic because "vital" union, instructing readers to treat him, if they love him, as he treats the most valuable ancient texts, demanding "this fond reiteration of the oldest expressions of truth by the latest posterity, content with slightly and religiously re-touching the old material." And, he avers, such "re-touching," such reading and rereading, such interpretation and translation, is not idiosyncractic nor egoistic. In fact, to Thoreau it seems "the most impressive truth of a common humanity" (59).

Over the past century, Thoreau has fully emerged from the shadow of being considered Emerson's disciple. Yet, to see Thoreau emerge from under all shadows would create further literary problems. It would also deny Thoreau's belief in the "truth of a common humanity." He was influenced by all shadows that crossed his path, whether cast by beans or Daniel Webster, by pines or Margaret Fuller, by political or religious or popular rhetorical problems, by Emerson or Hawthorne. Of all these shadows, these nimbi of influence, Hawthorne's is significant, in part because of his richly ambivalent relationship to Transcendentalism. With respect to *A Week*'s argument about literacy, a provocative but relatively unknown entry from Hawthorne's *Italian Notebooks* for 21 June 1858 is telling. Studying Michelangelo's "Fates" with a group of friends, Hawthorne contemplates the artistic problem of creating three separate figures that are nevertheless "united, heart and soul, in one purpose." His reading concludes:

But, as regards the interpretation of this, or of any other profound picture, there are likely to be as many interpretations as there are spectators. It is very curious to read criticisms upon pictures, and upon the same face in a picture, and by men of taste and feeling, and to find what different conclusions they arrive at. Each man interprets the hieroglyphic in his own way; and the painter, perhaps, had a meaning which none of them have reached; or possibly he put forth a riddle without himself knowing the solution. There is such a necessity, at all events, of helping the painter out with the spectator's own resources of feeling and imagination, that you can never be sure how much of the picture you have yourself made. There is no doubt that the public is, to a certain extent, right and sure of its ground, when it declares, through a series of ages, that a certain picture is a great work. It is so; a great symbol, proceeding out of a great mind; but if it means one thing, it seems to mean a thousand, and, often, opposite things.[2]

Thoreau shared all these critical values with Hawthorne. Criticism is a "necessity." Although conscious of the limitations of criticism, individuals are compelled to interpret an artist's works. Meaning arises from the interrelationship of the painting or text and its interpreters, and one can never be sure whether a particular interpretation issues more from the artist, the work, the interpreter, or a triangulation among the three. Moreover, a great work is one that seems "incomplete"; it not only demands interpretation, it not only provokes thousands of different interpretations, but a great work's meaning always remains imminent, elusive, and indeterminate, despite the thousand times it is read.

Hawthorne's reading of "Fates" is all the more provocative since Michelangelo's more famous anecdote makes the opposite aesthetic point. As the story goes, when Michelangelo was asked how he created "David," he presumably answered that he had only freed David from the stone. The image was already in the marble; the artist had only to carve away the excess rock. In sharp contrast, Hawthorne's reading of art's function stipulates that the language of a great work is not a coded message that can be deciphered; it does not hide a meaning to be freed. Instead, language is a hieroglyphic perpetually in the process of interpretation. Meaning is not settled argument; it is the process of eternal, universal reading. A great work remains a "great symbol" whose ultimate meaning is ever remote.

Note also the emphasis on a great symbol "proceeding out of a great mind." The gerund accents the idea that the Word is always *about* to be spoken, that meaning is ever *about* to be revealed. Of equal importance is the definition of "a great mind." On the simplest level, the great mind is the creator's. But the great mind that issues the "great symbol" is not only the artist, whether in his role of creator or interpreter of his or her work. The "great mind" is the composite of all those thousands of meanings that readers have found in the text. Moreover, the "great mind" also involves all those other minds that in the time to come will study the work—the individual painting or text, as well as all its commentaries and interpretations. Meaning is reading. *Walden,* as one example, will remain Thoreau's chief work, despite whatever may be Thoreau's or an individual reader's opinion; it has been deemed such by "the great mind" of more than a century of readers.

Hence, Thoreau most admires those writers who develop a language that provokes the great mind of reading. The very fact that there is "an endless dispute" among their interpreters is tribute to the language of writers like Plato, Pythagoras, Zoroaster, and Confucius (152). Their meaning is perpetually raveling. "In the very indistinctness" of their works, in the persistent elusiveness of their language, a "sublime truth is implied" but never resolved. Their language "hardly allows the reader to rest in any supreme first cause, but directly it hints at a supremer still which created the last, and the Creator is still behind increate" (153). They have created texts with gaps and margins for sufficiently wide interpretation that mirror the texts of nature that Thoreau describes. As Thoreau gazes upon the watery reflection of light filtering through trees, he relishes his reading experience most for its sense of perpetual remoteness. "For the most part we think that there are few degrees of sublimity, and that the highest is but little higher than that which we now behold; but we are always deceived. Sublimer visions appear, and the former pale and fade away" (291).

Thoreau is more rhapsodic than Hawthorne when making identical observations upon criticism, reading, language, and interpretation. However, many textual signals indicate that some of Thoreau's most passionate paeans were forced. Frequently *A Week* intimates that his praise for a language of desire may be the aesthetic equivalent of whistling in a graveyard to keep up one's courage. Of the many insinuations of his problems with language, two are especially interesting. One problem is that his critical ideal may be an attempt to make a rhetorical virtue out of a disappointing necessity. The "virtue" of his supreme rhetoric may be an oblique admission of defeat. One facet of this frustration is his awareness that he will be misread anyway, whether as a writer or as a person. Even if he did not use smoky, misty words to create a language of desire that provokes multiple, diverse interpretation, readers would still read him that way. In the "Thursday" chapter of *A Week,* he records how people seize the simplest clues to form their own interpretations. Because he is carrying an umbrella, people assume he is an umbrella mender. Because he is wearing a knapsack, people assume he is a tinker. Because he can close a window on a train, someone presumes he would like a job in a factory. Because of the sheer fact that he is wandering about the country-side, farmers assume he is seeking work as a transient laborer (303–4). It does not take much imagination to see that his description of real-life readers mirrors suspicions about literary ones. His countrymen might note his knapsack or his umbrella and fit those facts into their conceptual-izations. In like manner, his literary readers will be drawn to particular words and sentences that fit their own cognitive schemes. Misreading will occur whether Thoreau is taking a leisurely stroll in the country or painstakingly presenting "Thoreau" in a carefully constructed text.

The fact of misreading is paralleled by the frustration of writing. Meaning may be rhetoric's goal, but words are all a writer has. Words may be misread, and they are also inadequate to capture ideas even if misreading did not occur. Again and again, Thoreau records his disap-pointment over the limitations of words. He calls them "puny," insuffi-cient to the occasion. Even in the simple attempt to say what you feel to a departing friend, words fail you. How much more inadequate are words when you wish to sum up your life on your deathbed—or to describe just a part of your life in a book. "Have you any *last* words?" he asks. "Alas, it is only the word of words, which you have so long sought and found not; *you* have not a *first* word yet" (273). "The language" of his wild rhetoric "is not words but meanings," he avers at one point. "It is an intelligence above language" (273).

But could he always be sure that there was an intelligence beyond language? What was to distinguish a meaningful reading from a misread-ing or from ontological chaos? After all, he criticizes a language that is consummately private, mystical, and "unwordy." While his own rhetoric often promoted a kind of linguistic zen, he comments negatively on "those eastern sages" sitting and contemplating "Brahm, uttering in silence the mystic 'Om,' being absorbed into the essence of the Supreme Being, never going out of themselves, but subsiding further and deeper within; so infinitely wise, yet infinitely stagnant" (136). If "even virtue can become stagnant," so can an overly wild language. Yes, he praises Hindu scripture, and he says that "the reader is nowhere raised into and sustained in a higher, purer, or *rarer* region of thought than in the Bhagvat-Geeta," but he also suggests that its proper translator is the "Chairman of the East India Company" (137). He praises the "sublimity of conception" and "diction" of Oriental writings, but he will couple them with "the British dominion in India." He extols the pregnant possibilities of Buddhism, but he cherishes its clash with the more humanistic, practical, and didactic religion of Christianity, feeling that the battle of philosophies and rhetorics will issue forth "a new avatar." He demands that readers set down their Christ beside his Buddha, for in that collision meaning may be sparked (67). He sometimes instructs audiences to be adversarial, and he will confess that he exaggerates a point, challenging readers to surmise a truth somewhere around its exaggerated expression. He will provide gaps in his texts, daring readers to fill them with meaning.

Thoreau's rhetoric is never quite one thing or another. It is never totally wild or tame. It will utter neither only didactic statements nor only a "mystic Om." It will use a pellucid style and then counter it with inscrutable passages. It will describe a vision vividly, and it will praise a language full of smoke and mist. It will utter an explicit, idealistic maxim, and it will then dissolve the sentiment. As a literary artist, his rhetorical goal is to seem like a sculptor carving ice statues in August that melt even as they are being created.

Thoreau would object to that characterization, even though *A Week* provides ample evidence for it and even though the reader has been licensed to read broadly. After all, as a man of his times, his Romanticism persuades him to believe he is creating smoky truths in heaven, not ice statues in hell. He did not wish to be didactic like Longfellow, and he deviated from Emerson's belief in a divinely beneficent unity. Nevertheless, he frequently returns to a hoped-for concordance. Thus, he quotes Plutarch's comments on Plato about the "discordant parts" of music. He praises music's "want of tune," which "breaks forth into many extravagances and excesses." But he would like to think that discordance can be resolved, that harmony can be restored, that discordance "might be sweetly recalled and artfully wound up to their former consent and agreement" (175). In "The Service," where he cites the same passage, he boldly associates agreement with a "coward's" rhetoric, which reduces a thrilling, discordant music to "a nasal cant"—a "jingle, a jar" (*RP,* 11). But in *A Week* Thoreau makes the description more hopeful. He promises ultimate resolution into "a certain ineffable divinity," without explaining how those two warring adjectives—"certain ineffable"—can be harmonized.

Why else set pen to paper? If one writes only to be misread, to be unread, to be un-read, why take such pains in composition? Why not simply paint a blank canvas and display it in a museum? If a wild rhetoric erases the statements it has placed on a page, why not leave it unwritten? How does a writer avoid having his letters, like a scarlet "A," stand for "Anything"? Why not merely write an urgent-sounding message, like the message from the sea on the back of Melville's tortoise in "The Encantadas," that says inscrutably, "Memento * * * * *"? If his supreme rhetoric is "increate," as Thoreau says, leaving it to be uncreated, recreated, and un-created by other readers, why bother to create it? Crashing full against such hard rhetorical problems again and yet again, Thoreau offers many ways to frame them. To his credit, he seldom makes them reductive. In tribute to his own intellectual honesty and to the significance of the linguistic enigmas he encounters, he usually presents them in all their complexity. Often he emphasizes their profundity by revealing the very failure of his own frames. In the epigraph from John Cotton that begins "Wednesday," "language" can be substituted for "man" so that the epigram reads, "Language is man's foe and destiny" (235). Thoreau might be frustrated by the inadequacy of language, but it was all he or anyone had. One could choose but to write, even when aware of the insufficiency of one's words. As he soars aloft in abstruse reflections upon linguistic problems, he reminds readers of that casual sentence in "Tuesday": "As we cannot distinguish objects through this dense fog, let me tell this story more at length" (180).

Thoreau's wild rhetoric was not a means of resolving linguistic problems. Rather, it was one way to present those problems in all their gnarled complexity. When he offers a resolution, he subtly retracts it. Thus, he offers a fresh description of the trite idea that writers write because they must; then he erases the idea. As he stares in the "greenish eye" of the small bittern, he wonders what it has to say:

What a rich experience it must have gained, standing on one leg and looking out from its dull eye so long on sunshine and rain, moon and stars! What could it tell of stagnant pools and reeds and dank night fogs?

The answer is, it can tell nothing. All it can "say" is what Thoreau believes he reads in the bittern's dull yet "greenish eye."

In like manner, Thoreau can "say" nothing. He can only weave smoky patterns of words upon which readers will gaze and presume to find meaning. Readers will create their "Thoreaus," but they will not discover Thoreau. As he later says in *Walden,* Walden Pond may be "the landscape's most beautiful and expressive feature," it may be "earth's eye," but gazing into it, "the beholder measures the depth of his own nature" (*W,* 186). In *A Week,* departing from his usual tactic of making such points subtly, he bluntly interrupts to knit self-expression with his reading of the bittern's eye: "Methinks my own soul must be a bright invisible green" (236). Just as his musical truth has been modified by the irreconcilable yoking of "certain" and "ineffable," entry to his soul is introduced by "bright" and "invisible." Nature can say nothing, but Thoreau will read meaning into its eye; Thoreau can say nothing, but readers will read meaning into his "I."

And so, Thoreau resorts to a self-erasing language that makes self-expression more bright and invisible. Such language forces readers to confront the facts of their own reading experience as they imagine they are merely decoding Thoreau's words. And so, he stocks his prose with paragraphs that can be reconciled with other pronouncements only at the readers' peril. In "Tuesday," for example, he writes a passage that forces readers to doubt whether they grasp even his elementary rhetorical techniques. He complains that

travellers generally exaggerate the difficulties of the way. Like most evil, the difficulty is imaginary; for what's the hurry? If a person lost would conclude that after all he is not lost, he is not beside himself, but standing in his own old shoes on the very spot where he is, and that for the time being he will live there; but the places that have known him, *they* are lost,—how much anxiety and danger would vanish. I am not alone if I stand by myself. (184)

This is all well and good—and most comforting. Even if we set aside problems of writers being "beside" themselves when they dramatize portions of their selves in published form, and even if we blink at the question of how much anxiety we would indeed feel if we existed in our old shoes but the rest of the universe vanished before our eyes, we can still take comfort in Thoreau's assurance that we are never lost.

We can take such comfort, that is, if we read no further. However, the paragraph ends, "Who knows where in space this globe is rolling? Yet we will not give ourselves up for lost, let it go where it will." A declaration of pleasant faith transcending petty worries has evaporated into a defiant act of will. A limited problem of location has exploded into a cosmological conundrum of existential proportions. Our personal anxiety is soothed when we are told that the entire world is lost, that no one knows where he or she is going, and that the total universe might be rolling aimlessly about in the void of infinite space. What has seemed at first to be a word of solace looms into doomsday diction. What initially seemed comforting and clear had become disconcerting and linguistically confused. We are not lost on a personal scale because we are utterly lost.

That we are "utterly lost" is not a casual transcription. The bittern cannot "utter" its experience and wisdom, even granting it the intelligence to do so. Nature is dumb. It cannot utter its observations. If it did articulate its observations in the form of lessons, wisdom would be damaged, for the relation of facts would be perverted into schemata that would violate the narrative by forcing its data into "lessons." At times Thoreau would handle this paradox by simply delighting in language creation. He would thrill to the excitement of stringing words along an original pattern that produced an erotic pleasure. At other times, he enjoyed the opacity of words, delighting in books, paragraphs, sentences, and sometimes parts of sentences that would dissolve themselves. Yet as a creature of his culture, one part of him "knew" that the true "office of the scholar was to cheer and to guide."

He might thrill to the sheer game of the pine trees, showing now this side, now that of their tips. He might delight in the game of the loon teasing its pursuers (its pursuing readers) and constantly baffling them, thereby increasing their desire for intimacy by tantalizing them with meaning. He might enjoy ministerially issuing dicta, and then finding subtle ways to vitiate them. He might enjoy all these linguistic performances, much as magicians might enjoy the spells and illusions effected by their sleights of hand and their tricks of eye. But he wanted to be more than a magician, more than a humbug like Barnum, more than an illusionist, more than an entertainer, more than a seller of books the way Daniel Webster was a buyer of votes. He wanted to articulate Truth or, failing that, to articulate some truths. Language should do something more than weave cat's cradles of pleasurable reading experiences only to unweave them again, as though a linguistic manifestation of Sisyphus. He wanted more . . . but what was that "more"?

That "more" was a language of desire, always promising more than the writer could write, more than the reader could read. Although Thoreau would often hit upon this linguistic reality, he was always bothered by it. It remained his chief rhetorical agon. He wanted language to do more than it could, even though he was aware that it performed far less, despite the efforts he would take, devoting a decade to each of the books published during his lifetime. He wanted to guide, to direct, to control, to cheer, to instruct, even though he went to great lengths to critique these intentions. He could not escape his times. He could not accept language for what it was, with all its limitations, any more than he could accept reality for what it was. He constantly offered contrasts and alternatives to his era; he was also his era's fulfillment. Thus we arrive at the final paradox regarding that body of writings the world calls "Thoreau." Although he might praise his wild rhetoric in superlative terms, calling it his "mythology," his "universal language," his "Poetic truth," his "musicality," his highest fiction or his "supreme rhetoric," it was by no means supreme. Nor was it exclusively his. It was simply the most intellectually honest representation of his self, his culture, and his reality that he could create through his inherited language composed of inadequate words.

CHAPTER FOUR

Walden

1. "SCALPING THE SELF"

Let us begin by revitalizing a cliché: *Walden* is an "American classic."
Thoreau might have been prouder in some ways of *A Week,* but *Walden*
has become one of America's principal literary documents. Some could
argue that *Walden* is no more typical of the writer than his other works,
but the book clearly defines an American type. It is the book in which he
most allowed America to write through his pen. As *Walden* says early, "If
anyone designs to construct a dwelling house, it behooves him to exercise
a little Yankee shrewdness and sense lest after all he find himself in a
workhouse, a labyrinth without a clew, a museum, an almshouse, a
prison, or a splendid mausoleum instead" (*W, 28*). His first book had
been criticized for being a clueless labyrinth; his second would become an
American monument. The trick was how to keep the text from becoming
"a splendid mausoleum" as it became revered as an American classic.
Emerson said that Thoreau wanted *A Week* published in an inexpensive
form in order to ensure the widest circulation, but it had turned out to
be, as *Walden* describes, of too delicate a texture to have sold well.[1]
Walden would avoid that miscalculation. It would more consciously make
it seem worth a reader's while to buy the book, "or at least make him
think that it was so" (19).

    Walden is a consummate negotiation of private desire with public
demands, and Thoreau's assessment of market demands was sure. I do

not mean that he was merely "aiming to sell," as Greeley had advised. Nor do I intend value judgments that claim market demands made *Walden* "a better work—the one great one Thoreau wrote."[2] Instead, *Walden* is a special book within his canon, a text more willingly accommodated to the new genre of the "American Classic" for which the Young America movement of his age had been clamoring. More subtle than Whitman's and Franklin's overtures to be taken as archetypal Americana, *Walden* articulates an American experience as forcefully as either of these antipodal icons. *Walden* is a deliberate public act, a pubic performance.

A glance at some of his manuscript deletions over the ten years of *Walden*'s revisions makes that point obvious. He carefully toned down irreligious comments that had plunged him and other writers into much trouble with the censors of their age. He voluntarily tamed sentences that otherwise might have seemed heretical, himself acting the role that magazine editors like Caroline Kirkland had performed in domesticating his wilder essays. In a version of *Walden*'s "Conclusion" for 1852, he had daringly written, "I love to weigh, to settle, to gravitate toward {to drive toward God ⟨or the devil or whoever most⟩ [(interlined:) "whatever be the name of that which most"] strongly attracts, not to} hang by the beam of the scale and try to weigh less." By *Walden*'s publication in 1854, he had excised offensive allusions to the devil and the even more heretical references to "whatever be the name" of that which most strongly attracts. Instead, the passage would read more orthodoxly: "I love to weigh, to settle, to gravitate toward that which most strongly and rightfully attracts me." In negotiating his text as an American exhibit, "the devil" and "whatever be the name" of power were supplanted more civilly by "rightfully."

Identical self-censorship and textual domestication are at work in one of *Walden*'s most praised passages: the paragraphs explaining why "I went to the woods" in "Where I Lived, and What I Lived For." The published version asserts that he wanted to devour the marrow of reality and to render a true account of it. Should it prove to be mean, then he wished "to get the whole and genuine meanness of it, and publish its meanness to the world." Bold as that declaration sounds, it is tepid compared to an earlier version. Before 1849, before publishers began to beg the privilege of publishing *Walden,* he had been bolder. When he happened across life's meanness, he would not only publish it to the world, but he would "throw it in the teeth of the gods." Even more heretically, he would throw it in the teeth of "Him that made it."[3]

Even more originally, his drafts indicate that he had already noticed the rising phenomenon of the "moderate radical" as American icon. Wishing to honor its ideals, America would choose a radical to celebrate but not one too extreme for its growing mass culture to embrace. Perhaps Thoreau was responding to John Adams's elevation over Samuel Adams in the popular mind, as Martin Luther King would later be officially celebrated, but not Malcolm X. In any event, he took care to make his persona seem moderately radical, just as he had modulated his heretical statements. At the point when he prints his list of purchased foodstuffs, he had inserted a few lines that signal that, radical as this diet seems, it is not as extreme as others. He addresses readers of more "refined taste" than himself, "who abstain wholly from the vulgar practices of eating, drinking, and sleeping."[4] By the published version, the absurdity is tamed and the humor more subtle when *Walden* advises that only those readers with a "well-stocked larder" should embark on Thoreau's dietary regimen.

Another marketing necessity in the face of America's pell-mell transition from an agricultural to an urban environment was to effect a pastoral, idyllic, even arcadian aura. Nature must seem euphoric, and Thoreau must delete passages that portrayed nature in overly harsh lights. He could not afford such comments as his *Journal* observation that the eructation of Walden's frogs sounded like flatulence. He would also have to mute his experience with a dog that nearly drowned because it ventured too daringly over Walden's thin ice.[5] Certainly he would have to set aside from public perusal his account of saving a nest from the bite of his plough only to witness the young birds die from starvation and neglect because they were abandoned by their parents. It might be that he could let robins frolic within three feet of his hammer as he was building Walden cabin, but he would have to hide the fact that town boys smashed their eggs one day when he was off on a ramble.[6] The image of *Walden* as a sojourn into Arcadia would be rendered so effectively that readers would interpret it primarily as such for more than a century after its publication.[7]

While America's vanishing nature must seem arcadian, his effective persona had to exhibit that "Yankee shrewdness" mentioned in the opening paragraph. His persona would be a practical, down-to-earth idealist, an amalgam of Sam Slick and Swedenborg. All the kind words about his countrymen in his *Journal* and in early essays like "The Landlord" and "A Walk to Wachusett" would be pruned from *Walden,* and it would retain passages that depicted the "I" to be as socially tough as a laissez-faire capitalist or a Spencerian sociologist. It would deploy an economic language that makes its author seem as much a certified public accountant as a private idealist.[8] It would develop passages that ridiculed everyone from his former intellectual mentors to the luckless farmer John Field, whom he viciously characterizes as "Poor John Field!" in a passage that does not exist in any of *Walden*'s manuscript drafts. In his *Journal,* he might admire an Irishwoman who heroically cared for her family. In *Walden,* this representation of the feared "Irish Sea" surfaces as a greasy-armed lump. In the *Journal,* he might yearn to see reality through a strong woman's eyes, but misogyny and xenophobia would prevail in *Walden.* Women would be dismissed as petty annoyances in men's affairs. In one of the two pieces published as previews of *Walden,* a woman thwarts her husband's wish to sell Hollowell farm, and "every man has such a wife."[9] Apparently, an aristocratic tone of snooty no-shoes prejudice sold then as delicious Americana.

In like manner, *Walden* would avoid liberality. The *Journal* might opine that building the Welland Canal is as valuable as his own work, but *Walden* would insist that all business is degrading. The most blatant example is Thoreau's deletion of a lengthy Whitmanesque passage praising manual labor and the men who do it.[10] That five-hundred-word draft in 1847 delineates the working man's "nobility." Railroad workers are "healthy and sturdy working men" whose "rude wisdom and courtesy" Thoreau loves. They are "Greek-like men," the peers of Socrates and Cato, and like "Mustapha or Mamoud in disguise." They exhibit "a genuine magnanimity equal to Greek or Roman." Two years later, Thoreau revised his estimation upwards. His working man had come to exceed the noblest citizens of antiquity. Their magnanimity surpassed that of the Greek and Roman, and they were wiser than Socrates or Cato. In his draft for 1849, his railroaders had grown to become "older and of more worth than the sun and moon." Farmers also do well in *Walden*'s early drafts. One "who lived near the skirts of the wood would pay me a visit, and we took a sober view of or even review of the state of the world, and many times we felt that it was good for us to have come together."[11] The published *Walden,* the public *Walden,* the *Walden* as American

Classic would demand that he delete draft possibilities about the nobility of the American working class that would interfere with his tough, independent persona.

When creating an American classic that presented its author as an archetypal American, Thoreau would also erase references that were too personal. And so, some choice passages would have to go. Alek Therien's trick of sneaking up and scaring Thoreau out of his wits by shooting off a shotgun next to his ear would have to be abandoned. So would the episode when Thoreau plays a prank on his father, pretending that he has lost his father's ax through the ice only to reproduce it from behind his back, startling his old man that the ax entrusted to him has been returned in good shape.[12] In the famous ax anecdote that did survive *Walden*'s drafts, Thoreau brags about borrowing an ax and returning it sharper than before. He does the same with other tools of his civilization. He capitalizes on America's penchant for the conduct book and the how-to-do-it manual, only to warn readers not to follow his blueprints.[13] *Walden* begins like a contribution to America's extensive travel literature, but soon admits it is confined to Concord's environs. The text has the texture of an autobiographical record, seems to be yet another volume in America's library of the journal tradition, but Thoreau not only condenses the material into the cycle of a year; he feels free to import writings and observations that occurred years before and after the actual Walden experiment.

He pretends that telling his narrative in the first person is something new, but that point of view had long been a mainstay of journal writings of everyone from farmers and mountain men to ocean explorers. He borrows Franklinesque images and returns them dusted by an un-Franklinesque idealism. He scalds America's business enterprise and yet encodes much of his idealism in economic terms. He laments civilization's rape of the land, yet he confesses that "woodcutters, the railroad, and I myself have profaned Walden." He banks on his country's fondness for marginal figures like the hermit and the outsider, yet he reveals that he is no hermit and that he is quite willing to hold a civic sinecure, to be an employee of the railroad, or to "sit out the sturdiest frequenter of the barroom." He chastises America for its greed, but one of his earliest insertions admitted in bold clear pencil that greed was a vice "from which none of us is free."[14] He insists upon the importance of a wild solitude, yet the images he chooses are domestic or ambivalent; he says at one point that leaving the village to live in the woods was like leaving a "close prison or dungeon" to sit in "an open cage" and stare at nature through the bars. At another point, he flashes a curious sign about how we are meant to receive *Walden:* if some of us feel the author is "vainglorious" and sets himself "up above others" or apart from his fellow Americans, Thoreau whispers, "Finally I will tell them this secret, if they will not abuse my confidence—I put the best face on the matter."[15]

The best American face painted on *Walden* was not missed by the anonymous reviewer for the *Knickerbocker.* Almost in passing, the reviewer observes that Thoreau's "humbug" is much closer to "the gods we worship," while Barnum's narrative reveals the necessities we obey. In other words, *Walden* deftly mirrors aspirations that were as much part of his cultural situation as were Barnum's materialism, crowd manipulation, and popularity. While Barnum's ends are common as milk, *Walden* skims its culture's ideals, much as Thoreau's poet purports to skim the cream from Hollowell farm. Tellingly, the anonymous *Knickerbocker* reviewer adds that while Barnum represents "the crowd"—those masses of men who live such lives of quiet desperation that titillation is their main recompense, Thoreau will win few converts. And, Thoreau capitalizes on loneliness as one of his chief characteristics: he seems alone at Walden, or alone in *Walden,* despite the fact that he had more visitors than at any other comparable time; and *Walden*'s aloneness, aloofness, and solitude strike at a complex agony of American culture.

Tocqueville had to coin the term "individualism" in order to talk about the evolving American culture he witnessed, and Emerson had referred to individualism as a new obsession. All the Romantics devoted much attention to individualism, and words that address the phenomenon seem the theme of the era: orphan, bachelor, witch, Hawthorne's "outcast of the universe," Dickinson's "Nobody," Poe's "Apostate," Melville's "isolato." "Madness" obsessed everyone, in part because its most fundamental definition was predicated on one's ability to function acceptably in society, to be "a man of the crowd" as Poe would suggest. Hence, an early *Walden* sentence that was tamed for public consumption equated individualism with madness: "If I listen to the faintest but constant suggestions of my genius I see not to what extremes or insanity it will lead me.—And yet that way as I grow more resolute and faithful my road lies."[16]

The essential yang to the yin of individualism is the crowd, the "mass of man," as *Walden* says, the crowd that Thoreau told Emerson in a letter might prove literarily useful as something to hate but that was the one phenomenon worth seeing in New York; the crowd and the "hum of the city" were "something new and to be attended to," worth "a thousand Trinity Churches and Exchanges" (*Corr*, 107, 111). Individualism was deemed a source of power, and its power derived from the fact of the crowd—crowds that first began to appear in American painting in the 1850s and came to be represented as colorful, anonymous paint smudges in the 1890s. Crowds are unavoidable in American literature—the mob scenes around Hester's scaffold, Ishmael's tame reminder that he was "one of the crew," Whitman's collages of the *en masse,* the mobs that threaten Rip Van Winkle regardless of their politics, Clifford's suicidal impulse to join the political parade in *The House of the Seven Gables,* and even the groups of free thinkers in *Blithedale Romance* who appear in "knots" and "clumps."

America's increased valuation of the individual was a reaction to mass culture. Newly urbanized America intensely feared melting into the pot and privileged authors who seemed to escape this inevitability, whether by manipulating it as Barnum did or transcending it like *Walden*'s "Thoreau." One can, as it were, "read through" *Walden*'s pages to the cultural reality that lay beyond; the more insistent an aspiration to independence, the more powerful is the fact of the crowd. The louder an author insists we march to the music that we hear, the more fearful he is that all tunes are ground out by mass culture. The dread of the crowd would squeeze out beautiful and memorable images of the opposite, creating a persona that would "rather sit on a pumpkin and have it all to myself, than be crowded on a velvet cushion" (37).

Had Thoreau read the reviews of his first book, he would have noted one important lesson. A favorable review would focus on *A Week*'s comments advocating the "chastity" and "purity" of the individual who, even when longing for friendship, remains remote, untouchable, incapable of being elbowed even by a mob of one.[17] His portrayal of the self as an archetypal individualist in his second book would be increasingly valued as national journals and mass readerships grew during the nineteenth century. The year before going to Walden, Thoreau told Emerson that his days were filled "inventing machines for sawing his plumbago," whose chief use was in mass-magazine printing presses. About this time, cheap paper was also being developed, thereby making mass readerships possible. In short, the plumbago Thoreau helped produce went to ink massive machines to publish for mass audiences his eulogy of arch-individualism called *Walden*.[18]

This cultural paradox caused Melville to assert that "any mug who had his picture printed in the magazines" was a nobody.[19] Even Caroline Kirkland was noted for her sketches of pioneer life, which, while presenting her as a staunch individualist, poked fun at all the democracy around her, whether it surfaced as a girl's rancor at being called a maid or as a mob of Michiganders prancing around, faggots held high, demonstrating for a presidential candidate. On the popular level, 1850s America was fond of spreading the legend of prospectors like Dan Pound and Buckskin Joe Higginbotham, who purportedly turned their backs on the gold strikes they made, preferring the solitude of wandering in the wilderness.

In Cooper's novels, Natty Bumppo grows the more he claims he is a "man without a cross," even though he is in fact an instrument of colonizers whose settlements render his uncrossed role obsolete. Irving's Rip Van Winkle gains attractive power the more he seems apart from society, much as Ralph Ellison's hero in *Invisible Man* seems potent because he has just emerged from hibernation. Even in the acme of the genteel tradition, when Thoreau's reputation began to be established, writers as elitest as Henry James and as popular as Frank Stockton imaged withdrawal from the crowd as a source of power, and nature would be the signal for this withdrawal. The more insistently one advocates withdrawal, the more powerful is the fact of the crowd. Indeed, in the twentieth century it is difficult to name an author, whether Hemingway or Alice Walker, Updike or Faulkner, for whom this nexus of anxiety is not important. In "Wild Apples," one main point is that these fruits become increasingly delicious as they are made extinct by mass markets and standardization. The tangiest flavors cannot be tasted, and the impossibility inspires the desire to taste.

Walden exploits this American anxiety. To present it as a unique experiment in individualism, facts had to be juggled dexterously. Thoreau had to omit references that made him seem more involved in the human community. Thus, the crew of comrades who helped him raise Walden cabin is mentioned only incidentally (*W, 45*). He does not even allude to the antislavery society meeting at his hut—a fact that would give greater authority to "Resistance to Civil Government" and "Slavery in Massachusetts," but an episode that would detract from the "classic American persona" that he intended for *Walden* (*Life, 179*). Far from being a "landlord" who hosted social activists and housed fugitive slaves, *Walden*'s "Thoreau" must seem more aloof and independent. To embody "the gods we worship," 1850s America's aspiration toward individualism must be respected, filtered through this particular Thoreauvian pen inscribing *Walden:* as Thoreau said, "scalping the self" in the act of composition. As a literary creation, Walden cabin would be made to occupy a ground identical to Hester's cottage, precisely on the edge of both wilderness and civilization.

Walden represents Thoreau's most powerful agons, depicting his attempt to be most public yet most private. It portrays his desire to negotiate generously with public literary demands, while always drawing back at the last minute to remain integral, to have independent integrity. From an aesthetic point of view, *Walden* is all the more remarkable because it articulates many essential American points of view while seeming to speak in one voice. Instead of Whitman's strategy of admitting that his poetic voice was vast and contained multitudes, *Walden* utters these multiple voices while seeming to speak as one firm, unambivalent "I." This rhetorical tactic works so well that the text seems to fit whatever frame readers invent to portray the American literary experience, whether it be Vernon Parrington isolating the "Main Currents of American Thought" or Nina Baym defining the quintessential "American Imaginative space" as "an ambiance of isolation, alienation, defiance, and apology."[20]

In *Walden,* Thoreau said it is difficult to begin without borrowing, and his end is a rhetoric that emphasizes a melting, flowing, protean meaning. Narratively, Thoreau goes twice to Walden Pond, once as a cultural avatar on Independence Day, and again around the vernal equinox, emphasizing "the spring of springs" (40–41); just so, *Walden*'s language moves from "Economy" to the thaw, melt, and flow of "Spring." Ultimately, it will privilege language in which meaning is as "volatile" as "our perspiration toward the sun. The volatile truth of our words should continually betray the inadequacy of the residual statement. Their truth is instantly *translated;* its literal monument alone remains." He wants his text to spark as many possible translations as the voices it utters. In "Conclusion," he laments that "in this part of the world it is considered a ground for complaint ["complaint" meant "offense" in 1853] if a man's writings admit of more than one interpretation."[21] And America has responded to this rhetorical ambition. American readers have borrowed as freely from *Walden* as Thoreau borrowed from American culture to create the text.

Yet there is an obvious problem in this cultural quid pro quo. What limits must be set on the possibility of translation? How does one define the typological difference that distinguishes "many possible meanings" from a willful distortion of the text? Sherman Paul cites Thoreau's *Journal* observation that he cannot get close to nature: "Away behind and behind is she and her meaning." Thoreau comments, "I never saw to the end, nor heard to the end; but the best part was unseen and unheard."[22] Paul reads this comment as a lament that correspondence between the actual and the real could not be maintained, but I read the conjunction "but" as a signal for a different idea, not a reinforcement of the previous. In my reading, Thoreau says that the best part is unseen and unheard, and he sought to create a rhetoric that was true to that aching personal and philosophical agony.

Should Paul demur at my reading, I would cite another *Journal* passage for support:

> My loftiest thought is somewhat like an eagle that suddenly comes into the field of view, suggesting great things and thrilling the beholder, as if it were bound hitherward with a message for me; but it comes no nearer, but circles and soars away, growing dimmer, disappointing me, till it is lost behind a cliff or cloud. (10:128–29)

I would point to words like "somewhat," the images of remoteness like eagle, cliff, and cloud, the posing of different readers ("me" and "the beholder"), and the emphasis on thrill as superior to disappointment, and would argue that this passage describes Thoreau's wild rhetoric and the power in the language of desire. Probably, Paul still would not be convinced. Indeed, he would probably take the same text as further support for his reading. Most likely, we would cite academic structures, diachronic differences in criticism, and argumentative coherence to account for our different translations.

As long as the limits of our debate are kept within the frame of Thoreauvian scholarship and academic rules, the reasons for our different readings can be resolved—and the problem ignored. But we are talking about *Walden* as an "American classic," and America reads more broadly than academics do. One interesting way the twentieth century has of avoiding the question of misreading Thoreau is to grant authority to readers who have gained fame or esteem. While this method reveals how readers can borrow from "Thoreau," it still does not address the problem of what limits on translation exist or how loosely his texts may be honestly interpreted. He wants his words to allow "more than one interpretation," but is there one they will not license?

Fortuitously, no less an establishment institution than the National Bank of Detroit screened a television advertisement precisely when I was gnawing on this problem. Its expensive advertisement opens pompously with a voice-over quoting from "Conclusion" while the words appear on the screen: "If one advances confidently in the direction of his dreams, and endeavors to live the life which he has imagined, he will meet with a success unexpected in common hours" (323). The video portion begins with a boy traipsing through the woods, pausing to skip a stone over a pond. The stone caroms off the water to splash a multicolored phantasia of dreams in the sky—a new car, a two-story house, a motorboat, and other such emblems of middle-class success. The car is a family car, not a sports car. There is no jet nor acred mansion. The "dreams" remain solidly middle-class, materialistic, and family oriented. The bank helps families realize their dreams; together they fulfill the meaning of Thoreau's exhortation. Clearly, this reading is "wrong," and Thoreau's attacks on materialism can be cited to justify that opinion as something more than a value judgment. By the time this book is published, the bank's advertisement will be off the air, but other willful misreadings of the icon "Thoreau" will be available. American culture will continue to exploit its icon, will warp its sentences to suit different times and other purposes. Probably an entire book could be devoted merely to these attempts to accommodate the icon "Thoreau," to render its "moderate radical" even more moderate.

From a rhetorical point of view, the bank's choice of quotation is intriguing. It could have chosen passages more apt to its theme. It could have selected Thoreau's *Journal* entry for 7 September 1851: "I do not so much wish to know how to economize time as how to spend it, by what means to grow rich" (2:469–70). The bank might also have cited *Walden*'s paragraph: "I intend to build me a house which will surpass any on the main street in Concord in grandeur and luxury, as soon as it pleases me as much and will cost me no more than my present one" (49). In fact, dozens of statements are more appropriate to the National Bank's aim and would require less manipulation. But the bank chose the dreams quotation, a passage written in "open" language. There, Thoreau does not tell what he means. He does not specify a grand house nor the less specific concept of growing rich. He does not even clarify whether we can achieve our dreams. He promises only that our success will be "unexpected." The other, seemingly more apposite passages can be resolved through informed and basic readings. A reader can prove that by "rich" Thoreau means riches of the spirit, not materialistic wealth, as demonstrated by his careful definitions of cost and life. If forced by the "bank reader" to be more basic, more "bottom-line," more crude in argument, a reader can expose the joke about his grand and luxurious Concord house by pointing out that the mansion would have to cost no more than twenty-eight dollars, twelve-and-a-half cents.

"Bank readers" warp, manipulate, and distort Thoreau's sentences to conform to their own intentions. They have done so ever since Thoreau became a cultural icon, and they will continue to do so as long as he remains one. Perhaps it is a cultural necessity that more conservative elements of a nation must try to absorb its more radical icons. Bank readers are manipulative, sly, and cunning. But are they dishonest? Thoreau had written in his *Journal* for 6 March 1841 that "an honest misunderstanding" can be the ground for future communication. If he creates a rhetoric that encourages readers to read beyond his words, if he develops a language filled with gaps inviting readers to fill them with interpretation, then by what criteria does one distinguish "an honest misunderstanding" from a dishonest understanding? Is the only recourse to Roman law (as opposed to Occidental), where intention is crucial to a determination of the accused's innocence or guilt?

If intention be the criterion, then how does one resolve those perennial examples in which individuals quite sincerely interpret Thoreau in ways that seem wrong to other qualified and sincere Thoreau readers? Such examples range from the family in Buffalo claiming to be Thoreauvians who were sued for refusing to mow their lawn, to individuals who vehemently disagree on whether Thoreau was a political radical or an aristocratic snob. The loose translations by Melville, Lowell, Robert Pirsig, John McPhee, Edward Abbey, and, in an odd way, B. F. Skinner may be excused as poetic license, but the same problem of translation is well known in critical studies.[23] Leon Edel, who insists that a sense of *Walden*'s voluntariness is essential to an accurate reading, may find it hard to read past Victor Friesen's dedication to his parents, who "practiced Thoreau's simple rural economy *through necessity* and enjoyed doing so" (my emphasis).[24] It is not unusual to encounter two respected Thoreau scholars directing readers to approach Thoreau in radically different moods. Thus, one limns Thoreau as "a classic introvert," while another insists that many of his writings are quite "outer-directed."[25] The same paradox exists on a textual level. Of three who have studied *Walden's* revisions most intensely, one says that its successive drafts merely flesh out and expand his original intentions; another that they become increasingly more didactic in the manner of Longfellow or Whittier; the third, that they become increasingly ambiguous in the manner of Hawthorne or Melville.[26]

Many other examples may be cited, from the most prosaic to the most complex, but they would be redundant. The main point is that in Thoreau's wild rhetoric reading is all-encompassing, possible readings are all but infinite. Just as his various selves include both idealism and business routine and involve both "time and the world" and timelessness, and just as the number of "radii" that can be drawn "from one centre" is infinite, so the number of possible readings is endless (11). The text is endlessly possible. His long, painstaking revisions of *Walden,* as with his first book, guarantee to make it so. Readers are asked to read "deliberately" and to read in a liberated way.

Thoreau the rhetorician would be intrigued at the banker's reading. He would be interested in how much one could extend or distort one of his axioms. He would be fascinated, as he says in "The Landlord," at how far a reader (a proprietor or an expropriator of his text) could make one of his sentences travel. As textual landlord himself, Thoreau would entertain even the tallest or silliest tale or translation, even those that seem to defile his sentences. Michael West has pointed out the scatological dimension of Thoreau's claim that he enhanced the value of Walden by "squatting" on its shore, that he himself "has profaned Walden."[27] By a close parallel, even readers who seem to profane *Walden* by casting their excrescence of an intentionally distorted translation are valuable. Even a vulgar defilement of the text enriches it. Indeed, every reading does. Every translation, no matter how sincere or true to what seems to be Thoreau's meaning, is an excrescence and a distortion. Even Thoreau's own precis/critique of what *Walden* means would be a warping of the text. Even the idealistic, empathetic, and well-intentioned reader is also a banker reader. Every reader is all readers, and all squat on the text. Or, to express the same idea more delicately: "Could a greater miracle take place than for us to look through each other's eyes of an instant?" (10).

Thoreau might enjoy witnessing the wildest readings of his text, might be amazed to see how broadly his words could be translated. However, the agony of his rhetoric is that he could not revel in chaos. Possible readings might be infinite, but some order must exist to structure infinity. The random stars must be made to seem a zodiac. Some organizational principle must operate to prevent "many ways" of reading from becoming *any* way of reading. Although he might often sound like the most radical postmodern theorist, he could never quite convince himself that a text without principle was any more desirable than a "Life without Principle." That agon seems to lie behind passages such as that describing his failure with his tailoress. Thoreau cannot succeed in getting her to make the clothes he requests. Because she obeys other authorities, she refuses to follow his orders, "and I find it difficult to get made what I want, simply because she cannot believe that I mean what I say, that I am so rash" (25). Too "rash," too extreme, admittedly extravagant in his rhetoric, somehow he cannot force tailoress/readers to take him seriously or to read his instructions literally. They persist in translating him loosely, even when he shouts, *"I am far from jesting"*—when he recommends living in a coffin-like railroad toolbox "six feet long by three wide" (29). Whereas the "banker reader" cuts Thoreau's textures to fit his own patterns, the tailoress reader presumes she knows better what pattern Thoreau really means.

In this famous anecdote, Thoreau virtually throws up his hands at her misreading. What is one to do, he wails, with such willful misreaders who distort his patterns, his orders, his messages and meanings? Thoreau's answer comes immediately. His method is to exchange roles. He turns his misreader into an author and becomes the attentive reader of her intentions. Hearing her "oracular sentence, I am for a moment absorbed in thought, emphasizing to myself each word separately that I may come at the meaning of it, that I may find out by what degree of consanguinity *They* [i.e., the authorities] are related to *me,* and what authority they may have." Thoreau converts even his worst reader into a provocative author, and in the act of deferring author-ity to her by becoming her reader, he reserves the power of granting authority to the role of reading.

In a further turn of the rhetorical screw, Thoreau, after authorizing his "worst" readers, lambastes his presumed best. He tweaks readers who think that, through care, wit, and diligence, they have penetrated into the interior of his textual house. They have merely stepped onto his porch, and his text involves an infinite series of porches. At the midpoint of "Economy," he confides, "The house is still but a sort of porch at the entrance of a burrow" (45). Early in "Economy," he had explained that his rhetorical business necessitates "some obscurities, for there are more secrets in my trade than in most men's" (17). He would gladly reveal those secrets, and never paint "No Admittance" on his textual gate. Secrets are "not voluntarily kept," but an effective rhetoric demands obscurities. A language of desire that makes his meaning seem secret and private is "inseparable from [the] very nature" of his wild rhetoric.

Indeed, the paragraph that precedes his reader-author role reversals in the famous tailoress anecdote images Thoreau as a Salome—teasing, exciting, yet denying his most conscientious readers. Careful readers can, he promises, strip away that "false skin" of misreadings, hasty readings, misdirections, and missed signals and come to a true understanding of the author's meaning—an honest understanding instead of "an honest mis-understanding" (24). Such Thoreau promises, but he interrupts to raise a communicative barrier. Although he wishes never to paint "No Admit-tance" on his gate, readers cannot enter his textual house. He warns that a final garment cannot be removed. The act of public authorship, the reality of scalped selves, must be remembered. Strip down Thoreau's rhetoric as we may to bare the essence of his soul, we must stop, Thoreau says, at his shirt, layering the metaphor by making it plural: "But our shirts are our liber or true bark, which cannot be removed without girdling and so destroying the man."

The script-tease becomes supreme with the puns on *liber*. Readers can penetrate to the true man and his meaning only so far as the liber, or book. Moreover, Thoreau has stated that his main goal was to live "deliberately." He read his tailoress deliberately, and requests his best readers to do likewise, scrutinizing every syllable, resorting to every extra-authorial cultural source to determine the author's meaning. The script-tease becomes further complicated when the author has his most heroic reader and thinker, "the old philosopher," "walk out the gate empty-handed without anxiety." With great effort of will, conscientious readers can force themselves to become Thoreau's heroic readers and leave his text "empty-handed," having nothing to show for their efforts save the pleasure of the hunt. They can pride themselves on the achievement, except that in the next paragraph Thoreau complains about readers who will not believe that he means what he says. With good reason, conscientious readers might suspect they have been tricked more subtly and more completely than banker and tailoress readers.

The same game is at play with *Walden*'s most-quoted statement: "The mass of men lead lives of quiet desperation" (8). The sentence is famous largely because it sounds so aphoristic. It is an ideal selection for Bartlett's *Familiar Quotations*. It seems a tailor-made proverb that a tailoress might suitably cross-stitch into a sampler. But Thoreau does not let the sentiment lie. He obscures it by adding, "From the desperate city you go into the desperate country, and have to console yourself with the bravery of minks and muskrats." The persona that has seemed so cheerfully confident about discovering a true way to live suddenly sounds almost as desperate as the rest of humanity.

So much for an otherwise fine epigram. As the proverb dissolves, it entails wider ramifications. With the adage, readers are in control; they are "on top of" the author's meaning, clear about what he utters. In its dissolve, however, readers are trapped in the text, imprisoned by ambiguities, denied interpretive certainty. If they simplify the dissolve by claiming that it criticizes halfway commitments, then Thoreau's emphasis on "sojourning" is called into question. If they reason that Thoreau means "you" should go farther into the country, then they have to blink at Thoreau's ridicule of those who go to California to start life anew, or at his description of the Collins's cat, who ventured too far from home and so became a dead cat at last. Thoreau's explicit meaning is left up for grabs. *Walden* uses essential cultural myths, the linguistic currency of the realm, to launch sentences that ultimately float, hover, and dissolve. He borrows axes and axioms and returns them sharper and stranger than before. The whole of *Walden* is like the motto Thoreau borrows to begin "Resistance to Civil Government," which he simply extends and exaggerates until its once explicit meaning becomes arcane and oracular.

Walden's main defense against misreading is to demand perpetual rereading, as though its meanings were always "in the mail" and never quite delivered. *Walden* allows readers to squat temporarily on an epigraph or a theme, but they are instantly prodded to keep moving. Reading is a process of constantly travelling, marching, stepping to distant music. Reading in *Walden* involves an aesthetic sojourning. It is an eternal exploration of meaning. Late in his revisions, Thoreau decided to change the classic dictum "Know Thyself" to the less definite, less settled, more open process: "Explore Thyself." *Walden*'s text insists upon persistent exploration; even previously colonized territory must seem fresh and be revisited.

Hence parody, exaggeration, puns, strained metaphors, a language of desire, and all the other techniques of creating an "open" text are practiced. With *Walden,* this was especially essential since, next to pieces like "The Landlord," *Walden* was his most public text, his most negotiated presentation of the self as an American avatar. While his addresses generally insist upon an adversarial audience, *Walden* says it is "idle, if not desperate" to place "one's self in formal opposition to the most sacred laws of society" (322). As *Walden* specifies, he is extremely concerned that "I speak within bounds" (30). Or, as he suggests in "Conclusion," *Walden* is his most public "yarding" of the self. Since the text is so public in exploiting myths, themes, and anxieties of his culture, his wild rhetoric must be subtly deployed. It must seem less wild than in *A Week* or "Night and Moonlight." In literary projects like his *Journal* and *A Week,* he felt free enough to say wildly, "Give me a sentence which no intelligence can understand." He tames the wild statement in *Walden,* making it all the more complex rhetorically: "It is a ridiculous demand England and America make, that you shall speak so that they can understand you" (324).

The following sections of this chapter will approach *Walden*'s wild rhetoric by three routes. I will begin with those two extracts published as previews, whose aim was to make readers "think it worth their while" to purchase and peruse *Walden* upon its publication. Next, I will examine parody as the essential narrative strategy by which Thoreau could remain true to the infinite possibilities of the self within the bounds, limits, and yarding of his self as an American avatar. Finally, I will study Thoreau's wild rhetoric as it centers on reading as a process of "unreading." In a sense, I will attempt to clarify *Walden*'s "ridiculous demand" that we understand it.

2. FEEDING READERS

No one reads *Walden* for the first time. Conditioned by icons, even new readers have been strongly influenced about how to respond to this American classic. They have been saturated with images of Thoreau as a hermit, a social critic *cum* reformer of men's lives, and a skilled spokesman for nature. Virginal readings are denied us. The closest we can come to a fresh reading is to examine the two extracts Thoreau published to orient readers to his forthcoming book. This strategy will bring us no closer to a "first reading," but it will help clarify the rhetorical strategies intended in *Walden*.

On 19 November 1848, Horace Greeley advised Thoreau that the best way to advertise a book as to publish extracts in magazines (*Corr, 233*). His recommendation came at the opportune time when Thoreau was completing the third and fourth drafts of *Walden*. The next year, Ticknor and Fields offered to publish the book at their own expense. Declining Ticknor's generous offer, Thoreau chose to refine *Walden* through four further drafts over the next five years. Finally, he submitted two extracts to Sartain's *Union Magazine,* the publication that had earlier printed "Ktaadn." "A Poet Buying a Farm" (the first three and the fifth paragraphs of "Where I Lived, and What I Lived For") and "The Iron-Horse" (paragraphs 5–13 of "Sounds") appeared in July 1852. As selective samples of the book that would be published two years later, these extracts offered specific clues about how readers might approach *Walden*. In the first place, both pieces are humorous in a genteel way. Although among *Walden*'s funniest pages, they do not indulge in harsh satire or scatalogical whimsy. Readers might smile at Thoreau's attempt to make his loss of ten dollars seem a profit in "Buying a Farm," but they are spared descriptions about squatting on the land or strolling through the fields with a bottleful of yeast discharged on his pants (63–64). They would also be alerted to Thoreau's fondness for puns; even the "buying" of the title is a pun since the poet gives the farm's purchase a bye.

Readers of "Buying" would also be introduced to qualifiers and reversals as blatant as its puns. Even the seemingly limpid advice that readers "live free and uncommitted" is ushered in by the gloomy qualifier, "As long as possible." The theme at first seems clear: a poetic vision licks the cream from the landscape, whereas the farmer tastes only skimmed milk. However, a closer reading reveals that the theme is not quite so explicit. Although casting the sketch as a first-person narrative, Thoreau has not said that *he* has succeeded in skimming the cream of the experience. Instead, he says that he has frequently seen "a poet" accomplish this reading. As a reader, this poet is superior to the farmer, is probably a reader like Thoreau, but the poet and narrator have been distanced from each other. The rhetorical effect is to allow *Union* readers to feel superior to the farmer, to feel like the poet, or to feel like the "I"—a reader somewhere between the two levels. Rhetorically they can feel smug, proud, or like Tantalus—conscious of the best way to read experience, but aware that they do not always live up to that standard.

In the final 1854 draft just before *Walden*'s publication, Thoreau decided to insert a paragraph into "Buying a Farm." The burden of this added paragraph is that he is quite willing, "like Atlas, to take the world on my shoulders." That point becomes the main focus of "The Iron-Horse," where Thoreau professes that he is as much "an employee of the railroad" as Ishmael was "one of the crew."[1] Elsewhere in *Walden*, he states that he does not believe that the best rhetorical strategy is to stand in formal opposition to society like the highway bandit, Mirabeau. In this preview, he instructs readers that *Walden*'s narrator is not a voice crying out from an eremetic wilderness. Rather, the narrative voice is culturally complicitous. The speaker is very much part of commerce; he is a "citizen of the world" (119).

Framed as a member of the business community, the narrator also admires the future of America, a fate as inevitable as the locomotive's name, *Atropos,* suggests. He will not permit his vision nor his ears be "spoiled by its smoke and steam and hissing," but he appreciates commerce's "enterprise and bravery," its "steady and cheerful valor," its energy, its persistence, and its "miracles"—values that he often esteems in nature. In fact, Thoreau insists that commerce, "unexpectedly confident and serene, alert, adventurous, and unwearied," is a part of nature. "It is very natural in its methods withal, far more so than many fantastic enterprises and sentimental experiments," a statement that can make modern readers wonder whether the Walden experiment falls within that category. Indeed, when Thoreau does issue *Walden,* he will immediately follow "The Iron-Horse" extract with a paragraph that insists that the distinction between nature and civilization is false. The sounds made by the railroad, by the hum of commerce, by a wandering band of minstrels, by cows in the field or redbirds in the woods are "at length one articulation of Nature" (123).

Thus, readers primed by Thoreau's two previews before encountering *Walden* would have very different reading experiences from modern ones who begin with "Economy." Ur-readers, as it were, would not enter the text presuming that Thoreau preferred nature or that he was trying to escape civilization. Nor would ur-readers be biased by that other great facet of the Thoreau icon: that he was an ardent social reformer if not a cultural anarchist. Modern readers who begin with page 1 and read *Walden* through linearly would catch hints of this idea, especially in rhetorical asides such as his thought that he is not at all "certain it is desirable" that everyone should be transformed into philosophers (56). But ur-readers would have the point thrust before them more bluntly. In "The Iron-Horse," Thoreau says without concession or qualifier: "I confess, that practically speaking, when I have learned a man's real disposition, I have no hopes of changing it for the better or worse in this state of existence" (120–21). Guided by that sentence, an ur-reader might well weigh who is the satirical butt of the John Field episode that concludes "Baker Farm." Is it the unsuccessful farmer lured from worry only to fail equally at play and sport? Or is the target more properly the ineffectuality of the narrator's own reform-minded sentences? "Practically speaking," Thoreau has no illusion about his ability to reform men or their institutions. Aesthetically speaking, however, reform, along with the theme of nature, provides fine material to weave into his text. Nature is not distinct from civilization, nor is reform possible, but they can make a fine story, can supply a good read.

Good reading is, of course, the ultimate theme of both these extracts. The poet skimming the cream is one example. Another is "Thoreau" in "The Iron-Horse." He makes fun of books, particularly those that are (ironically enough) autobiographical: "written tales of real life, high and low, and founded on fact!" (120). He laments the waste of processing torn sails and worn-out clothes just to make paper for such books. Rather than read them, Thoreau prefers to read the rags: "This car-load of torn sails is more legible and interesting now than if they should be wrought into paper and printed books."

In the previous chapter, called "Reading," Thoreau describes many varieties of literacy. "Easy reading" and "little reading" closely resemble the books of high and low life in "Iron-Horse." But another kind is superior, is a kind of book-reading more like his reading of rags, wherein the text is a hieroglyphic that the reader must translate. "Tiptoe reading" is the name Thoreau bestows upon this activity; its participants must be always on the alert for words that shine like stars, whose meaning is perhaps as remote. Indeed, "Reading" opens with a transcendental reading that can be experienced only through books and that is superior to rag-reading. Reading an ancient text, "a corner of the veil from the statue of divinity" is raised, and personality is transcended: "I gaze upon as fresh a glory as [the original author] did, since it was I in him that was then so bold, and it is he in me that now reviews the vision" (99). Reader and author are united in communication. Like Moses allowed to gaze upon God, readers can lift the veil of language to gaze upon the "glory" of linguistic communion. Time and place, personality and culture, messages and categories are dissolved in the act of transcendent reading.

Good readers can achieve this miracle of communication, but rhetoric must provide the opportunity. *Walden* specifies two crucial frames for this rhetoric—persona and language. When *Walden* was finally published, Thoreau had decided to introduce the pages that had been printed earlier as "The Iron-Horse" with a paragraph that highlighted the fact that the "Thoreau" of *Walden* was a literary construct, a fictionalized self. While others went to society and the theater for amusement, Thoreau went to Walden, where his life, as he punningly underscores, "never ceased to be novel. It was a drama of many scenes and without an end" (112). The "Thoreau" of *Walden* is but one dramatized version of his many possible selves; it was one narrativized "mode of life" of the many lives he could have lived during those two years, two months, and two days at Walden. It was like a tightly framed shot, as photographers say, seen in that tiny three-inch mirror he took with him as one of the essentials to lead a life of simplicity at the pond (65).

Unlike *A Week on the Rivers*, where the self was frequently so diffuse that it was not possible to determine precisely which voyager was experiencing the incidents narrated, the self of Walden is tightly framed, closely cropped, and more narrowly bound as one avatar of American selfhood. The virtue of that rhetorical experiment is that, as in his remarks on chastity, power would derive from small compass. Like Walden, where the drop could be the ocean, where the pond could focus a nexus of ideas more surely than in the unfenced wildness of the Maine Woods or the well-trodden sands of Cape Cod, the self in *Walden* would gain rhetorical power through circumspection.

By speaking rigorously "within bounds," he could speak more vigorously without bounds, could bound more springily. Typically, in *Walden* a circumscribed statement provides the platform for a wilder, more exaggerated statement. Hence, a meticulous, Franklinesque catalogue of food expenses would augur the advice not to attempt this diet unless you have a "well stocked larder." The list of essentials he took to Walden, including the "looking-glass three inches in diameter," would be followed by praise for the ritual of the busk. Detailed instructions about how to live his way melt into admonitions not to "adopt *my* mode of living on any account," which then melt into expressions of desire that there be "as many different persons in the world as possible" and that "each one be very careful to find out and pursue *his own* way" (71). In the quotation about his persona being a "novel" and its record a "drama," the point has been, after all, to give readers a sense of "many scenes and *without an end*" (my emphasis). And, he defines that stereotype of early Victorian America—the "good *man*" (read "good writer")—not as one who feeds readers but instead as one who tantalizes them (74). At the least, he does not "stand between any man [reader] and his genius [interpretation]" (73). At his most provocative, he offers an "example which leaves them far behind" (75).

"Solitude" is an extended example of rhetorical power gained through a bounded self-image. Its explicit theme argues that "Thoreau" is never less alone than when alone and that when alone, he is alone like God. But as the theme is developed, explicitness becomes complicated. Its author prefers solitude, even though he could "sit out the sturdiest frequenter of the bar-room." He is alone at *Walden*, but he has more visitors than at any other time. He is far removed from civilization, but his "nearest neighbor is a mile distant," about as distanced as the farms along what he describes as the "crowded shore" of the St. Lawrence River in *A Yankee in Canada*. More subtle than these obvious paradoxes is a powerful and beautiful passage. Justifying, even sanctifying America's desire for solitude the more it became a mass culture, Thoreau writes:

> I am no more lonely than a single mullein or dandelion in a pasture, or a bean leaf, or sorrel, or a horse-fly, or a humble-bee. I am no more lonely than the Mill Brook, or a weathercock, or the north star, or the south wind, or an April shower, or a January thaw, or the first spider in a new house. (137)

The passage's beauty and power depend largely on its contradictoriness, its unlikeness, its erasure of posited theme. The specialness of a single mullein or dandelion stems from such being extremely rare. Remarkable for their proliferation and "community" and commonness, they are seldom seen alone. Moreover, Thoreau obliquely tames his image of wildness. By gratuitously adding the phrase "in a pasture," he has domesticated his opening emblems of solitude and independence.

Indeed, all his images of solitude are social. Not just any brook, but the miller's, vital to the town's development; not any star, but the freedom-pointing star for fugitive slaves whose symbolism *Walden* frequently mentions (e.g., p.71) Every example in this panegyric to solitude has a domestic context. Even the weathercock evokes civilization's attempts at regulating nature's wildness through calibrations of time or direction. Lastly and most beautifully of all comes the concluding image of "the first spider in a new house." No more powerful simile of solitude has ever been written, but its evocation of aloneness is predicated on a manmade structure awaiting the imminent arrival of friends, visitors, family, and tax collectors.

Solitude's images are potently beautiful because they are mixed, impure, impossible. Aloneness is blended with society, wildness with domesticity. Even if one achieves an ultimate solitude, one then becomes alone like God, responsible for all creation. Conversely, one does not have to strive for aloneness. Our individuality is an obvious reality. Even close friends are as far apart as "dwell the two most distant inhabitants of yonder star." Realistically, our aloneness is inevitable. Thoreau asks, "What sort of space is that which separates a man from his fellows and makes him solitary?" His answer is blunt: "I have found that no exertion of the legs can bring two minds much nearer to one another" (133). Legs cannot, but rhetoric can. At least it can create the illusion that the inevitable space that separates us can be bridged. And the most effective rhetorical arch that can be spun between author and audience is a language that permits readers to feel they have "a little world all to myself," that "the horizon is never quite at our elbows" (130).

That language definition is encoded in his paragraph on "nextness" (134). The rhetorical situation is not one where two minds become one, where the reader has received the author's message intact and clear. Writer and reader are not united; rather, they share an approximate communication, they stand next to each other in attempting to create meaning. Amid the fact of our individual isolation, this rhetorical situation creates the impression that we experience a shared power in our longing to communicate, that we are *almost* able to span the space between us. "Nearest to all things is that power which fashions their being. *Next* to us the grandest laws are continually being executed. *Next* to us is not the workman whom we have hired, with whom we love so well to talk, but the workman whose work we are." From a theological or cultural perspective, that workman could mean God or society; in a rhetorical context, the workman is the reader. Thoreau does not feed readers ideas. Rather, he offers an imagistic menu that, as we study it, rewrites itself in a mysterious tongue. He is more like Tantalus's gods, offering fruits that grow more deliciously desirable the more they elude our grasp. Two of his most frequently offered linguistic fruits are presented through the extended metaphors of beans and berries.

His passages on huckleberries stand out so vividly that they have been taken to stand for his writings and his life. Emerson, for example, depicts him chiefly as a "fine captain of a huckleberry party."[2] Huckleberries are often privileged over other wild fruits, as when he opens "Housewarming" by ransacking nature, collecting grapes for their "beauty and fragrance" more than for food, wild apples for their tang and dietary variety, and chestnuts chiefly for their bouquet. He avoids cranberries, whose growers are like Hawthorne's Bartram in "Ethan Brand," heedlessly measuring "them by the bushel and the dollar only." Nonetheless, cranberry farmers are as much cognoscenti of markets as the basket-weaving, *Walden*-weaving "Thoreau," who knows that a strong demand exists "to satisfy the tastes of lovers of Nature" in cities like Boston and New York (238).

The quest for huckleberries opens "The Ponds," the chapter many believe to be *Walden*'s most beautiful. After rhapsodizing over huckleberries, it extols a silent companion whose mute presence is "a psalm." Then it pictures Thoreau playing his flute over the waters, awaiting a responsive echo. Next, after outstaying a family until they have all gone off to bed, Thoreau goes off to fish and imagines that he, in another famous *Walden* image, has caught "two fishes as it were with one hook." After that well-known image, the text breaks (again a typical rhetorical tactic) before taking up his hymn to Walden Pond as a metaphor for the self and as "Earth's eye."

When he opens this rhetorically complex development, his signals to readers are as precise as his instructions in "Buying a Farm" and "Iron-Horse." Before venturing out for huckleberries, venturing farther than Walden's environs, venturing "still farther westward than I habitually dwell, into yet more unfrequented parts of the town," this pilgrim has had to detach himself from the complicity with civilization admitted in "The Iron-Horse" and in the insertion on Atlas to "Buying a Farm." He is propelled upon his quest because he has had "a surfeit of human society and gossip" and because, in fair quid pro quo, he has "worn out all my village friends." Ravenous for huckleberries in the absence of satisfying or fulfilling social contact, he happens across an abundance nature provides. He not only eats many hand-to-mouth, but he also lays up "a store for several days." Despite the fact that he will luxuriate in huckleberries for days after he had collected them, he insists that their "fruits do not yield their flavor to the purchaser of them, nor to him who raises them for market." In a floridly worded sentence, he pontificates that "the ambrosial and essential part of the fruit is lost with the bloom which is rubbed off in the market cart, and they become mere provender" (173). The same problem also pertains to prose aimed at the market; its bloom will be rubbed off by accommodation and compromise.

Thus far, the paragraph's meaning, though complicated, can be unraveled, but it becomes more complex when Thoreau turns positive. If one cannot experience the essential taste by buying them or by growing them, then how is one to know them? "If you would know the flavor of huckleberries," Thoreau begins to respond—and we anticipate a recommendation that we venture into uncultivated nature and pluck them ourselves. Instead, he concludes the sentence by advising, "ask the cow-boy or the partridge." Short wisdom could the partridge supply; the cowboy not much more. We have only Thoreau to tell us, and he demurs. But we know better. We sense that he has given us a clearer description than could a cowboy or a partridge, than could a purchaser or grower of huckleberries. We readers know better than our author—precisely the rhetorical situation he has arranged. We scent the bloom he has cunningly cultivated.

He shortly reinforces the rhetorical point when he shifts from berries to fishing as a transcendent experience. Having linked his eloquent persona with the audiences of his silent companion and the family he has outlasted, he almost catches "two fishes with one hook." The image means to unify sky and water, idealism and reality, but cautious phrasings ("It seemed as if"; "as it were") signal that this fusion is only metaphorical. Synthesis has not occurred, but the illusion is almost palpable. This suggestive, literary quality is consonant with the point of his fishing description. It is the act of fishing, not the catching of fish that matters; it is the act of reading that is significant, not the capture of meaning. What Thoreau most values is the "dimpling of the surface," the "slight vibration along" his fishline, and the sense of "life prowling about" his hook.

Instead of desiring to catch "perch and shiner," he is most keen to experience the illusion that he "is communicating by a long flaxen line with mysterious nocturnal fishes which had their dwelling forty feet below." When he does catch a fish—or, when it snags him—it is merely "some horned pout squeaking and squirming to the upper air." From all the kinds of fish he could have landed, he chooses to cite one he considers among the ugliest and most repulsive.[3]

To succeed as a tantalizing author and not a mere feeder of his readers, Thoreau has to give the sense that big, beautiful fish lurk somewhere near the ends of his lines. He must use language that keeps readers fishing, without allowing them to settle for a string of shiners. He wants words like berries whose bloom has not rubbed off in the market cart. He wants word-berries to whet desire, to create the idea that communication can take place, without making language like manna that feeds his readers. That he shuns the latter is clear considering all the images of satiety in *Walden*—Thoreau tiring of human society and gossip, outlasting a family until all its members have gone off to bed, wearing out all his village friends. He wants "reading" always to remain a verb—always "reading," not "a reading." His first book had been too wild, like huckleberries. Readers respond, then and now, with feeling that the book is too loosely structured, too much an idle ramble. *A Week* failed to give readers enough of a sense that fish and fruits lie within their grasp. His lines did not tremble enough with the illusion that fish nibble at their ends and that readers could yank them "sqeaking and squirming into the upper air" if only they pulled more adroitly. *Walden* would avoid that rhetorical error.

Walden gives us beans. Along with wild berries and mysterious nocturnal fish, *Walden* offers readers a diet of cultivated beans, an extensive crop intended for the marketplace, always meant to be traded. As late as "Version F" (1853–54), he had thought to title a chapter simply "Beans," and evidence indicates that he believed the chapter was of special importance. An early titles list indicates that he thought "Beans" might lead off *Walden*'s second part. Later in 1854, he changed the title to the more genteel "The Bean-Field," but the switch did not fool *Walden*'s contemporary readers. In fact, the anonymous reviewer for the *Knickerbocker* magazine was so intrigued by the scatological dimension of Thoreau's beans that he or she devoted more attention to flatulence than to his or her perceptive characterization of Thoreau as a "Yankee Diogenes."[4] The

reviewer quips that the *Walden* persona would be roiling in his tub like
Diogenes, railing against society, if he did not have to eat beans. "The
Bean-Field" does read like a complementary essay to the satires of "Economy," and its mood expands from that of the "conscience of Concord" to
that of what Perry Miller has called "Consciousness in Concord."[5]

Instead of criticizing others' labors and instead of preferring dreamy
images of consciousness, Thoreau lands ideas in "The Bean-Field" and
spreads them out to dry. The result is one of *Walden*'s most direct, honest,
and frustrating chapters. From the outset, the patterns seem out of kilter,
the images askew. The man who exemplifies a life of simplicity grows "so
many more than I wanted." Why raise them at all? "Only heaven knows."
In mixed metaphor, growing beans is a Herculean labor from whose soil
he derives strength like Antaeus. Even *Walden*'s roles of a superior "I"
among lesser others are reversed; travelers sit at their leisure observing
the sweaty, foot-blistered, "laborious native of the soil." At the beginning
of the chapter, passing gossips decry, "Beans so late! peas so late!" By
chapter's end the narrator's principal advice curiously vindicates the gossips: "But above all, harvest as early as possible." Even the function of his
Walden experiment is confused. At one time it is the typical "connecting
link" between civilization and the wilderness; at another, it has become
more tame, and his bean field is only "at the other end of the town." Most
unsettling of all is the number of enemies Thoreau incurs and the variety
of life he displaces. His specified foes include crows, frosts, skunks, woodchucks, the brown thrasher, red mavis, worms, and cool days. When not
trying to destroy these enemies, he inadvertantly disturbs a host of plants
and animals on every other page: blackberries, johnswort, "sweet wild
fruits and pleasant flowers," grass, spotted salamanders, Roman worm-
wood, pigweed, sorrel, piper-grass, and even "the ashes of unchronicled
nations." This rampage goes on while he persistently marvels that "such
kindredship is in nature."

Of course nothing remains simple in *Walden*. Even the most basic
phenomenon looms into metaphor. And so it is with beans. His crop
invites allegory, whether his beans are taken to stand for food or politics,
"porridge or voting." Bean growing soon leads to one of *Walden*'s unfor-
gettable passages, in part because it involves one of Thoreau's most
horrendous puns. Without any hint that he means sarcasm or irony, he
presents himself slashing weeds in his field on "one of the *great* days"
when he hears the militia practicing in Concord "as if all the village was a

vast bellows, and all the buildings expanded and collapsed alternately with a din." He avows that sometimes their volleys and music created "a really noble and inspiring strain." While he is hunting a skunk or chipmunk to cut in half and "exercise my chivalry upon," this martial music inspires Thoreau to wonder why we should "always stand for trifles" like mere chipmunks. He is inspired to bloody thoughts of murder, if not cannibalism, "as if I could spit a Mexican with a good relish."

Loathesome thoughts result from "a really noble and inspiring strain that reached these woods, and the trumpet that sings of fame." Meanwhile Thoreau works to make the earth say "beans" instead of "grass," and the chapter bares anxiety about his desire to utter exhortations that have "a really noble and inspiring strain." While he reiterates the standard theme that taking a position limits opportunities, the burden of "The Bean-Field" is much darker. This chapter suggests that taking any position not only limits possibilities but creates hatreds. Engaging in even so ordinary and seemingly innocuous an activity as growing a crop of beans causes enemies, disrupts life, and leads to emotions that can inveigle individuals into murderous and cannibalistic inklings. Unlike the sun that beams indifferently on beans and grass alike—indeed, unlike the sun that makes no distinction between "weed" and "plant"—the simple cultivator cultivates enemies, violence, discriminations, and hatreds.

As in "Resistance to Civil Government," his ideas are loosely woven; general principles are left for others to particularize in the light of specific sociopolitical circumstances. Times will change, and Thoreau hopes that general truths will remain applicable, even though "The Bean-Field" is *Walden*'s most direct confrontation with the practice of "apprehending particulars derived from universal principles."[6] His beans are like those paper pellets that the philosopher bounces off others' chests in the introductory sketch of Sherwood Anderson's *Winesburg, Ohio*. Thoreau's beans were not meant to be consumed. They were meant to be traded, to be exchanged, while he acknowledges that the selling of beans was "the hardest part of all." Beans were meant to be swapped, and bartering this simple legume entailed trading off the chapter's complexities with readers.

Cultivating beans involves Thoreau's equivalent to Occam's razor: "the invidious hoe." As soon as he begins to make the simplest distinctions, he not only raises havoc with the environment that he generally loves, but he creates distinctions that lead to hatreds, even to roasting a Mexican on a spit and devouring him with relish. And this author, who seemed to make such clear distinctions between a noble, rustic, independent "I" in "Economy" and the multiform failures of civilization, reveals that all distinctions, even the "most noble and inspiring" ones, are unfair and artificial, if not fatal. Himself capable of civilization's worst traits, he warns, "By avarice and selfishness, and a grovelling habit, *from which none of us is free,* of regarding the soil as property, or the means of acquiring property chiefly, the landscape is deformed, husbandry is degraded *with us,* and the farmer leads the meanest of lives. He knows Nature but as a robber."

Every reader is a "a robber reader." Even the most sincere and well-intentioned who attempt to harvest the growth of his writings and store their beans of meanings in some thesis-constructed barn appropriate the soil of his texts. "Most men," Thoreau says, "I do not meet at all; they are busy about their beans." And Thoreau is busy with his. One cannot look upon a text or a field and not try to "appropriate" it, to make it one's property, to give it order, structure, and coherence. Readers must perforce defile the soil, must make an orderly field, and they feel especially encouraged to do so since this chapter offers a text of virtually almanac wisdom that also conforms to the formulas of the conduct book and the self-improvement manual. But Thoreau still hopes that a nondiscriminating reading experience is possible. He still has faith in the "subtile and ineffable quality" of his prose. He continues to believe that readers, even when acting as "robber readers," can see through the masks of language. He did not relinquish the desire that his readers treat all thoughts, even his own, as servants to their own, and not slaughter them like oxen or approach them like slaves, even though he excised that assertion from an early draft.[7]

In a later draft, he allowed other expressions of his rhetorical ambitions to last to publication. He quotes Evelyn's agricultural advice and directs it toward literacy as a mutual engagement of writer and reader: he comments that there is "no compost or laetation whatsoever comparable to this continual motion, repastination, and turning of the mould with the spade," and this image represents his linguistic ideal of fertile communication. In that ideal, readers, instead of harvesting beans, will be attracted to "power, or virtue (call it either)." Thus the utmost distinction of reason's "invidious hoe," the discrimination between power and virtue, is dissolved. He values readers who can transform a "kernel or grain" of truth into an unharvested growth, who can transmute a *"granum"* into "*gerendo,* bearing." He idealizes readers who not only enhance the value of his textual field by squatting on it, but who can more expansively water it and make it green. He most appreciates readers who can transcend the chapter's cultivator role, readers who can achieve a "continual motion, repastination, and turning of the mould" with the spades of their reading experience.

Thus, in the concluding pages of "The Bean-Field" he expresses his hope that "these beans have results which are not harvested by me." Initiating a series of presumed rhetorical situations, he presents his authorial self as the grower who cultivates a textual crop that readers long to harvest. As author/grower, he must do his best simultaneously to encourage and to frustrate a final harvesting lest his "noble and inspiring" strains be taken to justify one determined, settled translation or another. Therefore, he centers on a rather specious etymology, although it makes sense considering the rhetoric he espouses, that the spike of a plant or a proverb will promise *speca*—that is, "hope" or "bearing." His prose will engender thought, hope, or fertile possibility among his readers. They will come away from his text "bearing." In that rhetorical sense, "The Bean-Field" concludes with abstracted advice to those whom Thoreau imagines as his idealized reader, the "true husbandman" who relaxes from the "anxiety" of interpretation while striving to read truly. To succeed in that interpretative endeavor, a reader will have to be willing to relinquish "all claim to the produce of his fields, and [sacrifice] not only [his] first but [his] last fruits also." That is his imagined readers' sacred art and calling. It is an elevated role, a role as frustrating as it is idealized.

Thoreau sweated in his bean field, blistering his feet and enduring the acrimony of passing villagers and friends. He sweated ten years over eight drafts of *Walden* manuscripts, depriving himself of time to roam the woods. He worked "in fields [of beans and language] if only for the sake of tropes and expression, to serve a parable-maker one day." Thoreau toiled to provide the expressions from which his idealized readers would create parables. A language of paradox, ambiguity, oxymoron, indirection, and exaggeration provided the widest and richest fields for reader interpretation.

3. PARODIC *WALDEN*

Immediately after Thoreau became established as a major American author, readers were impressed by his variety of voice. In 1906, Bradford Torrey marveled at how he could sound variously like a "poet, idealist, stoic, cynic, naturalist, spiritualist, lover of purity, seeker of perfection . . . , free-thinker and saint."[1] The idealistic spokesman for social reform who attracted Gandhi and King could change his pitch to sound like "the comedian at Walden Pond"; the intense voice insisting upon a spartan existence could mellow to tones more appropriate to a gentleman of leisure. One focus of recent Thoreau scholarship has been to study the rhetorical means by which these various voices have been created.[2] In his other works, Thoreau's disparate voices are usually kept separate, but in *Walden* they are blended into the same text as one way of preventing an American classic from becoming "a splendid mausoleum." The playful mood of "Natural History of Massachusetts" would be unsuitable for the angry, exasperated voice of "Slavery in Massachusetts." The rage in his John Brown essays would not fit "The Landlord." Among his books, the persona of *Maine Woods* is an initiate, a tyro, or a "chaplain in the army," and in *Cape Cod* it is a hard-hearted, reserved, laissez-faire individualist.[3] But in *Walden*, the persona seems both the strong individualist in *Cape Cod* as well as the self-deprecating, fallible person who laments that his seeds of virtue did not sprout. *Walden*'s persona both proudly proclaims his independence and admits he is an employee of the railroad. It insists, "I am I," while also demonstrating the variety of his "I's," a host of "I's" that ultimately includes all of "we" and even, finally, "they."

Scholarship has generally concentrated on untangling *Walden*'s voices. One scholar will privilege the voice—reminiscent of Theodore Parker, George Ripley, and the young Emerson—that speaks for idealism, love of nature, and social reform in the clear, confident tones of the Transcendentalist, holding forth self-assuredly like the famed Chanticleer of *Walden*'s epigraph. Another will select passages that concentrate on Thoreau's doubt and indecision. Walter Benn Michaels, for one, argues that the parable inserted in 1852 about the traveler who, misled by a boy, becomes mired in a bog vitiates Thoreau's confident assurances that there is a solid bottom everywhere.[4]

These differing views arise in large part from the history of *Walden*'s drafts. First delivered as a lecture, "Walden" called upon the adversarial audience that worked so successfully in his other lectures. He would not lecture upon the Sandwich Islands, but upon issues of dire importance "to every one of you" seated in the auditorium. But Thoreau quickly began to add contrasting voices, particularly one more concerned with mystery and ambiguity than fact and assured statement. As early as 1847, he began to import material that would emphasize what he called "the Protean character of things." At the very end of his lecture draft— probably just before he left the pond—he added his requirement that "all things be mysterious and unexplorable, that land and sea be infinitely wild, unsurveyed and unfathomed by us because unfathomable" (317–18). To borrow Thoreau's animal imagery, he quickly imposed the red squirrels' "vocal pirouetting" (310) upon Chanticleer's cocksure crowing.

Rather than search for passages in which the voice speaks *either* as the self-confident lecturer *or* as the doubting, ambiguous artist, this section focuses instead on crucial occasions when his various voices merge. *Parody,* with its etymology as "counter-song," is the best term for this aesthetic phenomenon, although not in the popular sense, nor in the generic meaning of Mikhail Bakhtin. Instead, *parody* is intended more along the lines investigated by recent critics as a rhetorical strategy in which the text is made multivocal.[5] According to this theory, the parodied text is awarded added authority by virtue of the fact that it has been deemed worthy of being parodied. Its authority, having been tested by the parodic countertext, grants the author greater license to make his text even more extreme, knowing that its extreme statement will be counterbalanced by its parody, a technique that would attract a writer like Thoreau, concerned about being able "to exaggerate enough even to lay the foundation of a true expression," a rhetorician whose aesthetic goal was *"Extra vagance!"* (324). In a sense, I reduce *Walden's* famous epigraph (reproduced in *Walden's* text): "I do not propose to write an ode to dejection, but to brag as lustily as chanticleer in the morning, standing on his roost, if only to wake my neighbors up." In an almost semiotic clarification, my reduction reads, "I do not propose . . . but to brag." After all, the epigraph invites compression, with its redundant assertion that calls attention to an *artiste-poseur* at work, "standing on his roost." My reduction presents Thoreau proposing so that he can brag, and exaggeration is the ultimate end of this proposal. Thoreau uses the explicit langugage of proposition in order to develop another kind of language, an indeterminate language of desire.

And so, I concentrate on the voices whose proposals are swept up against brags and exaggerations and countercurrents or countervoices. I will attend to his proposing "primary voice," not because it is most important, but because it is the cocksure adversarial voice heard in his lectures and reinforced by a century of readings that have typecast Thoreau under one category or another: a reformer, a radical, a Jeffersonian, a nature lover, and so forth. Along with his primary voice of chanticleer crowing, he was wont to insert a red squirrel's pirouetting, which undercut the boast—a countervoice that left his text indeterminate.

The physicist Niels Bohr has said that every great truth has its countertruth. Rhetorically, one might add that a truth can be made to seem true if poised against its countertruth. Unlike Hegel, where thesis sparks antithesis, resulting in synthesis, Thoreau is noted for puns and oxymorons, but they lead to a higher rhetorical aim. As the most economical form of linguistic transactions in which verbal values are not only exchanged but suspended in the moment of pun recognition, puns call attention to the limitations or play of language.[6] Disrupting order, they interject confusion; rupturing structures, they intimate a higher truth beyond language. Since Sartre, it has been obvious that a statement of truth is an inadvertent admission of doubt, but the turnabout should be fair play: a cunning rhetorical development toward doubt should mean the reassertion of truth or "depth" or "profundity." At the very least, it should give the impression of "sincerity" or "seriousness."

Generically considered, puns and oxymorons fit Thoreau's texts nicely, especially when they are viewed as collapsing boundaries of classification and division. If nothing else, parody shares power. If you mock the president, you enhance his prestige even as your mockery is bruited by the media. In parody, positions easily seep into their opposites. Two or more negations buttress the fortress being undermined. Since not an autobiography, *Walden* might be classed as an historical novel, and that classification raises a rich irony since the cognate but antithetical attitudes of "history" and "fiction" are evoked. One scholar has sung the praises of rhetorical indeterminacy because, while it does not allow language to communicate truth except through implication, it frees the text and its readers to exercise power.[7] This idea is reinforced by Thoreau's two-year hiatus in developing *Walden*'s drafts after 1849. Immediately upon resuming his drafting of *Walden*, Thoreau's *Journal* emphasis was on force and power and subtle nocturnal influences in communication. Thus, for

7 September 1851, he confesses that "I am prepared not so much for contemplation as for force and expression." He continues to value precise description, but only as it leads to an indelible impression always reminding readers of an infinite beauty that is always remote, communicable only through a "true exaggeration."

His rhetorical ambitions were further complicated by the fundamentally parodic nature of Transcendentalism. It is no surprise that, having rejected Greeley's ready-cash requests for essays on Transcendentalists, Thoreau instead wrote a provocative essay on Carlyle, who continues to be esteemed as "one of the most important Victorians."[8] As a recent critic explains, Carlyle's language remains valued largely because it transcended the local concerns of his Victorian epoch by obfuscating apparently simple ideas in symbolism that aspires to impenetrability. Evan Carton has studied the quintessential remoteness that informs Emerson's themes, even those as intimate as friendship. After all, Transcendentalism, whether Carlylian or Emersonian, presumes that our real selves are but cartoons of what we can be and that our actions parody our aims. Thus, bragging is the only idealistic truth. Exaggerations, even cartoons, are the most accurate expression of our ambitions and aspirations. Reality becomes a mirage, and only hyperbole and crowing verge on true expression (*J,* 9 February 1852).

Within that rigorous yet ephemeral philosophical framework, parody was a refreshing out for the writer who delighted in moving his mystic pen through creamy paper. Parody always presumes *vis-a-vis* instead of *versus.* Thoreau's chanticleer could seem as urgent as a rooster destined for the chopping block or as cagey and comic as Chaucer's Chaunticleer. In fact, his assertion that he will not propose an ode to dejection is parodic. The assertion involves his refusal to be fashionably morose as a poet, his negation of negativity. He is an "anti-Jacques," if one considers Shakespeare's *As You Like It,* an eremetical persona that refuses to mope. Therefore, Thoreau is fond of following assertion with the subjunctive mood. After he has traipsed through Massachusetts's mountains finding nothing to inspire his pen, he chastises nature and asserts that "we condescend to climb the crags of earth." But he follows this *Journal* entry for 23 May 1854 with a subjunctive phrasing: "Man *should be* the harp articulate."

Multitudinous examples of a Transcendental insistence on the ideal over the real exist, despite the fact that language is the only communicative "real" we have. And so, on 3 February 1841 he says that one's imagined life *must seem* superior to the one led. In the same entry, he remarks that his public, published life *must seem* on "a higher plane than that occupied." A "higher plane" than idealism exists, a rhetorical plane that might be called space, silence, the subjunctive mood, or Melville's "pondering repose of IF." Frequently in Thoreau's writings, his traveler pursues a path that leads to a cliff where he delights in a panoramic view so vast and diverse that it cannot be framed without doing injustice to the whole. These descriptions can be emblems of his rhetoric, which pursues the path of a certain proposal or a specific idea only to culminate in silent wonder or indeterminacy. Thus, he pursues the slogan of the Democratic party as it expands to mean that government is best when it does not govern at all. Finally, his governmental trail culminates in a clifftop conception that he has often "imagined, but not yet anywhere seen."

In the *Walden* paragraph immediately after his most famous emblem of desire (the missing hound, bay horse, and turtle-dove), Thoreau experiments with the "if possible," or the "possible if." A standard Franklinesque maxim that it is wise to rise early is extended until it reaches a philosophical cliff beyond which one cannot farther travel. In his extension, he urges us, "To anticipate, not the sunrise and the dawn merely, but, if possible, Nature herself!" (17). Cast as a sentence fragment and capped by an exclamation mark, the sentiment's own grammar and punctuation asperse its message. The interruptive insertion of "if possible" calls attention to the fact that the desire is not possible. Indeed, were it possible, then much of the primary voice's text, which has insisted upon harmony with nature, would have to be rejected.

Having reached a speculative cliff, Thoreau makes the statement even wilder, so extreme that the vision spills beyond its frame. The proposal is dashed to pieces, much as in Wendell Phillips' toast, which he admired, that the Constitution be dashed into a thousand pieces. Having expanded that vision until it transcends any possible frame, he concludes the idea with a passage that is truly a "passage"—that is, it promises passage to an understanding beyond the limits of communal, public language. He writes, "It is true, I never assisted the sun materially in his rising, but doubt not, it was of the last importance only to be present at it." Although he says it was of the "last importance," the rhetorical effect is that it was of the first importance. If "the sun" means reality, then Thoreau's biological-cultural presence is at one and the same time crucial and supererogatory. If "the sun" intends a rhetorical situation, then readers are likewise privileged and deflated. They note meaning's rise, and thus their observations are essential, or they are insignificant —as insignificant as the sun or the creation upon which it shines. There is no "last importance," no "final meaning." The impossibility that launches the paragraph culminates in the injunction to "doubt not." Even doubt and impossibility must lead to possibility. Even indeterminacy must not be final.

Over the past century and a half, readers have established the primary voice of "Thoreau" as the voice derived from his most famous texts: *Walden* and "Resistance to Civil Government." That cultural decision is a useful way to discuss the phenomenon of the text called *Walden* as its primary voice is challenged by its countervoices. The self-parody that opens the chapter called "Brute Neighbors" is an interesting case in point. Since this form of parody is most consonant with conventional definitions, it should serve as a useful transition to more subtle parodic varieties contained in Thoreau's sketch of his ideal artist—the Artist of Kouroo from *Walden*'s "Conclusion"—and the complex parodic functioning that opens "Where I Lived, and What I Lived For," which has obvious links with the Artist of Kouroo sketch.

Walden's primary voice is so strong that it can overwhelm its countervoices, causing them to slip past readers. One classic example is Bradford Torrey's lament that Thoreau was not "one of those gentler humorists who can sometimes see themselves, as all humorists have the gift of seeing other people, funny side out." Had Thoreau been able to engage in self-deprecating humor, Torrey believed, his writings would have been "richer, freer, more expansive, more various and flexible." Of course, Thoreau was indeed capable of self-parody, probably for the very ends Torrey describes, and no clearer case exists than the seven paragraphs that open chapter 12; "Brute Neighbors."[9]

In this seven-paragraph sketch, Thoreau departs from the first-person autobiographical mode and creates the third-person roles of "Hermit" and "Poet" as though he were writing a script for a mock melodrama or burlesque. Casting himself in the role of "Hermit," Thoreau pretends to be confused as to whether his seemingly fine thoughts are truly a "budding ecstasy" or simply a case of "the dumps." He presents himself as a petty conman who sends his Poet "friend" (probably Ellery Channing) off to do the dirty work of digging worms, all the while instructing him on the proper way to dig bait. In short, Thoreau depicts his friend and

210 THOREAU'S WILD RHETORIC

himself as though someone as unsympathetic as Judge Hoar or as disrespectful as Sam Staples were penning the burlesque instead of Thoreau, a hostile attitude that apparently persists to the present day.[10]

Perhaps part of the reason Thoreau included this self-parody was to compensate for the inimical audience he imagined for his lecture version of *Walden* and to provide the anonymous book-buying audience with a glimpse of how some of his townspeople viewed him. But more important rhetorical strategies are involved, and they entail questions not only of theme and content but also of facts about when the parody was created and where it was placed. In 1847, Thoreau had intended to follow "Higher Laws," with its discussion of diet that centered on fishing, by beginning the next chapter with the simple admission, "But practically I was only half-converted by my own arguments, for I still found myself fishing at rare intervals." Thematically there might have been no compelling reason for expanding this single sentence into a seven-paragraph parodic sketch; the original version served just as well. For thematic purposes, that admission was sufficient to qualify his idealistic assertions, and it provided the countervoice sounded in other parts of *Walden,* as when Thoreau listed how little he ate but whispered to readers not to follow this restricted diet without having a well-stocked larder in reserve. Not until the fifth draft of late 1852–1853 did Thoreau begin to create the elaborate seven-paragraph parody that would take the place of this single sentence.[11]

The timing of this alteration from simple admission to parody at the start of chapter 12 is significant, for it corresponds chronologically with changes Thoreau was making to chapter 11, "Higher Laws," a chapter that, as the manuscripts show, caused Thoreau a great deal of effort. The basic material of "Higher Laws" was present in early drafts even when the chapter went under the working title "Animal Food," but in the fifth draft Thoreau began to intensify statements and make them so extreme that the alterations may comprise a difference in kind as well as degree. That is, in the same draft, while Thoreau felt free enough to indulge in self-parody, he was also adding sentences to "Higher Laws" like, "We are conscious of an animal in us, which awakens in proportion as our higher nature slumbers. It is reptile and sensual, and perhaps cannot be wholly expelled; like the worms which, even in life and health, occupy our bodies. Possibly we may withdraw from it, but never change its nature" (219). Similarly, Thoreau added *Walden*'s most troubling sentence to this fifth draft, writing that "Nature is hard to overcome, but she must be overcome." After the ample love for nature in all its varieties that Thoreau has demonstrated in the text, this single sentence jars; in its extreme statement, it seems, ironically, somehow un-Thoreauvian.

The main point entwines the fact of compositional simultaneity and the text's multivocal quality. At the same time and in the same draft, Thoreau was pushing his serious statements to their furthest bounds in "Higher Laws" while also engaging contrarily in whimsical, deprecatory self-parody that was to be placed immediately after "Higher Laws" and to open "Brute Neighbors." These are not separate moods, each isolated from the other; rather, they produce an interchange of rhetorical strategy. Knowing that self-parody would immediately follow his most didactic chapter—knowing, as it were, that a wink would follow moralistic threats—Thoreau was at liberty to make the text of "Higher Laws" as extreme as he might. Parody coupled with sententiousness could help the text leap conventional rhetorical bounds to reach the aesthetic goal of *"Extra vagance!"* [12]

While obvious markers exist to signal that "Brute Neighbors" opens with burlesque, a more subtle parodic technique is at work in the Artist of Kouroo sketch in *Walden*'s conclusion. Traditionally the sketch has been taken as a parable of Thoreau's ideal artist or possibly as a self-portrait. Sherman Paul claims it proves Thoreau's personal success at aiming to live in "the eternal present"; Frederick Garber interprets it as Thoreau's victory over the ever-returning cycles of the seasons insofar as "his work has redeemed him out of time, so that he has no need of liberating release into one more spring." [13] These interpretations clearly address the text's primary voice, which calls for a striving after perfection, an experience of perennial youth, a victory over time, and a transcendence of social/historical factors such as friendship, culture, and race. This clearly established primary voice, however, is interrupted by a counter-voice, which is emphasized because it articulates the only question posed within the tale. Two-thirds of the way through the parable, the "real" author intrudes into his sketch to ask, "But why do I stay to mention these things?" and the intrusion occurs precisely at the moment when the finishing stroke is about to be put to the "ideal" artist's perfect work.

That intrusion—that "imperfection" in the tale of perfection—accomplishes the multivoice function of parody. It distances the voice of the real author working his pen from his idealized model; it links the author more closely to his reader than to the Kouroo artist meditatively perfecting his stick (topos for pen?), oblivious to family, friends, and cultural/historical audience; it images an actual artist struggling with his material, extremely conscious of his craft, ever inspecting it for flaws, as opposed to the idealized artist's smooth and easy perfection. The primary voice calling for perfection and transcendence remains intact, but the whispered aside of the interruptive question puffs it to a level remote, ethereal, precious but a trifle fantastical.[14]

As with self-parody in "Brute Neighbors," placement of the idealized sketch is crucial. Occupying the eleventh paragraph of Walden's "Conclusion," the parable is a gate that swings the text from primary voice to countervoice. Before the parable, the primary voice is dominant; after it, the countervoice prevails. Before Kouroo's story appears, the text exhorts readers to be Columbuses bravely exploring the soul's uncharted regions, or to be at least the biggest pygmies possible. At any rate, they should be on the march, stepping to the music that they hear, however measured or far away. After the idealistic tones of this primary voice have been firmly situated, qualifications and reservations follow, and the imagery becomes less heroic after paragraph 11. Post-Kouroo allusions are to a hanged tinker, the traveler mired in a bog, a man living in a hollow tree, and Thoreau living in the angle of a leaden wall. Imagery is insectival, limning the author as a "spider" and as "the human insect" who analogizes themes of rebirth and salvation with images of "the seventeen-year locust" and the "strong and beautiful bug" gnawing its way loudly through an apple-tree table.

The primary voice certainly has not been silenced, nor was it intended to be; its echoes can be heard even in the less heroic imagery and allusions of the conclusion's closing paragraphs. However, the text has indeed become multivocal. Post-Kouroo material clearly comments parodically on the unreserved boasts of the conclusion's first ten paragraphs, but it also serves as serious parody in that it challenges the power of the primary voice and tests how loudly its confidence can echo within more negative language. Conversely, the primary voice speaks back, imposing its authority upon the parodic mode. Such values as "strength" and "beauty," previously represented by Columbus and Hercules, pine trees and Walden Pond, persist and are reincarnated in the less lofty and less conventional images of hanged men and bugs. The ideal represented by the artist of Kouroo, though remote and perhaps unattainable, is borne by the conscious artist struggling with his material, intruding into his tale, interrupting his text with serious parodic insinuation—enriching his work by imperfecting its perfection.

The parable of the idealized artist represented in the Kouroo sketch has been linked with *Walden*'s second chapter, "Where I Lived, and What I Lived For." Sherman Paul, for one, comments that Thoreau "began with his desire to live in the eternal present, and 'Where I Lived, and What I Lived For' and the concluding fable of the artist of the city of Kouroo described his success."[15] While Paul's link is thematic, striking stylistic parallels exist between *Walden*'s second chapter and its "Conclusion." Both chapters offer identical allusions, such as references to exotic models, to the importance of foundations beneath airy dreams, to pygmies, to Spartans, and to mud. Similarly, parody plays an important role, but in a way different from the other two cases that have been studied, and its development is part of *Walden*'s evolution.

Starting with paragraph 15, the last eleven paragraphs remain virtually intact from the 1846–1847 version that was still considered as a lecture, with the idea of a book a mere possibility. They are without parody, and, as usual with Thoreau's lectures, they engage the audience adversarially, challenging it with direct, unmitigated assertion, particularly at paragraphs 16 and 17, with their emphasis on living deliberately and their doctrine of simplicity. But the chapter's first fourteen paragraphs are a quite different matter. The first five were composed in 1852, long after Thoreau had left his cabin and three years after he had declined Ticknor's offer to publish *Walden* at the firm's expense, and these chapters appeared as a separate essay in *Sartain's Union Magazine* for August 1852. However, the remaining paragraphs, 6 through 14, contain much new material; what remained from the first draft was so heavily revised as to constitute new matter. For example, the pun on Thoreau's taking up residence on Independence Day was not made until 1852, and the insertion of Thoreau's self-image as Chanticleer was added to the sixth draft in 1853–1854. These new first fourteen paragraphs were added not only after Thoreau's famous discovery that the seasons formed a cycle but also after he began to enter doubts in his journal such as whether every simple yes or no were a lie; whether any scheme, even Christ's, vitiated idealistic teachings; and whether it might be a good idea to establish a Society for the Diffusion of Useful Ignorance to balance those associations that sought intellectual certainty.[16]

Clearly intended as a preface to the old material from the lecture draft of 1846–1847, where the confidence of the primary voice remains pure, these first fourteen paragraphs are structurally remarkable in their use of parody. As with the kouroo parable, they make use of textual interruption. As with the self-parodic skit that opens "Brute Neighbors," they offer a countervoice to more confident, definite assertions of the primary voice. However, the order is reversed: whereas parody follows immediately upon the primary voice in chapters 11 and 12 here parody interweaves with the text, helping to introduce the primary voice, which then speaks uninterruptedly in the last eleven paragraphs of "Where I Lived." A three-part structural pattern—Play, then Sentence, followed by Parodic Release—recurs four times in the introduction before the text is given over entirely to the primary voice in the chapter's second half. "Play" entails verbal or visual puns; "Sentence" echoes the primary voice and offers a moral or maxim or heroic call; "Release" of the reader from a possibly tendentious Sentence is achieved through conventional parodic devices such as zaniness, exaggeration, qualification, or carnival.

"Where I Lived" begins with an elaborate pun on "country seat," followed by the adage "a man is rich in proportion to the number of things which he can afford to let alone," after which the reader is released from the adage's ponderous profundity by the zany account of how Thoreau sort of "purchased" Hollowell farm and by his sexist comment on wives. Beginning with the space provided by the quoted poem, with its pun on "survey," the pattern is repeated through another four paragraphs until the next break in the text, with Thoreau punning on skimmed milk and riches, offering morals about "improvements" and being "committed," and then out-Catoing Cato by exaggerating a historical figure who is ambiguous in the first place.[17]

The pattern of Play, Sentence, and Release recurs a third time through paragraphs 7–9, beginning with a pun on the "accident" of Independence Day, pursued by the Sentence of morals like "Olympus is everywhere," followed by the undercut of Thoreau's being "caged" in his cabin. The pattern recurs a fourth, more elaborate time through the fourteenth paragraph. This final introductory pattern starts by echoing the pun on "seat" and introduces a beautiful visual pun that the pond seems "like a tarn high up on the side of a mountain, its bottom far above the surface of other lakes." That visual pun is mirrored more symbolically by distant hills that seem "true-blue coins from heaven's own mint." Then Sentences on the theme of rebirth symbolized by light and waking imagery march into the text: "Renew thyself completely each day," the morning is "the most memorable season on the day," darkness bears its fruit and is no less good than the light, "the day is a perpetual morning," and so forth. Then these inspiring sentiments are undercut by the last lines of paragraph 14, where Thoreau, complaining that "only one in a hundred millions" is alive to "a poetic or divine life," also suggests that he feels fortunate in that complaint. If he ever did meet "a man who was quite awake," then "how could I have looked him in the face?"

In these paragraphs, Thoreau passes carefully through many moods: the witty, clever punster; the intent, high-sounding idealist with his exhorting style; the zany village clown or the undercutting skeptic who parodically questions the Sentences of the text's primary voice. By intermingling parodic devices with the cherished values spoken for by his primary voice, Thoreau relieved the potentially stifling, restrictive, and exclusionary weight of his Sentences, the weight borne by "the minister, the school-committee" and even by Christ's scheme. By ingenious use of serious parody, he sidestepped the intellectual, psychological, and spiritual trap he described in "Economy": "So thoroughly and sincerely are we compelled to live, reverencing our life, and denying the possibility of change. This is the only way, we say; but there are as many ways as there can be drawn radii from one centre" (11). To the "Conclusion" of *Walden*'s sixth draft (1853–1854), Thoreau added that one reason he left Walden was because he had worn a path from his cabin to the pond and "others may have fallen into it"; through parodic techniques, he could rescue readers rhetorically from repeating the error of falling into a textual rut.

Thus, parody provided Thoreau with a rhetorical strategy by which his style and expression could sound free, expansive, and undogmatic while simultaneously remaining true to his profoundest aspirations, even presenting those ideals more intensely by virtue of parody's multivocality. Thoreau refined this technique during *Walden*'s last four drafts from 1852 to 1854. In late 1852–1853, he added a passage that could stand metaphorically for the aesthetic experience he hoped his readers would share —the famous description of his "pretty game" with a loon on the surface of Walden Pond, which is metaphorical if one casts the reader in the role of "I" and images Thoreau's textual meaning in the figure of the loon. For "I" and "you," read "reader"; for "he," the author or his text.

While he was thinking one thing in his brain, I was endeavoring to divine his thought in mine. It was a pretty game, played on the smooth surface of the pond, a man against a loon. Suddenly your adversary's checker disappears beneath the board, and the problem is to place yours nearest to where his will appear again. ... Again and again, when I was straining my eyes over the surface one way, I would suddenly be startled by his unearthly laugh behind me. But why, after displaying so much cunning, did he invariably betray himself the moment he came up by that loud laugh? (235)

Thoreau provides the answer to his own question: so that his mind may "live wild and free though secret" (277). Attempting to share his most intimate thoughts with strangers, to remain elusive while inspiring readers, to provide a glimpse of the self as "a mass of thawing clay" (307), he offers a representation of the self closest to that nature he discovered in the early 1850s—forever familiar, forever new. A parodic style prevented the meaning of his profoundest thoughts from becoming ossified, settled, or stale. In *Walden*'s last four drafts of 1852–1854, much material was added to emphasize thaw, melt, flow, change, process; the development of parody provided the text with rhetorical possibilities to match the added themes.

4. UNREADING "THOREAU"

Discussion of *Walden* keeps curling back to Thoreau's page break on page 16. Before that break, *Walden*'s aim has been to define its reading audiences and to clarify how most lead frivolous or desperate lives. After the break, Thoreau tells that he would never paint "No Admittance" on his gate, he offers his emblem of desire in the hound, bay horse, and turtle-dove, and he launches the Walden experiment parodically as a kind of town business, sinking "well-nigh all my capital" into it. The paragraph that immediately follows that crucial textual break invents a fascinating rhetorical situation:

If I should attempt to tell how I have desired to spend my life in years past, it would probably surprise those of my readers who are somewhat acquainted with its actual history; it would certainly astonish those who know nothing about it. I will only hint at some of the enterprises which I have cherished.

That two-sentence paragraph has two cynosures: reading and narration. Those "acquainted with its actual history" will be surprised at its fictionalized appearance. Familiar with some of the facts, they will marvel at how different these facts look when filtered through narrative structures.

Moreover, historical readers seem at a disadvantage to those who have no facts to come between them and the story. Readers unacquainted with the experiment's reality are either better readers, or they can look forward to a more powerful and exciting reading adventure: they will experience astonishment, whereas historical readers will only be surprised. Furthermore, the paragraph makes clear that the narrative is incomplete. As in *A Week*, where Thoreau says his text captures all but the most significant thoughts and events, *Walden*'s narrative strategies can "only hint at" his meaning; indeed, his narrative can hint at only "some of the enterprises which I have cherished."

This highly complex rhetorical situation has occurred earlier; in fact, it replicates the strategy deployed in *Walden*'s second paragraph. For that matter, the main purpose of *Walden*'s opening three paragraphs is to establish and to satisfy three principal reading attitudes. The straightforward first paragraph reads rather conventionally as a journalistic record or an autobiographical account. Although facts have been bent to achieve narrative purposes, the paragraph's plain style communicates information directly. Its meaning is clear, whether creative or factual—whether creatively signaling readers to receive the event as an experiment and to imagine the author as a sojourner in civilized life, or bluntly describing details of the experiment. The rhetorical mode of this paragraph is rooted in the American tradition, reminding one of William Bradford's wish to record history simply and earnestly in a plain style.[1]

The third paragraph is likewise clear and traditional, but its tone differs greatly from the first. Its satirical material is harsh, and the plain style has been transformed, invoking exaggeration, hyperbole, and exotic allusions. Still, the paragraph's intent is sharply defined: a forceful criticism of the way most people masochistically misspend their lives while following "normal routine." Rhetorically, the most interesting point is its treatment of the reading audience. The first paragraph had positioned its readers as the main point of address, inviting them to partake directly of the message almost as though sharing a meal. But the third paragraph situates readers in the margin of the text, as though asking its readers to hold Thoreau's coat while he rolls up his sleeves and wades into battle. The text posits those "who are said to live in New England" or "in this town" as the principal point of address, thus freeing book readers to choose when they wish to place themselves safely at the author's elbow off to the side of the text and when to seat themselves in the lecture audience as the target of attack. This clever rhetorical strategy is nevertheless conventional, a technique long established in satire. Readers are sure exactly how they are intended to receive this paragraph's messages and how to respond to its rhetorical signals.

Although different in tone and intent, the first and third paragraphs are similar in that they emerge from established literary modes and present messages clearly. However, the intervening paragraph is markedly different. While the first paragraph may sound as traditional as Bradford's history and the third may be as familiar as Swift's satire, this middle paragraph is in a different mode. Like the paragraph on page 16, it is unconventional, puzzling, ambiguous. It retracts a statement as soon as it is made, withdraws a declaration as soon as it is uttered, and qualifes assertions to the extent that readers doubt whether an assertion has been made. In sharp contrast to the clarity and "sincerity" of the other two paragraphs, the second paragraph pushes beyond contradiction and oxymoron toward indeterminacy, leaving readers to guess tenuously how they should take any given sentence. The first paragraph makes one feel that speech-act theory, which stresses the idea that a writer has a definite message to convey, would be an appropriate approach. The third paragraph may reward an analysis like Bakhtin's of Menippean satire or Bercovitch's of the American jeremiad. But this second paragraph is the kind that makes Thoreau sound to some interpreters like a poststructuralist in a department full of New Critics.[2]

Indeterminacies abound from the paragraph's opening sentence, even when considering only one rhetorical essential such as the reader's relationship to the text. The author apologizes for having to bother with details about his affairs; he regrets the autobiographical report that has become *Walden*'s most appealing feature. The text suggests that its "best readers" are those who are superior to autobiography. They "who feel no particular interest in me" are granted a privileged reading relationship, are empowered even to pardon their author. These superior readers are elevated "above" the main matter of the text, despite the fact that its author has obviously taken great pains and, as the record of the reading response has demonstrated, has wonderfully succeeded in making the account of his life in the woods intriguing, fascinating, and delightful.

Walden's principal audiences are variously described in later paragraphs as those who are shackled to materialism by "golden and silver
fetters" or as the "mass of men" who lead lives of quiet desperation. But
this second paragraph defines a very different audience: "Perhaps these
pages are more particularly addressed to poor students." In contrast to
the distinct delineations of other possible audiences, this sentence is more
slippery. It begins with a qualifying "perhaps" and ends with "poor
students," which could mean poor economically, as in a financially-strapped
version of Emerson's American scholar, or poor in an intellectual sense,
as in those "poor studiers" of the text who warp it to fit their own theses.[3]
Finally, the paragraph concludes with the Carlylean metaphor of Thoreau's
coat. In this trope for *Walden*'s philosophy, Thoreau trusts "that none
will stretch the seams in putting on the coat, for it may do good service to
him whom it fits."

Readers cannot be sure just how big this makes them. The metaphor
may present the author in a modest mood, assuming his readers are larger
than he, but it also suggests that the author is larger than his readers
who, after all, might be merely those pygmies in *Walden*'s conclusion
who could never stretch the seams of Thoreau's woven work. The latter
seems all the more possible since the metaphor is preceded by the author's
complaint—in which the author poses as a reader—that he has never
read a true book of a true life. Yet even that interpretation is slippery, for
one is not positive which lack this author/reader called "Thoreau" more
laments: the absence of "a simple and sincere account" or of a man who
"has lived sincerely." One cannot even be sure whether the complaint is
more aesthetic or philosophic.

Amid this swirl of indecision and rhetorical complexity, one point
remains clear. The paragraph promises that Thoreau will either speak
from or fill that gap of a "sincere account." He will make some readers
feel as though they were "kinsmen" addressed from a far "distant land," a
distance necessitated by time and space and, more significantly in rhetorical terms, a distance represented by the inscribed pages of the text that
stand between reader and author, while simultaneously providing the
bridge by which reader and author can entertain the illusion of kinship,
communion, communication. Thus, in a paragraph that seems so thoroughly to dissolve itself, one message emerges clearly. Nonetheless, that
message emerges from an absence, a lack, an existing gap. The promise

of a sincere account of a life sincerely lived remains precisely that—a promise, a possibility that can be entertained only in the transitory act of reading.

Walden's first three paragraphs, with their intermixture of rhetorical modes, resemble Hawthorne's idealization of a kind of writing he sketched when he and Thoreau were friends and neighbors: "To write a dream, which shall resemble the real course of a dream, with all its inconsistency, its eccentricities and aimlessness—with nevertheless a leading idea running through the whole. Up to this old age of the world, no such thing has ever been written."[4] *Walden* proffers many "leading ideas" that are confidently asserted and clearly articulated by its primary voice. Its author does believe firmly that many waste their lives, that the railroad rides upon us, that nature is rejuvenating, that materialism exacts a dear price, that thought and self-discovery are worthwhile pursuits.

Still, these "leading ideas" are often wrapped within cloaks of obscurity. Certainty frequently leads to uncertainty. Even simplicity can become highly complex. *Walden*'s longest chapter might detail in extreme precision how economically one may live but the postmodernist Thoreau advises no one to undertake a dietary experiment unless there is "a well stocked larder" in reserve (61). *Walden* clearly extols the crucial value of leading a virtuous life and praises the desire to sow the seeds of "sincerity, truth, simplicity, faith, innocence, and the like," but "The Bean-Field" confesses, "Alas! I said this to myself; but now another summer is gone, and another, and another, and I am obliged to say to you, Reader, that the seeds which I planted, if indeed they *were* the seeds of those virtues, were worm-eaten or had lost their vitality, and so did not come up" (163–64). Thoreau includes many jarring notes in the text of *Walden,* telling readers that he "caged" himself in the woods (85) and narrating the anecdote about the Collins's cat who, like Thoreau, takes to the woods but becomes a wild cat, and "a dead cat at last" (44). I have already mentioned how the story in *Walden*'s conclusion about the boy who misleads a traveler into becoming mired in a bog casts doubt on all of Thoreau's other assertions that there is a solid bottom everywhere. In fact, while the leading idea of *Walden*'s "Conclusion" is clearly meant to inspire readers to step to the music that they hear and to lead more heroic lives, the inspirational message is mixed. Precisely how much is one meant to be encouraged when told, "Love your life, poor as it is. . . . It is not so bad as you are"?

Thoreau's famous aphorism about building castles in the air may represent his ultimate confrontation with the limits and indeterminacy of language. Although his famous air-castles image clearly urges readers to work hard to place solid foundations beneath their dreams, this inspirational passage in introduced by the sentence, "In proportion as he simplifies his life, the laws of the universe will appear less complex, and solitude will not be solitude, nor poverty poverty, nor weakness weakness" (324). A rigorous linguistic interpretation of this statement would translate it to mean that words do not mean what they say; if poverty does not equal poverty, then *love* does not mean love. Even a conservative translation would read that the author's language is private, independent of the public language his culture has constructed. Dictionaries, thesauri, glosses, commentaries, midrash, or other repositories of cultural discourse will not much help in translating meaning. Fittingly, Thoreau begins the next paragraph, "It is a ridiculous demand which England and America make, that you shall speak so that they can understand you. Neither men nor toad-stools grow so." This interweaving of rhetorical modes, particularly the blending of "leading ideas" with dreamlike dissolves, of assertions with infinite qualifiers, of clear sentences with the perpetual sense of their imminent erasure, is the crux of that writing that we call "Thoreau."

Essentially this interweaving consists of three rhetorical strands. Some statements are confidently urged, their maxims forcefully proposed. Other passages are more suggestive, less explicit, and more open. *Walden*'s concluding image of the sun as a morning star is one example. Still other sections dissolve as they are read; seemingly crystal-clear sentiments melt into obscuring fogs. In fine, some statements are said, others unsaid, still others un-said, and often these three rhetorical effects are deployed simultaneously. The closest Thoreau comes to anticipating this articulation of language is when he refers to three fundamental linguistic presentations as the "halloo, the whisper, and silence" (*PJ1*,61). His "halloo" bespeaks the confident assertions of his primary voice, his "whisper" calls into question an assertion just made, and his "silence" renders any textual meaning indefinite and indeterminate.

A writer less interested in the boundaries and limits of language— whether naturalist, social reformer, satirist, or moralist—might avoid this last rhetorical mode in order to seem as clear as possible, but Thoreau experimented with the possibilities of language, more so in *Walden* than in "Slavery in Massachusetts" and his John Brown essays, less so in

Walden than in works like "Moonlight" and his first book, *A Week on the Concord and Merrimack Rivers*. In *Thoreau's Complex Weave*, Linck C. Johnson has demonstrated that in its initial drafts *A Week* was much more structured, coherent, and accessible than in its final version. *A Week*'s revisions were carefully aimed at making the text more silent than a "halloo" or a whispering image. In its draft evolution, *A Week* became less conventional, less easy to follow, less easily comprehensible. *Walden* blames a certain kind of reader for these narrative dissolves, for the un-saying of meaning, for the pains Thoreau spent recasting his message to make it at once more sincere and more elusive. Of course, by "reader" I mean Thoreau's conception of his reader or, to put it more accurately, his attempt to create an idealized process of reading.

This idealized reading activity, imagined and then blamed for the rhetorical necessity of silence, was discussed in chapter 1 in terms of the linguistic theories of Bushnell, Kraitsir, and others, primarily at Harvard. However, Thoreau's language theory was more radical, and it antedates theirs. Publishing their most influential books in 1846 and 1849 respectively, Kraitsir and Bushnell may have encouraged Thoreau's own linguistic explorations as he paused for several months before undertaking the final three revisions of *Walden,* but he had settled many of their crucial issues for himself by 1842, when he published "Natural History of Massachusetts," writing that "Nature is mythical and mystical always, and works with the license and extravagance of genius. She has her luxurious and florid style as well as art" (*Writings*, 5:125). Pushing beyond the Kantian or Hegelian need to yoke opposites in synthesis, Thoreau went so far as to suggest an equation of chaos with beauty, of wildness with aesthetic pleasure.

By the time he had prepared "Walking, or The Wild" as a lecture in 1851, he began to suspect that

in literature it is only the wild that attracts us. Dullness is but another name for tameness. It is the uncivilized free and wild thinking in *Hamlet* and the *Iliad*, in all the scriptures and mythologies, not learned in the schools, that delights us. . . . A truly good book is something as natural, and as unexpectedly and unaccountably fair and perfect, as a wild-flower discovered on the prairies of the West or in the jungles of the East. Genius is a light which makes the darkness visible, like the lightning's flash, which perchance shatters the temple of knowledge itself. (*Writings*, 5:231)

This language theory ranges far beyond Kraitsir's and Bushnell's, with their emphasis on metaphor, paradox, and oxymoron. Rather than seeking a synthesis of multiple dictions, Thoreau's theory involved a true "contra-diction": a use of language to create an impression of meaning that is immediately called into question or rendered into unmeaning—a positing of a temple of knowledge that is promptly rent. Others reasoned that paradoxical language could convey the highest meaning, but Thoreau had developed the idea that the highest rhetoric created a meaning that poked gaps in its own decodability. As he wrote in a letter to Emerson for 12 February 1843, friends communicate most effectively when "we communicate like the burrows of foxes, in silence and darkness, under ground. . . . How much more full is Nature where we think the empty space is than where we place the solids!—full of fluid influences. Should we ever communicate but by these? The spirit abhors a vacuum more than Nature" (*Corr*, 87). By deliberately placing "silence," "darkness," and "empty space" in his text, the literary artist could more forcefully provoke readers to attempt to fill the text's vacuum, to strive to span or stop its gaps. The highest rhetoric offers "solids" of meaning that the reader can study and understand, but it also provides "empty space" that provokes readers to try to plug it with material whose provenance lies outside the text.

Walden is as much a language experiment in a "natural style" as it is a record of "Life in the Woods." A natural style, like nature itself, speaks in many dictions, in a variety of styles. It can sound florid and plain, Egyptian and New English. At another rhetorical level it involves an eloquent silence, "the silence of a dense pine wood," as Thoreau told Daniel Ricketson (*Corr*, 599). On that level, a natural style resembles the most artificial of aesthetic forms; the writer goes to nature for the same reason that "men go to the opera because they hear there a faint expression of this news which is never quite distinctly expressed" (*Corr*, 300). Thoreau admired this natural style even in the speech of children, representing them as those closest to nature's speech, furthest from a learned diction or a public language. He told Emerson in a letter for 10 February 1843 that his young daughter was already proficient in this natural style.

And like the gypsies she talks a language of her own while she understands ours. While she jabbers Sanskrit, Parsee, Pehlvi, say "Edith go bah!" and "bah" it is. No intelligence passes between us. She knows. It is a capital joke,—that is the reason she smiles so. How well the secret is kept! She never descends to explanation. It is not buried like a common secret, bolstered up on two sides, but by an eternal silence on the one side, at least. It has been long kept, and comes in from the unexplored horizon, like a blue mountain range, to end abruptly at our door one day. (Don't stumble at this steep simile.)

Query: what comes of the answers Edith thinks, but cannot express? She really gives you glances which are before this world was. You can't feel any difference of age, except that you have longer legs and arms. (*Corr*, 83–84)

In describing Edith's natural style, Thoreau emphasizes many points. Untutored Edith already intuits the bases of all languages, she utters a private language that antedates all public discourse, and she speaks most provocatively in silent glances, enjoying her unspoken rhetoric in good humor. More properly, Thoreau does all this, for it is, after all, his own translation of Edith's silent meanings and intuitive stylistic gifts that he presents as "hers"—we would say the "author's" or the "translator's." In entertaining Edith as author, Thoreau makes himself his own idealized reader, a reader who is coauthor, filling Edith's silent glances and linguistic silences with meaning, empowering her nonstatements with significance.

One should note how Thoreau intrudes upon his own presentation of Edith's rhetoric through parenthesis, a technique he exploited in his more public works. After describing this young child's silent meanings and natural style in metaphors borrowed from nature, he jokes and puns. After creating a beautiful simile, he calls attention to the fact that it is a simile, he labels it "steep," and he warns Emerson not to stumble over it. After conveying a very difficult, abstract idea in graphic terms, he chooses to give three signals that cast doubt upon how seriously one is to take the idea. That is, after narrating how Edith's inscrutable secret is rhetorically effective because it seems "bolstered up" by "an eternal silence on the one side, at least," Thoreau adds his joking parenthesis, which un-makes the statement by removing the end wall of his paragraph and substituting what he would call a bolstering silence.

In short, after carefully describing the rhetorical power of Edith's indeterminacy, Thoreau renders even that idea of indeterminacy indeterminate. To achieve a similar effect, he often uses varieties of intrusion throughout *Walden*. Perhaps the most apt example occurs in his Artist of Kouroo sketch when he interrupts ideal sketch of his time-transcendent artist to ask, "But why do I stay to mention these things?" Impatience intrudes upon patience, a care for time upon timelessness. The "leading idea" of the perfect artist has been qualified by an interruptive practicing artist. The temple of a thought has been cracked, if not shattered.

The logical question to be posed is, Why should Thoreau be so concerned about unmaking assertions? Why should he strive with such pains to become the "Unsayer of Concord" in an age of Melvillean nay-saying and Emersonian aye-saying? What purpose is served in spending ten years rendering indeterminate texts like *Walden* and *A Week*, which seem superficially so confident and self-assured? Several reasons pertain. The most obvious is the Transcendental commitment to thinking over thought, to process over product, to being over system—the sort of phenomenon that has caused the editor of Thoreau's poetry to remark that he was much more interested in the theory of poetry than he was in the production of poems (*Poems*, vii). That poets should be "liberating gods" became a Transcendental maxim soon after Emerson uttered the aesthetic goal. Proverbs like "every thought is a prison" imply that even that thought is a prison. With the Transcendental stress upon intuitive reason over analytical understanding, Thoreau could proclaim, "Give me a sentence which no intelligence can understand." He would concur with Emerson that Man Thinking is superior to the mere thinker, and he would persist in his belief that, although it is a profound service to proffer noble precepts to live by and to pinpoint the errors of life's normal routine, liberation from any settled thought, even the most noble, is the highest morality.

This explanation is too pat, almost a textbook definition of Transcendental aesthetics for sophomores, but it leads to a more interesting point. When discussing Kraitsir and Bushnell's theory of language, I stated that their emphasis was on biblical exegesis. Thoreau did not share their orientation. While the Bible was their text, his was nature, and he had concluded early in his writing career that nature, inspiring though it may be, was so vast and complex that it stood apart from human systems of meaning, and it eluded attempts to understand it. Trying to console Emerson over the tragedy of his young son's death, Thoreau (who had recently lost his brother) wrote that "the old laws" of nature prevail in spite of pestilence and famine, genius and virtue, or the death of loved ones. "Nature is not ruffled by the rudest blast—the hurricane only snaps a few twigs in some nook of the forest" (*Corr*, 64). To Blake a few months before *Walden*'s publication, he explained that there was neither higher nor lower, "no up nor down in nature," only expansion (*Corr,* 311). In "Walking, or The Wild," he wrote that "Nature is a personality so vast and universal that we have never seen one of her features" (*Writings,* 5:242). In *Walden,* he attempted to present readers with a text that mirrored the nature that Thoreau perceived. A pine tree might inspire, and so might a proverb; a frozen sandbank might melt, and so might a thought; a fog might evaporate into ether, and so might an idea; a bog might mire a traveler, and so might an exhortation the reader. Looking into the text of *Walden* fluidly reflects the vision Thoreau experienced when looking into nature.

As Thoreau delighted in the intense aesthetic pleasure of reading nature's text, so he felt an equally intense need to imagine idealized readers of his own texts. He enjoyed reading a loon, a chipmunk, or a battle between ants, but he could not expect them to read him. As he says in *A Week,* "It takes two to speak the truth,—one to speak, and another to hear. How can one treat with magnanimity mere wood and stone?" (267). His wild rhetoric was his utmost exertion to be magnanimous not merely to wood and stone, but to those others who occupy the same orbs of his existence—not his neighbors, biological or racial kinsmen, nor friends, but those potential communicants in the reading process called "readers," the receptors of his words, and the cocreators of meaning. I do not mean to ascribe psychological motive to Thoreau, being more focused here on his rhetorical ambitions. The need for a reader and the compulsion to work painstakingly on texts for ten years each, even declining *Walden*'s early publication in 1849, in order to present it to the public in what he considered its best rhetorical form were philosophically and aesthetically motivated. As suggested in the quotation from *A Week,* in order to express meaning, reading is as necessary as writing; reader and writer are collaborators in attempting to create a thought through the inadequate vehicle of words, especially when their communication transcends the dictionary definitions or public representations of those shared words.

One of Thoreau's most poignant expressions of literacy as a communal act occurs in his *Journal* for the summer of 1845:

When I play my flute tonight earnest as if to leap the bounds that narrow fold where human life is penned, and range the surrounding plain—I hear echo from a neighboring wood a stolen pleasure occasionally not rightfully heard—much more for other ears than ours for tis the reverse of sound. It is not our own melody that comes back to us—but an amended strain. And I would only hear myself as I would hear my echo—corrected and repronounced for me. It is as when my friend reads my verse. (*PJ2*, 167)

Thoreau's emphasis on "echoes," "other ears," the "reverse of sound," "amended strains," and "repronouncements" attests to the importance he grants the reader/listener. Without another reading, the message does not communicate, meaning does not occur. Without the reader/listener, the writer cannot, as Thoreau seriously puns, "leap the bounds that narrow fold where human life is penned." By freely translating, readers can enable the writer finally to "range the surrounding plain" and liberate meaning from explicit statement. As Thoreau expresses in his earliest *Walden* notebook, the reader can help free the text from literal meaning in order to achieve a universal language, using the ineffability of words to suggest "the inexpressible meaning that is in all things" (*PJ2*, 178). By believing in a loving Echo, Thoreau could rescue the text from Narcissus's fate. Or, to express the idea less pretentiously, entertaining the conception of a reader who reads beyond words enabled Thoreau to feel justified in un-saying his statements in the interest of suggesting a more abstract truth than could be suggested by a didactic message or an image of moral signification.

That "universal language," of course, meant communication as Thoreau intended the term, a constant looking through words (in both meanings of "through") as opposed to the settled perception of an idea, a perpetual process of interpretation and translation of possible meaning. As he wrote in his *Journal* for spring 1846, echoing his request in *Walden*'s second paragraph that readers pardon him when he undertakes to respond to autobiographical questions, "If you would not stop to look at me,—but look whither I am looking and further—then my education could not dispense with thy company" (*PJ2*, 239).

It is therefore no surprise that much of *Walden* is preoccupied with descriptions of Thoreau's conceptions of a variety of imagined readers: its first two dozen pages, many intermittent references, an entire chapter titled "Reading." Just as *Moby-Dick* may be approached as an intermixture of various writing styles from different genres and phases of literary history, *Walden* may be studied as an interweaving of different reading experiences. When most concentrated, the reader's relationship with the writer can be described as warfare or as communion—in "Visitors" as a hostile activity where the author threatens to put a "bullet" of thought into the listener's ear, in "Winter Visitors" as a friendly relationship wherein reader and writer peacefully wade "so gently and reverently" that "the fishes of thought were not scared from the stream" but "came and went grandly, like the clouds which sometimes form and dissolve there."

Perhaps the most profound of these reading experiences is presented in *Walden*'s famous passage:

> I long ago lost a hound, a bay horse, and a turtle dove, and am still on their trail. Many are the travellers I have spoken concerning them, describing their tracks and what calls they answered to. I have met one or two who had heard the hound, and the tramp of the horse, and even seen the dove disappear behind a cloud, *and they seemed as anxious to recover them as if they had lost them themselves.* (W, 17; italics mine)

As the most glossed passage in all of Thoreau's works, it testifies to the power of Thoreau's "leading idea." Scholars have searched diligently to discover what these three animals represent. Treating them as emblems in a personal equation, many have tried to make them stand for explicit losses, approaching them as allegories like those in which Thoreau's coat represents fashion and Walden Pond "earth's eye." But when one of Thoreau's readers asked the "meaning" of this parable, he responded, "I suppose we all have our losses."[5]

He supposed much more than that. The text invites readers to read this parable as an allegory, but it also presents a metaphor of desire. The passage seems specifically autobiographical, yet it is simultaneously a universal and abstracted intimation of that generalized sense of a revelation always imminent but never quite realized, a discovery always promised but never quite grasped by the words that have pointed toward it. It is, as Harrison Blake remarked, a letter posted but never quite delivered. Yet one crucial signification is rarely glossed: the miracle of attempted communication, the fact that anonymous others, readers who are strangers, should feel anxiety as intensely as the author to recover losses, to reach toward an understanding, to aspire toward communion and communication. Others whom the author has never met, more powerfully than those he has met, are as desperate to capture meaning as he is to convey it. The desire for communication is a marvel whose awesome power is as "telling" as one of Edith's silent glances, as eloquent as the hush of a pine woods.

Lest this conclusion seem too conclusive, Thoreau's miraculous communication should be balanced by its darker side in order to preserve its dynamic tension. If communication as he defines it is a miracle, then it is an agonized miracle. Discovering that others share one's losses may create a sense of communion, but it is an aching community of unsatisfied and unsatisfiable desire. Asking readers to "look whither I am looking and further" may articulate a rhetorical ideal, but it clearly involves anxiety over the loss of an author's control and authority. Silence may be offered as a supreme discourse, but it would take a determined reader not to associate silent communication with an ultimate and total silence, a transcendent meaning with meaninglessness. And Thoreau was as intelligent a reader as any. His *Journal* entry for 21 January 1853, an entry recorded when he was putting his final touches to *Walden,* illustrates this closing point. In *Walden,* where he has put "the best face on the matter," reasonably straightforward statements tend to lead to bright and pleasant imagery. Simple criticisms move toward positive depictions, such as when he takes the dank and warped boards and lays them in the sun to be purified before building his cabin. In those simpler rhetorical modes, where an explicit message need only be articulated clearly, even potentially sinister events can be treated amusingly and delightfully, whether these events have Thoreau wanting to devour chipmunks raw or to spit Mexicans with relish or describing how a soldier blasted by a cannonball might not care much about fashion.

In contrast, Thoreau's deliberations upon silence often lead to more anxiety-ridden delineations. His "natural style" can bring him to a state of mind like that evoked by the silent nature he discovers atop Ktaadn in *Maine Woods,* an ultimate blankness that he regards not in terror nor despair but in puzzlement, a final wall of nature and language with which he knows not what more to do except to turn his back and begin his descent. "Man was not to be associated with it. It was Matter, vast, terrific,—not his Mother Earth that we have heard of, not for him to tread on, or be buried in,—no, it were being too familiar even to let his bones lie there—the home this of Necessity and Fate" (70). As with nature, so with Thoreau's natural style when it confronts linguistic silence in his *Journal.* Beginning positively enough by referring to "a fertile and eloquent silence," he continues to praise silence as a supreme rhetoric. "I wish to hear the silence of the night, for the silence is something positive and to be heard," he says, insisting even more emphatically that "silence alone is worthy to be heard. Silence is of various depth and fertility, like soil." And he concludes this paragraph with joyful sentiments: "The silence rings; it is musical and thrills me. A night in which the silence is audible. I hear the unspeakable" (*J,* 4:471–72).

But these thoughts, uplifting though they seem, are followed in the next paragraph by darker intimations. The silence that is deep and fertile "like soil" leads him to contemplate the grave. Night's beauty prods thoughts of ultimate night. Silence's purity reminds him of "the rotten-ness of human relations." Boasting that he "can easily read the moral of my dreams," he transforms his praise for eloquent silence into visions "full of death and decay," and he narrates how, "In the night I dreamed of delving amid the graves of the dead, and soiled my fingers with their rank mould. It was *sanitarilly, morally,* and *physically* true" (472). It was also the ultimate wall of language.

Thoreau's "Perfect Play"

This book has traced the main contours of Thoreau's venture into rhetoric. Early in his career he became dissatisfied with the limits of explicit language. Although adequate for quotidian messages, it could not express what he felt were higher meanings. It could convey his decision not to pay his tax, but it failed to do justice to the ideals of truth, goodness, love, and beauty that lay behind his decisions. He hoped that a wild rhetoric had more linguistic power, that a language of gaps and indeterminacies, filled with smoky words, could more adequately suggest those higher truths.

While his wilder rhetoric evaded the limitations of explicit language, it also raised complex communicative problems, not the least of which was the paradox that if a problem were solved, then its solution would demean the integrity and power of the issue. His language of desire, which constantly affirmed the remoteness of meaning, could be as frustrating as explicit prose. The vacuums he valued in his texts could be taken for vacuousness. His linguistic triumph could be construed as an admission of defeat. Often he was content to pleasure in the puzzling game of language, but just as often he felt that he should be doing more, that he should be guiding readers to a more certain truth. When particularly frustrated by one of language's problems, he resorted to the vast, never-ending process of literacy, not as a solution but as a way to better frame the problem. Echo alone could save the writer from a narcissistic doom.

The act of perpetual reading remained his ultimate response to the linguistic walls he confronted. And so, his texts are salted with a galaxy of rhetorical situations, involving robber-readers, banker-readers, tailoress-readers, adversarial readers, companionable readers, misreaders, poor-student readers, easy-readers, transcendental readers, conservative readers, idealized readers, on and on. These readers were not imagined to be different people, for each person performs many reading roles when scanning a text. Rather, they were linguistic functions conceived in order to triangulate communicative problems. Like a language of calculus, they bracketed the possibilities of meaning within a given situation.

This book has concentrated on Thoreau's language as he presents himself as a creative writer. Fittingly, the book concludes with an example of how he performed when he assumed the critic's role. Usually his critical essays focus on literary style and the creation of persona (as in his reviews of Carlyle and Raleigh) or on a mystical philosophy (as with his pieces on Orientalism). But his essay "The Sphinx" approaches the question of textual meaning and linguistic power through a variety of critical methodologies.

Thoreau devoted many days to a line-by-line close reading of Emerson's "The Sphinx" and wrote the fruits of his speculation in an entry of around twenty-three hundred words recorded in his *Journal* for March 7-10 1841 (*PJ1,* 279–86). While the stated aim of the entry is to explicate a poem, his criticism truly centers on the sphinxlike quality of language. Its main problem is a language that speaks in riddles, a tormenting language that threatens to devour those who fail to decode its mysteries but laughs at those who believe they have solved its enigmas, a teasing language that baffles its readers but will not let them go. This sphinxlike language arises from the ashes of linguistic failure. Perhaps one can intuitively resolve the mysteries of life within his or her own soul, but one cannot properly express the truth of these soul-felt mysteries. One can only stutteringly articulate one's own inadequate attempts to express truth beautifully by deploying what Thoreau calls a style of "skill and inscrutable design," of "Daedalian intricacy." He confesses, "Man can only tell his relation to truth, but render no account of truth." Often using "sincerity" to stand for his desire to communicate a significant thought powerfully, he is constantly aware that he cannot effect that communication through the public language of words.

Writers are forced to a language that glorifies the riddle as the only way of suggesting the power and authenticity of its mysteries. A sphinx-like language stresses the mystery of mankind—the knowledge "only that he is, not what—nor whence." Once they pierce the necessary mask of persona, readers will perceive that authors are like the sphinx in that they have no individual existence but are "allied to and brood over all." Once they penetrate the guise of an author's wisdom—the necessary artifice of valuing authors, of authorizing authors, because they must seem to have something urgent to say—readers arrive at the writer's supreme confession that he ultimately resides at a zenlike plane of what Thoreau calls "complete uncertainty—and a renunciation of knowledge." Thus, Thoreau reiterates his writerly agon over language's inability to communicate profound truths. "It is a great presumption," he warns, "to answer conclusively a question which any sincerity has put. The wise answer no questions." Indeed, it is more than presumptuous; it is wrong. "To rest in a reply—as a response of the oracle—that is error." It is not only wrong; it is vicious: "A truth rested in stands for all the vice of an age." Finally, more objectively, "Each understands all—for to see that we understand—is to know that we misunderstand." Still, from philosophical failure comes linguistic power. A sphinxlike language depends upon smoky words, dissolving statements, and spontaneously melting thoughts. It is replete with gaps, contradictions, oxymorons, self-erasures, and indeterminacies. Unable to communicate except through tongue-tied, dictionary-bound, stumbling and faltering words, it makes its failure all the more obvious and poignant. Failing in its attempt to communicate—and by fixing our attention on that failure—a sphinxlike language intensifies the desire for communication.

Thoreau describes his language of desire in terms that Harrison Blake echoed when commenting upon Thoreau's correspondence. Blake had remarked that no matter how often he read and reread Thoreau's letters, they continued to give the impression that their meaning had not yet arrived, that his meaning was "still in the mail," still on the way, still in the process of being sent. Fifty years before Blake's comment, Thoreau expressed his admiration in "The Sphinx" for a language that makes us "career toward [truth] eternally" and does not "degrade" transcendent "meanings to be intelligible to us." "We shall never arrive at . . . meaning, but it will ceaselessly arrive to us." Indeed, he hoped that a language of desire is "kindly" and restores "health" because it demands that each rereading be a "revolution" that topples any settled "truth" gleaned from previous readings.

Blake had learned one of his friend's lessons about rhetoric, but it is not clear whether he had mastered a more complex issue. The linguistic paradigm of Thoreau's youth posited the idea that a "profound," "eternal," or "transcendent" truth existed in the universe, a communication model that Thoreau frequently worked from in order to develop his wilder rhetoric. In the quarrels about language among his contemporaries, this model was not questioned, although they argued whether truth resided in the soul or in the heavens. Emerson, for one, extended this model when he suggested that the power that excites truth, goodness, and beauty existed not in nature (nor in the heavens) but in man or in a harmony of both. Thoreau would extend this suggestion to insinuate that, while an eternal truth may be enjoyed as a private experience, the only shared sense of a transcendent truth was *in* language. The impression of a profound truth existed only in the smoky words, the thawing sentences, the self-dissolving statements of a transient, fluctuating language of desire. The only communication of truth through language was in the creation, recreation, and uncreation of meaning in the unending process of reading. In "The Sphinx," Thoreau reasons, "The truth we seek with ardor and devotion will not reward us with a cheap acquisition." Any acquisition or settled interpretation is "cheap," and "truth" exists only in the process of perpetually seeking it. Truth occurs only in the protean activity of reading, in the visions and instant revisions of literacy.

When most optimistic, Thoreau calls this process of reading and unreading a "perfect play." A sphinxlike language of desire can produce "pleasant songs" that not only compensate for but are more beautiful than wisdom or knowledge. "Poetry is the only solution time can offer," and Thoreau's sense of "poetry" is like Henry James's definition of the Romantic as the articulation of the unknowable. This "perfect play" must be imperfect to be perfect. Even his joy at poetry's solution must be unresolved. The riddle of language must be respected and embodied in all its mysterious mists in order to retain power. And so, Thoreau concludes his four-day *Journal* criticism by drawing a line and adding a coda that directly addresses his readers: "You may find this [critical essay] as enigmatical as the Sphinx's riddle—Indeed I doubt if she could solve it herself." Of course, the author's admission that he cannot resolve language's mysteries has the rhetorical effect of enticing readers to hope that perhaps *they* could find the clue to the labyrinth.

The coda "concludes" his criticism only in a technical sense. Actually, it unravels his argument, making it less conclusive. Readers who read "with ardor and devotion" must read further in their quest for meaning. They might want to read at least the single-sentence entries for the day before and the day after "The Sphinx." For 6 March 1841, they would read, "An honest misunderstanding is often the ground of future intercourse." For 11 March 1841, the day after Thoreau has praised the "pleasant songs" of a sphinxlike language, they would be told, "Every man understands why a fool sings." Do you understand what Thoreau means? Does that make him a fool? Or you? Can we sing songs only through a foolish understanding? An Emily Dickinson poem begins, "Finding is the first Act, / The second, loss, / Third, Expedition for / the 'Golden Fleece.' " Thoreau's wild rhetoric is a cunningly wrought prose of "Daedalian intricacy" that offers "delicate textures" to attract readers. Some value certain elements of his texts, others prize different features. Regardless whatever value has been found, his language involves loss. His wild rhetoric finds power in that loss as a way to intensify desire, to enkindle the hope that writer and reader could correspond if only they practiced more "ardor and devotion." If only we read his letters more closely, or more often, or read more of his writings, or more interpretations of other readers, or more writings by authors he has read, somehow we could arrive at a settled understanding of what he means. Some of us will pretend that we have in fact achieved such an understanding. Then the "Expedition" can end, the searching cease, the frustration rest. In that hubristic moment when readers pose as "some Oedipus," proud about having "solved" one of language's enigmas, the Sphinx of language "will go dash her head against a rock."

Like Walt Whitman a year after *Walden,* Thoreau offered a bible to the world, but it was a bible written in the language of "liquidation" that Kraitsir, Bushnell, and other linguists were defining in Thoreau's day. His was a bible whose maxims led to myth, whose certainties raveled into indeterminacies. His messages, enjoyments, beautifully articulated sentiments, humorous quips, and precisely registered rages entice readers to a "First Finding" only to instruct us that this finding is far more complex and mysterious than supposed—that ultimate meaning lies beyond the communication of language or exists only in the gap-filled weave of words. In Dickinson's poem, she fears that readers will soon weary of language's inadequacy. Eventually, they may wonder what is the point to this eternal game. Frustrated, they may decide that if a poetic wild rhetoric is the only solution, then it is also idle, if not a fraud. They may come to feel that "finally, no Golden Fleece—/ Jason—sham—too."

As a rhetorician who valued myth and the intangible music of language, Thoreau would note that Jason is certainly a fiction. He exists nowhere save in words. And yet, none can deny the power of his myth. Perhaps Jason's power would even diminish had he a reality outside words, much the way some readers have proclaimed *Walden* a sham simply because its mythic and "real-life" dimensions do not always agree. He would also witness readers who would turn away from his first book, dismissing *A Week on the Rivers* because it did not offer a sufficiently coherent structure, did not provide a clear enough grounds for a "first finding." But an equal danger lurked with readers who mistook first findings for ultimate ones and denied the "hypaethral" quality of his texts, a language that left his textual constructions open to the skies. Such readers would be denied the experience of rereading and unreading, not to mention a second, third, or fourth reading. He hoped his wild rhetoric could provide the material for a pleasurable and perhaps truthful weaving and reweaving of perpetual interpretation, of endless translation, of eternal reading.

In his 1980 novel *Disappearances,* William Wiser's protagonist, called "Critic," confronts a character called "the Poet" who offers him many oracular and wise sayings. The Poet's final note commands, "Finish my poem for me, Critic." Thoreau's poem is still being finished, will never be completed as long as people read his works. The closer we come to the "heart" of his writing, the more obvious looms the mysterious aura that hovers about the body of his texts. In his *Journal* for 9 February 1852, Thoreau insists that the only permanent vision is "a constantly varying mirage" (*J,* 3:291). As Richard J. Schneider has elucidated, *Cape Cod*'s principal theme is illusion, misperception, and how "mystery, power, and silence" are "at the heart of things."[1] Thoreau also characterizes some of Cape Cod's residents as first-finding readers who shout "*Ne plus ultra,* (no more beyond), but the wind bore to us the truth only, *plus ultra* (more beyond), and over the Bay westward was echoed *ultra* (beyond)."

As it comes time to stop shouting *plus ultra* and to say *vale* ("enough" and, one hopes, "sufficient"), I close with one last parable. In 1842, Thoreau transcribed the following passage into his *Journal:*

The researcher is more memorable than the researched. The crowd stood admiring the mist and the dim outline of the trees seen through it—when one of their number advanced to explore the phenomenon, and with fresh admiration all eyes were turned on his dimly retreating figure. (*PJ1,* 414)

I now cease to be the researcher of *Thoreau's Wild Rhetoric* and become merely its author. The book's new researchers are those chance readers who search its mists for further meaning about this poem being written called "Thoreau."

Be assured that Thoreau's admiring eyes are upon you. After all, has he not said so?

Notes

Introduction: Problems

1. Taylor Stoehr, *Nay-Saying in Concord: Emerson, Alcott, and Thoreau* (Hamden, Conn.: Archon Books, 1979), 156. Joseph Wood Krutch, Introduction to *Thoreau: Walden and Other Writings* (New York: Bantam, 1962), 2. *Some Unpublished Letters of Henry D. and Sophia E. Thoreau: A Chapter in the History of a Still-Born Book,* ed. Samuel Arthur Jones (New York: Marion Press, 1899), xxiv.

2. For a discussion of Thoreau's parody of guidebooks for young men and self-help manuals, see Leonard Neufeldt, "Thoreau's Enterprise of Self-Culture in a Culture of Enterprise," *AQ* 39 (Summer 1987): 246. In *Critical Essays on Henry David Thoreau's "Walden",* ed. Joel Myerson (Boston: G. K. Hall, 1988), Robert A. Gross discusses Thoreau's parody of agricultural reform in "The Great Bean Field Hoax: Thoreau and the Agricultural Reformers," 193–201; Linck C. Johnson studies self-improvement and house pattern books in "Revolution and Renewal: The Genres of *Walden,*" 215–27; and Joel Meyerson points out other fine works on pattern book parody, 9.

3. Walter Harding, *The Variorum Walden and the Variorum Civil Disobedience* (New York: Washington Square Press, 1968), xix. See also Harding's "Five Ways of Looking at Walden," in *Critical Essays on "Walden",* 93–94.

4. The passage is reproduced as it will appear in a forthcoming volume of the Princeton *Journal;* for a more "standardized" version, see *Journal* 3:340–41.

5. Harold Bloom, *Agon: Towards a Theory of Revisionism* (New York: Oxford University Press, 1982), 166–76.

6. Emerson, "Thoreau," in *The Complete Works of Ralph Waldo Emerson,* ed. Edward Waldo Emerson, Centenary Edition (Boston: Houghton Mifflin,

1903–1904), 10:449–85. For a discussion of Emerson's view of Thoreau as absolutist, see Leonard Neufeldt, *The House of Emerson* (Lincoln: University of Nebraska Press, 1982), 124–31.

7. Contradictory epigraphs in Lawrence Buell, *New England Literary Culture: From Revolution through Renaissance* (New York: Cambridge University Press, 1986), 319. Different views of the social Thoreau: Walter Harding, *The Days of Henry Thoreau* (New York: Knopf, 1965) and Leo Stoller, *After Walden* (Stanford: Stanford University Press, 1957); Richard Bridgman, *Dark Thoreau* (Lincoln: University of Nebraska Press, 1982) and Mary Elkins Moller, *Thoreau in the Human Community* (Amherst: University of Massachusetts Press, 1980), For reasons they explain, editors have chosen to publish Thoreau's essay as "Walking" and "The Wild," a decision Thoreau approves in a letter to his publisher; see Charles R. Anderson, *Thoreau's Vision: The Major Essays* (Englewood Cliffs, N.J.: Prentice-Hall, 1973), 23, and Leo Marx, *Excursions* (New York: Corinth Books, 1962), xiii.

8. See Richardson's intelligent effort to make this choice about Thoreau's militaristic language; *Life,* 72.

9. See MMPI Survey of Everett and Laraine Fergenson in *Thoreau's Psychology: Eight Essays,* ed. Raymond D. Gozzi (New York: University Press of America, 1983), 79–94.

10. I am aware that traditionalists will label this methodology "revisionist," "New Americanist," or, more safely, "post-structuralist," while post-structuralists will wonder why so much time is spent on traditional interpretations of Thoreau, and both camps will puzzle at my taking all reading experiences as seriously as theirs, including those of gift-book publishers, popular magazines, and even commercial advertisements. Yet I believe that this approach strikes more directly at the kind of rhetorical problems that confronted Thoreau and writers like him. Some may wish to call it "auto-deconstructionist," since it exposes its own assumptions along with the ideologies of others, or even "self-deconstructionist," but I prefer the simpler and, in a time already fraught with ample terminology, more accessible characterization: Problem Criticism. Readers trained to the perspectives provided by Roland Barthes, Michel Foucault, Gilles Deleuze, Jacques Derrida, and other theorists that reached America in the 1970s and 1980s will quickly recognize their influence in this study, but the single scholar I would submit as this book's methodological exemplar is Jean Starobinski, who employs a problem-oriented criticism in order to capture and to convey a sense of writers in flux. See his *Montaigne in Motion* and *Jean Jacques Rousseau: Transparency and Obstruction,* both translated by Arthur Goldhammer and published by the University of Chicago Press, 1985 and 1988 respectively.

11. *Life,* 348. See also Thomas Woodson's provocative essay "The Two Beginnings of *Walden:* A Distinction of Styles," *ELH* 35 (1968): 440–73. Woodson argues that, like Whitman's poetry, "*Walden* stands as an archetypal American book."

12. I mean "pure" in the sense of genre, referring to Thoreau's refusal to idealize,

digress, editorialize, or to include any other mode of writing than travel narrative; *A Yankee in Canada* was published the year before *Walden; Writings,* 5:20.

13. John Carlos Rowe, *Through the Custom-House: Nineteenth-Century American Fiction and Modern Theory* (Baltimore: Johns Hopkins University Press, 1982), 24.

14. In *Agon,* Harold Bloom discusses Valentius and the Gnostic idea of Kenoma, which, in contrast to Hegelian synthesis, articulated "a cosmos of mirrors that mirror only nothing or the void" (61); Julie Ellison, in *Emerson's Romantic Style* (Princeton: Princeton University Press, 1984), argues that dialectical language can more profitably be traced to Friedrich Schlegel than to Hegel because of Schlegel's emphasis on the *"indissoluble* antagonism between the absolute and the relative" (6–10).

1. Thoreau in Time

1. TRANSCENDENT TRANSLATION

1. Thoreau, *Huckleberries,* ed. Leo Stoller (The Windover Press of the University of Iowa/ The New York Public Library: 1970), 30.

2. To Thoreau, the icon "Socrates" would be the idealistic truth-seeker, not the neofascist as characterized by I. F. Stone, *The Trial of Socrates* (Boston: Little, Brown, 1988).

3. Thoreau, "A Plea for Captain John Brown," *RP,* 131; "Slavery in Massachusetts," *RP,* 91–109.

4. That is, a scholarly edition true to Dickinson's "packets" presentation and a readerly edition that conforms to publication conventions seem irreconcilable, as R. W. Franklin demonstrates in *The Editing of Emily Dickinson: A Reconsideration* (Madison: University of Wisconsin Press, 1967).

5. *Some Unpublished Letters of Thoreau,* ed. Jones, 49–50. See history as a form of translation in Thoreau's "Dark Ages," *EE,* 143, and *PJ1,* 414. In his "Martyrdom of John Brown," Thoreau chose to include a long poem called "The Soul's Errand," perhaps because its authorship (Raleigh?) was debatable (*RP,* 140–41). For *Prometheus Bound,* see K. P. Van Anglen, *Translations* (Princeton: Princeton University Press, 1986), 3–53.

6. Jefferson Humphries, *Losing the Text: Readings in Literary Desire* (Athens: University of Georgia Press, 1986), xvi.

7. Recent studies include Richardson, Buell, and Edward Wagenknecht, *Henry David Thoreau: What Manner of Man?* (Amherst: University of Massachusetts Press, 1981). Of continuing value are Harding's *Days,* Leo Marx's *The Machine in the Garden* (New York: Oxford University Press, 1964), and Richard Lebeaux's *Young Man Thoreau* (Amherst: University of Massachusetts Press, 1977). As more specialized studies, Taylor Stoehr's *Nay-Saying in Concord* and James Armstrong's "Thoreau, Chastity, and the Reformers," in *Thoreau's Psychology,* demonstrate that Thoreau's reform ideas regarding

sex, diet, temperance, and so forth would appear rather moderate when contextualized with his era, even though they seem extreme to modern readers.

8. As much as I admire Richard Poirier's *The Renewal of Literature: Emersonian Reflections* (New York: Random House, 1987), I can understand reviewers' complaints that his treatment of Emerson is not sufficiently contextualized by the discourse of Emerson's times; see, for example, Denis Donoghue, "Whose Trope Is It Anyway?" *The New York Review of Books,* 25 June 1987, 50–52.

2. LIKENESS TO GOD

1. For "clerisy," see Lewis P. Simpson, *The Man of Letters in New England and the South: Essays on the History of the Literary Vocation in America* (Baton Rouge: Louisiana State University Press, 1973), 3–31; and Michael T. Gilmore, *American Romanticism and the Marketplace* (Chicago: University of Chicago Press, 1985), 43–48.

2. C. H. Faust, "The Background of the Unitarian Opposition to Transcendentalism," *Mcdern Philology* 35 (February 1938): 300–1, 322–24.

3. René Wellek, "The Minor Transcendentalists and German Philosophy," *New England Quarterly* 15 (1942): 652–80. Although its metaphorical style may make it difficult to follow, a remarkable study of philosophers who greatly influenced the Transcendentalists and whose language depended on "occlusion, tremorings, hoverings, and tunnelings" in creating their texts is by John Sallis, *Spacing: Of Reason and Imagination in Texts of Kant, Fichte, Hegel* (Chicago: University of Chicago Press, 1987), xiv–xvi, 24–25, 64–66, 106–15.

4. It could be argued that, as in the modern era and in antebellum America, language was equally in crisis after World War I. Called "Crisis Theology" and "Dialectical Theology" in Europe and "Neo-Orthodoxy" in America, this movement also repudiated literalism and emphasized paradox and contradiction. Tracing its roots back to Kierkegaard, who flourished in Thoreau's times, its adherents included Karl Barth, Martin Heidegger, Karl Jaspers, Reinhold Niebuhr, and other illustrious minds.

5. William Ellery Channing, "Unitarian Christianity" and "Likeness to God," in *Selected Writings of the American Transcendentalists,* ed. George Hochfield (New York: Signet, 1966), 33–44, 54–66.

6. *Selected Writings of the American Transcendentalists,* 408–9.

7. George Ripley, *Discourses on the Philosophy of Religion Addressed to Doubters Who Wish to Believe* (Boston: James Munroe, 1836), discourse 6; for a fuller discussion of Ripley's part in this debate, see Henry Golemba, *George Ripley* (Boston: Twayne, 1977), 29–48.

8. Richard Whately, *Elements of Rhetoric, Comprising an Analysis of the Laws of Moral Evidence and of Persuasion, with Rules for Argumentative Composition and Elocution,* ed. Douglas Ehninger and David Potter (Carbondale:

Southern Illinois University Press, 1963), 207, 211–12, 365. See also James L. Golden and Edward P. J. Corbett, Introduction to *The Rhetoric of Blair, Campbell, and Whately* (New York: Holt, Rinehart and Winston, 1968). For Thoreau's Harvard education, see Richard H. Dillman, "Thoreau's Education in Rhetoric and Composition," *TJQ* 13 (July and October 1981): 49–62. Thoreau's examination on Whately: *Life*, 13.

9. Philip F. Gura, *The Wisdom of Words: Language, Theology, and Literature in the New England Renaissance* (Middletown, Conn.: Wesleyan University Press, 1981); an essay from this book appears in *Critical Essays on Thoreau's Walden*, ed. Joel Myerson (Boston: G. K. Hall, 1988). Peter Carafiol, in *Transcendent Reason: James Marsh and the Forms of Romantic Thought* (Tallahasee: University Presses of Florida, 1982), says Coleridge required "a new sort of reading" (87) and that Marsh and others assumed scriptural interpretation was "necessarily imperfect" (177). For a discussion of ritualistic discourse, see Sacvan Bercovitch, *The American Jeremiad* (Madison: University of Wisconsin Press, 1978). Catherine Albanese stresses the Transcendentalist emphasis on a religious language of motion: *Corresponding Motion: Transcendental Religion and The New America* (Philadelphia: Temple University Press, 1977). Larry R. Long has described how freely Thoreau paraphrased quotations, sometimes to the extent that the original is barely recognizable: "Thoreau's Portmanteau Biblical Allusions," *TJQ* 9 (July and October 1979): 49–54.

10. Gura, 53; quotation below, 63; on p. 184, Gura cites other critics (Michael West, David Skwire, Richard Poirier, Stanley Cavell) who have studied Thoreau's language; see also Robert D. Richardson, Jr., *Henry Thoreau: A Life of the Mind* (Berkeley: University of California Press, 1986), 292–95. Thoreau also ridiculed writing that was too organized, using the same terms as Bushnell of "firstly," "thirdly," and so forth.

11. Barbara Packer's "Origin and Authority: Emerson and the Higher Criticism" is a cogent discussion of this dilemma; see *Reconstructing American Literary History*, ed. Sacvan Bercovitch (Cambridge: Harvard University Press, 1986), 67–72.

12. Provocative discussions of these issues can be found in John Hollander, *The Figure of Echo* (Berkeley: University of California Press, 1981) and Richard Poirier, "Originality," *Raritan: A Quarterly Review* 2 (Spring 1983): 24–44, and *The Renewal of Literature: Emersonian Reflections* (New York: Random House, 1987), 20–36, 185.

13. William Batchelder Greene, *Transcendentalism (1849) and Equality (1849)* (Delmar, N.Y.: Scholars' Facsimiles and Reprints, 1981), 10–15. Greene makes an interesting observation: "So the word Transcendentalism relates not to a system of doctrines but to a *point of view;* from which, nevertheless, a system of doctrines may be visible" (14).

14. Poirier, *Renewal*, 68–75.

15. Charles Ives, "Thoreau: Nature's Musician" (1920), in *Henry David Thoreau:*

A Profile, ed. Walter Harding (New York: Hill and Wang, 1971), 120. Ives was responding to attacks on Thoreau by Robert Louis Stevenson, Mark Van Doren, and others, as well as by Lowell.

3. A CONSTITUTIONAL LANGUAGE

1. The Duke of Wellington's comment in 1831 that "the only thing I am afraid of is fear" seems a more literal antecedent for Roosevelt's quotation, whereas Thoreau's proverb seems to echo Montaigne: "The thing of which I have most fear is fear." See Montaigne, *Essays,* book 1, chapter 17.
2. *Huckleberries* (see chap. 1.1, n. 1), 28.
3. Anne C. Rose, *Transcendentalism as a Social Movement, 1830–50* (New Haven: Yale University Press, 1981); Edward H. Madden, *Civil Disobedience and Moral Law in Nineteenth-Century American Philosophy* (Seattle: University of Washington Press, 1968), 96–98; Michael Meyer, *Several More Lives to Live: Thoreau's Political Reputation in America* (Westport, Conn.: Greenwood Press, 1977).
4. Walter Harding, *A Thoreau Handbook* (New York: New York University Press, 1959), 132.
5. Leonard Neufeldt has a fascinating discussion of Thoreau's attempt to purify the terms of the Republic's legacy so that government could function as the Founding Fathers intended; "Henry Thoreau's Political Economy," *NEQ* 57 (1984): 359–83. In his two forthcoming books, Neufeldt will analyze how Thoreau's language is contained by his culture, particularly with respect to three forms of discourse in his culture—republican, moral-aesthetic, and economic. Oxford University Press published the first of these books as *The Economist: Henry Thoreau and Enterprise* (1989).
6. B. L. Packer, *Emerson's Fall: A New Interpretation of the Major Essays* (New York: Continuum Press, 1982), 1–7.
7. An exhibit celebrating Davy Crockett's two-hundredth birthday was held 17 August 1986 at the National Portrait Gallery in Washington, D.C. In 1955, when the Crockett craze was in full swing, Murray Kempton punctured many of the myths in his four-part *New York Post* series called "The Real Davy."
8. *Huckleberries,* 3. Leo Stoller claims Thoreau was working hard toward completion of this manuscript from January to March 1861, on the eve of the Civil War.
9. Douglass, "Slavery in Massachusetts," *RP,* 144; Webster, 97. "Resistance" was first printed in Elizabeth Peabody's *Aesthetic Papers* in 1849 and was given as a lecture before the Concord Lyceum on 26 January 1848. Curiously, at the same time that Thoreau was becoming an icon sufficient to be credited as the source for Roosevelt's proverb about fear, in *The Devil and Daniel Webster* (1937), Stephen Vincent Benet was apotheosizing Webster

as an archetypal orator who could out-orate Satan and persuade even America's villains to dream of freedom.

10. See chapter 5 of John Locke's *Second Treatise of Government* (1690), titled "Property."

11. Lincoln Caplan, extract from his forthcoming book, which appeared as "Annals of the Law: The Tenth Justice," *New Yorker,* 10 August 1987, 30. Some fascinating studies of the Constitution as language and icon appear in *Laws of Our Fathers: Popular Culture and the U.S. Constitution,* ed. Ray B. Browne and Glenn J. Browne (Bowling Green, Ohio: Bowling Green State University Press, 1987), particularly Ross J. Pudaloff's "Education and the Constitution: Instituting American Culture," 23–41; Ailene S. Goodman's "Mythical Animals and the Living Constitution: Interpreting Tradition," 66–87; and Alan Ira Gordon's "The Myth of the Constitution: Nineteenth-Century Constitutional Iconography," 88–109.

12. Michael Kammen, *Spheres of Liberty: Changing Perceptions of Liberty in American Culture* (Madison: University of Wisconsin Press, 1986), 5, 74, 172.

13. Kammen, *Spheres,* 169, 10, 3. Of course, a number of author-centered "strict constructionists" disagree with this argument, particularly those followers of Leo Strauss (d. 1973): Walter Berns, Martin Diamond, Thomas Pangle, Morton Frisch, Charles Kesler, Edward Erler. In *Taking the Constitution Seriously* (New York: Simon and Schuster, 1987), Walter Berns says, "There is nothing obscure about the text [of the Constitution and its elaboration in the *Federalist Papers*] or nothing so obscure as to defy a search." Of course, the Straussians also disagree with each other about authorial intentions.

14. George B. Hutchinson has taken an interesting approach in trying to link Transcendental style with national crisis in *The Ecstatic Whitman: Literary Shamanism and the Crisis of the Union* (Columbus: Ohio State University Press, 1986).

15. Seward cited in Alfred H. Kelly and Winfred A. Harbison, *The American Constitution: Its Origins and Developments* (New York: Norton, 1963), 368; Perry Miller, *The Life of the Mind in America: From the Revolution to the Civil War* (New York: Harcourt, Brace and World, 1965), 224–25.

16. Brook Thomas, "*The House of the Seven Gables:* Reading the Romance of America," *PMLA* 97 (1982): 200.

17. Kammen, *Spheres,* 78.

18. James Russell Lowell, "The Progress of the World" (1886), in *Latest Literary Essays and Addresses* (Cambridge: Riverside Press, 1893), 179.

19. Descriptions of many hermits are included in Carl Sifakis, *American Eccentrics* (New York: Facts on File Publications, 1984).

20. William H. Goetzmann, *The American Hegelians: An Intellectual Episode in the History of Western America* (New York: Knopf, 1973), 7–14. Concord School of Philosophy's 1883 edition of "The Service" is housed in the Pierpont Morgan Library, New York.

21. Georg Lukacs, "On the Romantic Philosophy of Life: Novalis," in *Soul and Form,* trans. Anna Bostock (Cambridge: MIT Press, 1978), 58. Joseph J. Ellis, *After the Revolution: Profiles of Early American Culture* (New York: Norton, 1979), 221.

22. Kammen, *Spheres,* 100. George Frederickson, *Inner Civil War: Northern Intellectuals and the Crisis of the Union* (New York: Harper & Row, 1965). John Higham, *From Boundlessness to Consolidation: The Transformation of American Culture, 1848–1860* (Ann Arbor: University of Michigan Press, 1969).

23. In his diary the day after Samuel Adams's death in 1803, Reverend William Bentley referred to the popular idea of Adams as the "Cato of the American Revolution" because he called for a return to the simpler, more honest life. Of course, it is now established that Thoreau and Manlius Stimson Clarke performed "A Greek Dialogue. 'Decius and Cato' " for Harvard classes on 13 July 1835; which part Thoreau took is not certain. Furthermore, "Cato" in Thoreau's times would call "Cato's Letters" to mind, those newspaper essays by John Trenchard and Thomas Gordon in 1720–1721 that provided many political phrases for the writers of the Constitution. Michael Kammen, *A Season of Youth: The American Revolution and the Historical Imagination* (New York: Oxford University Press, 1978), 99–100, 234; *Spheres,* 30.

24. William L. Howarth, "Successor to *Walden?* Thoreau's Moonlight—An Intended Course of Lectures," *Proof 2. The Yearbook of American Bibliographical and Textual Studies.* (Columbia: University of South Carolina Press, 1972), 89–115. Richardson, 324–26, 331, 375. "Dispersion of Seeds" manuscript with John Brown broadsides (dated 2 December 1859, Concord) in the Berg Collection, New York Public Library.

25. I am assuming that the red bird is a political emblem, but its link with "election days" may be as "accidental" as Thoreau's going to Walden on Independence Day. However, redness was connected with radical politics, as when a character is called a "red Republican" in *Uncle Tom's Cabin* for his "levelling ideas" about society.

4. "THE ASTONISHED EYE"

1. Millerites twice predicted the end of the world in the 1840s. Slater Brown, *The Heyday of Spiritualism* (New York: Pocket Book, 1972) offers a fascinating account of the more extreme religious movements. Whitman, *Song of Myself,* canto 51.

2. Frederick Douglass, "Contradictions in American Civilization," *Frederick Douglass: The Narrative and Selected Writings* (New York: Modern Library, 1984), 364.

3. Webster, "An Address at the laying of the Corner-stone of the addition to the Capitol," as quoted in Kammen, *Spheres,* 65. Margaret Fuller expressed the

opposite opinion in *Summer on the Lakes in 1843,* hoping that ethnic plurality would be preserved like a mosaic, not a melting pot.

4. James Russell Lowell, "Progress of the World," 179.

5. Joseph J. Ellis, *After the Revolution,* 213.

6. John Delaware Lewis, *Across the Atlantic* (London, 1851), 24. For many sources regarding Barnum, I am indebted to Neil Harris, *Humbug: The Art of P. T. Barnum* (Chicago: University of Chicago Press, 1973).

7. In late August 1843, Barnum had advertised a free buffalo hunt, but had arranged for a rebate from the ferry operators who transported the crowds, Thoreau among them, from Manhattan to the hunting grounds in New Jersey; his profits derived not from the hunt—which proved to be a fiasco, with bison bogging down in the swamp—but from the transportation fees.

8. Harris, 216; the next two quotations also from Harris, 292, 285.

9. *The Annotated Walden,* ed. Philip Van Doren Stern (New York: Bramhall House, 1970), 172. James Russell Lowell, *My Study Windows* (Boston: James R. Osgood, 1871), 202.

10. Review in *Knickerbocker* 45 (March 1855): 235–41; quoted in *Toward the Making of Thoreau's Modern Reputation,* ed. Fritz Oehlschlaeger and George Hendrick (Chicago: University of Illinois Press, 1979), 13; reprinted in *The Merrill Studies in Walden,* ed. Joseph J. Moldenhauer (Columbus: Charles E. Merrill), 8–14, and in *Critical Essays on Walden,* ed. Meyerson, which reprints all known contemporary reviews; see also *Pertaining to Thoreau,* ed. Samuel A. Jones (Detroit: E. B. Hill, 1901), 75–88. For character types, see Mary Sue Carlock, "I Celebrate Myself and Sing Myself: Character-Types in Early American Autobiographies, 1840–1870" (Ph.D. diss., Columbia University, 1958), 5.

11. Harris, 54, 57, 216.

12. Harris, p 77.

13. Harris, 23.

14. See Michael T. Isenberg, *John Sullivan and His America* (Carbondale: University of Illinois Press, 1987).

15. Orson S. Fowler, *The Octagon House: A Home for All* (1848). Introduction by Madeleine B. Stern (New York: Dover, 1973); Mark Twain wrote *The Adventures of Huckleberry Finn* in an octagonal study apparently based on Fowler's plans (vi). See also Steven Fink, "Building America: Henry Thoreau and the American Home," *Prospects: An Annual of American Culture Studies* 2 (1986): 327–65.

16. The closing words to section 2 of Karl Marx's and Friedrich Engels's *Communist Manifesto* (1848) also seem to posit a liberated, participatory reader: "The free development of each is the condition for the free development of all." A favored motto of Aeschylus, whom Thoreau translated, was "I harbor hatred against all gods." See also Constance Rourke's *Trumpets of Jubilee* (1927) for a fictionalized account of Barnum. In linking Thoreau with agricultural reforms through parody, Robert A. Gross briefly compares Thoreau

with Barnum, in "The Great Bean-Field Hoax: Thoreau and the Agricultural Reformers," *Critical Essays on Walden,* 193.

2. *Thoreau in Form*

I. TROPHIES OF THE SELF

1. Sharon Cameron, *Writing Nature: Henry Thoreau's Journal* (New York: Oxford University Press, 1985), 23; Laurence Stapleton, *Henry David Thoreau: A Writer's Journal* (New York: Dover, 1960), ix.
2. William Bysshe Stein, "Thoreau's *A Week* and OM Cosmography," *ATQ* 11 (Summer 1971): 24.
3. Rowe, *Custom-House* (see intro., n. 13), 39.
4. Thoreau's poetic relation to the haiku is discussed in *The Winged Life: The Poetic Voice of Henry David Thoreau,* ed. Robert Bly (San Francisco: Sierra Club Books, 1986), 78.

2. THE *JOURNAL*

1. The *Journal's* draft status is exemplified by anthologies that offer *Journal* samples, sometimes without even bothering to date the entries; for example, *Thoreau: Walden and Other Writings,* ed. Joseph Wood Krutch (New York: Bantam, 1971). For a discussion of the *Journal* as Thoreau's preeminent genre, see Sharon Cameron, *Writing Nature,* 23.
2. Cameron, 5, 48. Sherman Paul, *The Shores of America: Thoreau's Inward Expansion* (Urbana: University of Illinois Press, 1958), 339.
3. Ambrotype and Daniel Ricketson comment in Milton Meltzer and Walter Harding, *A Thoreau Profile* (Concord; Thoreau Foundation, 1962), 287.
4. Laurence Stapleton, *Henry David Thoreau,* ix.
5. *Walden's* subtitle, "Life in the Woods," had special meaning for contemporary readers familiar with autobiographies of "backwoodsmen" like John Russell, Jim Bridger, and Davy Crockett. "Life in the woods" was a location as distinct from the "backwoods" or "deep woods" as it was from metropolitan centers.
6. The interweaving of the *Journal* with Thoreau's essay "Life without Principle" has been mentioned by Cameron (157) and Richardson (434); see Bradley P. Dean's "The Sound of a Flail: Reconstructions of Thoreau's Early 'Life Without Principle' Lectures," (M.A. thesis, Eastern Washington University, 1984). Carl Hovde has written "Nature into Art: Thoreau's Use of his Journals in *A Week on the Concord and Merrimack Rivers,*" *American Literature* 30 (1958): 165–84, and Linck C. Johnson discusses this issue at length in *Thoreau's Complex Weave: The Writing of "A Week on the Concord and Merrimack Rivers," with the Text of the First Draft* (Charlottesville: University Press of Virginia, 1986). It should also be mentioned that Thoreau's *Journal* has usually appeared in procrustean form. Even his friend Harrison

Blake first offered the *Journal* to the public editorially tailored for public consumption around the cycle of the seasons. Tampering with Thoreau's *Journal* less than Thomas Wentworth Higginson and Mabel Loomis Todd did with Emily Dickinson's poetry, Blake nevertheless felt at liberty to "fix up" for the public what he personally considered a master text. The more complete, more accurate, and hence "truer" 1906 Torrey edition also offered the *Journal* in an editorially "correct" version, emending spelling and punctuation, smoothing out the paragraphs and prose, omitting what the editors of the current, authoritative Princeton edition would consider essential matters.

7. Marlene A. Ogden and Clifton Keller, *Walden: A Concordance* (New York: Garland Publishing, 1985), ix.
8. Jefferson Humphries provides an excellent description of this modern sense of the self in *Losing the Text: Readings in Literary Desire* (Atlanta: University of Georgia Press, 1986), xii.
9. Emerson, "Montaigne," *Collected Works*, 4:90, 96.
10. Richard J. Schneider argues that illusion and deception are the principal themes of *Cape Cod*, in *Henry David Thoreau* (Boston: Twayne, 1987), 93–108.
11. Cameron, 3.
12. A dozen years later, a letter indicates that Thoreau had read Ruskin's *Modern Painters; Corr*, 497.
13. John Burroughs, three-page holograph critique of Thoreau catalogued in A231 of the Berg Collection, The New York Public Library. The first national park was established in 1864, but the park movement flourished during Theodore Roosevelt's tenure as president.
14. *Huckleberries*, 27–29.
15. For a discussion of this temporary epigraph, see Ronald Clapper, *The Development of Walden: A Genetic Text* (Ph.D. diss., University of California at Los Angeles, 1967), 39.
16. Cameron discusses whether Thoreau was hermaphroditic or narcissistic as Miller claims (91).

3. CORRESPONDENCE

1. *J*, 3:106–7. Malcolm Ferguson places the "Says I to myself" statement in the *Tristram Shandy* tradition, particularly with respect to a small book by Edward Nares first published in 1811 called *Thinks-I-to-Myself: A Serio-Ludicro, Tragico-Comico Tale, Written by Thinks-I-to-Myself: WHO?* (Wilmington: R. Porter, 1812); "Thinks-I-to-Myself," *The Concord Saunterer* 7 (December 1972): 8–9.
2. *Corr*, 252; letter to Blake 20 November 1849. Letters specified in this section will be cited by *Corr*'s page numbers in parentheses.
3. After becoming established in 1848, Thoreau would become collectible Americana a generation later. Samuel Arthur Jones, for example, mentions

how *A Week,* which originally sold poorly at $1.25 a copy, had become worth eighteen dollars by 1899. See his *Some Unpublished Letters,* 29.

4. As Philip Fisher points out, this linguistic reference collapses the "carefully subdivided states of [tribal] civilization" and flattens the diverse tribes into the generic term "Indians," symbolizing the opposing other, the enemy. By 1850 America had ceased to distinguish among different tribes of Indians; *Hard Facts: Setting and Form in the American Novel* (New York: Oxford University Press, 1985), 32–37.

5. Linck C. Johnson, *Complex Weave,* 257. See also H. Daniel Peck, " 'Further Down the Stream of Time': Memory and Perspective in Thoreau's *Week,*" *Thoreau Quarterly* 16 (1984): 93–118. Johnson also recognizes Thoreau's reader-oriented rhetoric when he says, "The true test of *A Week* is whether its seeds will germinate in the lives of its readers"; *Weave,* 199.

3. Before Walden

1. EARLY WRITINGS

1. *American Literary Magazines: Eighteenth and Nineteenth Centuries,* ed. Edward Chielens (New York: Greenwood Press, 1986). Frank L. Mott, *A History of American Magazines* (Cambridge: Belknap, 1968). Perry Miller, *The Raven and the Whale: The War of Words and Wits in the Era of Poe and Melville* (New York: Harcourt Brace, 1956). Michael Gilmore, *American Romanticism and the Marketplace* (Chicago: University of Chicago Press, 1985). Kurt Heinzelman, *The Economics of the Imagination* (Amherst: University of Massachusetts, 1980). Leonard Neufeldt's and Stephen Fink's forthcoming books also address Thoreau's relationship with the literary marketplace.

2. D. F. McKenzie, *Bibliography and the Sociology of Texts: The Panizzi Lectures 1985* (London: British Library, 1986). As a related example, Shelley's "Hymn to Intellectual Beauty," which was first published by Leigh Hunt in the *Examiner* (January 1817), appeared in the immediate context of a long article dealing with political power and its abuse by the government. Hence, the word "power" in the poem would cause readers to think also of political power. Extracted from its magazine context, the poem would seem to mean power exclusively in a neoplatonic sense.

3. Thoreau delivered this lecture frequently in the 1850s, separated it into two parts in 1856, and then reassembled it for submission to the *Atlantic Monthly,* where it was first published posthumously in June 1862.

4. Walter Harding, *Days,* 141; Leo Marx, *Excursions* (see intro., n. 7), xii. Sherman Paul and Joseph M. DeFalco have taken "The Landlord" seriously. The latter, for example, admires the essay as a "tightly unified and coherent whole" and sees the landlord as an example of the Transcendental technique of transforming the commonplace into the sublime; " 'The Landlord': Thoreau's Emblematic Technique," *ESQ* 56 (Third Quarter 1969): 23–32.

5. "The Landlord," *Writings,* 5:196.

2. "NATURAL HISTORY"

1. Thoreau's narrative voices and personae have been a major concern of recent scholarship. As Charles R. Anderson has said, we must "learn to separate the actual Henry Thoreau, citizen of Concord, from the fictive character who is both the persona and the voice that speaks to us in the book," *The Magic Circle of Walden* (New York: Holt, Rinehart and Winston, 1968), 11; Richard Poirier pointed out that Thoreau scholarship had been split between thematic and stylistic studies, *A World Elsewhere: The Place of Style in American Literature* (New York: Oxford University Press, 1966), x, 36. Lawrence Buell has insisted on Thoreau as "the main character in an action of his own making" in *Literary Transcendentalism: Style and Vision in the American Renaissance* (Ithaca: Cornell University Press, 1973), 300–301. Further relevant studies include Steven Fink, "Variations on the Self: Thoreau's Personae in *A Week on the Concord and Merrimack Rivers,*" *ESQ* 28 (First Quarter, 1982): 24–35; Edward L. Galligan, "The Comedian at Walden Pond," *South Atlantic Quarterly* 69 (1970): 20–37; Ross Pudaloff, "Thoreau's Composition of the Narrator: From Sexuality to Language," forthcoming in *The Bucknell Review;* Edward Wagenknecht marks the trend to see the "I" as persona serving as both narrator and character in *Henry David Thoreau: What Manner of Man?* (Amherst: University of Massachusetts Press, 1981), 56.

2. Audience roles have long been a focus of Thoreau studies. Sherman Paul says audiences determined whether Thoreau treated his theme humorously or contemptuously, *Shores of America* (see chap. 2.2, n. 1), 309. Stanley Cavell feels Thoreau had to consider audience in order to establish authority as a speaker, *The Senses of Walden* (New York: Viking, 1972), 11; and he has provided a more broadly philosophical analysis of the connection between writing and the problem of the other in *The Claims of Reason: Wittgenstein, Skepticism, Morality, and Tragedy* (New York: Oxford University Press, 1979), Joseph Modlenhauer discusses a "hostile fictional audience" in "Paradox in *Walden,*" in *Twentieth-Century Interpretations of Walden,* ed. Richard Ruland (Englewood Cliffs, N.J.: 1968), 78; and Richard Bridgman explains how "society" changes from a lurking danger to an active evil during *Walden*'s revisions, *Dark Thoreau* (Lincoln: University of Nebraska Press, 1982), 100. William Howarth comments on "the mute other" of *A Week* in *The Book of Concord: Thoreau's Life as a Writer* (New York: Viking, 1982), 40, whereas Stephen Fink sees the reader as complicitous with the author, in "Variations on the Self: Thoreau's Personae in *A Week,*" 27, and in "The Language of Prophecy: Thoreau's 'Wild Apples,'" *NEQ* 59 (June 1986): 222, Fink argues that "the reading public, Thoreau's 'bovine foes,' have shaped his own 'wild' American self." The abstract reader is considered by John C. Broderick, who believed Thoreau's paradoxical style allows the reader to enter and leave the text, "The Movement of Thoreau's Prose," in *Twentieth-Century Interpretations,* 70–72, and by Richard Poirier, who claims

Thoreau's puns force readers to struggle for verbal consciousness, *World Elsewhere,* 77–84.
3. Some parallels between "A Winter Walk" and *Walden* include an idyllic woodsman's hut, a fish as a symbol of ideality, a fisherman seeming to melt into nature's clouds, a lake with no visible inlet or outlet being "earth's liquid eye; a mirror in the breast of nature"; *Writings,* 5:210–13.
4. Emerson, "Biographical Sketch," in *Excursions,* ed. Leo Marx, 10–12.

3. "RESISTANCE" AND *A WEEK*

1. "Resistance to Civil Government," *RP,* 63–90. Because my discussion involves close analysis of the essay's forty-five paragraphs, my parenthetical citations are to paragraph number.
2. *Week,* 5, 6, 9, 10, 12; further page citations will be given in the text. Scholarship on *A Week* is, of course, voluminous, and methodologies have been as diverse as approaches to the book. It has been assayed by Marxist and spiritual tests (respectively: Edwin Fussell, "Thoreau in His Time," *RLV* 39 [1976]: 157–70, and Jonathan Bishop, "The Experience of the Sacred in Thoreau's *Week,*" *ELH* 33 [1966]: 66–91). It has been studied for castration imagery and for cultural references (Richard Lebeaux, *Thoreau's Season* [Amherst: University of Massachusetts Press, 1984], 26–46; Linck C. Johnson, " 'Native to New England': Thoreau, 'Herald of Freedom,' and *A Week,*" *Studies in Bibliography* 36 [1982]: 213–20). In addition to studies already cited (Stephen Fink, H. Daniel Peck and, preeminently, Johnson's *Weave*), David B. Suchoff's admirable article should be mentioned: " 'A More Conscious Silence': Friendship and Language in Thoreau's *Week,*" *ELH* 49 (1982): 673–88. Suchoff reasons that *A Week*'s main theme is the "rift between the abundant meaning inherent in Nature and the possibility of poetic access to it."
3. Ontological distinctions are accomplished in the first two paragraphs of "Sunday" by recalling the doctrine of the "fall of man," the fact that at noon the memory of dawn's freshness cannot be preserved, the sight of bulrushes neatly standing "as if clipped by art."

4. A "CUMULATIVE TREASURE"

1. Examples of the rhetorical conflation "while one did this another did that" occur in *Week,* 116, 118, 123, 158, 172, and 353.
2. Nathaniel Hawthorne, *The French and Italian Notebooks,* ed. Thomas Woodson (Columbus: Ohio State University Press, 1980), 334–45.

4. Walden

1. "SCALPING THE SELF"

1. Emerson letter of 1847 as quoted in Michael Gilmore, *American Romanticism and the Marketplace* (Chicago: University of Chicago Press, 1985), 10.
2. Gilmore, 50–51.
3. Clapper (see chap. 2.2, n. 14), 872, 282.
4. Clapper, 200–201.
5. Huntington Library manuscript catalogued as HM 924, file 5, p. 59.
6. Clapper, 606.
7. See, for example, the opening pages of Joseph Wood Krutch's introduction to the Bantam edition of *Thoreau: Walden and Other Writings* (New York: 1962, 1971).
8. Marc Shell discusses the language of money as a discrete, highly complex art form within economic systems, *The Economy of Literature* (Baltimore: Johns Hopkins University Press, 1978), 58–62; Kurt Heinzelman studies the interrelationship of economic language and moral philosophy, *The Economics of the Imagination* (Amherst: University of Massachusetts Press, 1980), 70–85; Leonard Neufeldt's forthcoming books on Thoreau (Oxford University Press) should be a valuable addition to this vein of scholarship.
9. W, 82. The two extracts that previewed *Walden*'s publication were "A Poet Buying a Farm," which opens *Walden*'s second chapter, and "The Iron Horse," from the chapter "Sounds." Both appeared in *Sartain's Union Magazine* 11 (1852), 127 and 66–68, respectively.
10. Clapper, 399.
11. Clapper, 399–401; James Lyndon Shanley, *The Making of Walden, with the Text of the First Version* (Chicago: University of Chicago Press, 1957), 173.
12. Clapper, 501; too personal also was the poignant mention of how Concord rejected his course of lectures and his proposal for a public library; Clapper, 87–88.
13. Leonard Neufeldt discusses Thoreau's parody of guidebooks for young men and self-help manuals in "Thoreau's Enterprise of Self-Culture in a Culture of Enterprise," *AQ* 39 (Summer 1987): 231–51.
14. Clapper, 465; Shanley, *Making*, 183.
15. Clapper, 265, 854.
16. Shanley, *Making*, 190.
17. Lydia Maria Child, "Review of *A Week* and *Walden*," *National Anti-Slavery Standard*, 16 December 1854, 3; available in *Merrill Studies in Walden*, ed. Joseph Moldenhauer (Columbus: Charles E. Merrill, 1971), 7.
18. See, as a collateral example, John Klancher, *The Making of English Reading Audiences, 1790–1832* (Madison: University of Wisconsin Press, 1987). For plumbago, see Richardson, 144.
19. Melville letter, as cited in Gilmore, 4. James Russell Lowell's 1886 essay "The Progress of the World" makes interesting points about mass culture,

particularly the power of newspapers, in *Latest Literary Essays and Addresses* (Cambridge: Riverside, 1893), 179.

20. Nina Baym, *Novels, Readers, and Reviewers: Responses to Fiction in Antebellum America* (Ithaca: Cornell University Press, 1984), 13.

21. Clapper, 859–60.

22. Sherman Paul, "The Wise Silence: Sound as the Agency of Correspondence in Thoreau," *NEQ* 22 (1949): 527.

23. I refer to Melville's portrait of Thoreau in *The Confidence-Man* and Lowell's in *A Fable for Critics*. Skinner's *Walden II* is as notoriously loose a reading of Thoreau as is Gary Trudeau's Zonker with his Walden puddle in *Doonesbury*. Pirsig's narrator and son weigh Thoreau's sentences as they wheel west in *Zen and the Art of Motorcycle Maintenance*, and McPhee describes a Thoreau-like artisan who despises Thoreau in *The Survival of the Bark Canoe*. Edward Abbey camps with Thoreau in the wilderness in "Down the River," *Walden: Henry David Thoreau* (Salt Lake City: G. M. Smith, 1981).

24. Leon Edel, "The Mystery of Walden Pond," *Stuff of Sleep and Dreams: Experiments in Literary Psychology* (New York: Harper and Row, 1982), 47–65. Victor Carl Friesen, *The Spirit of the Huckleberry: Sensuousness in Henry Thoreau* (Edmonton: University of Alberta Press, 1984).

25. William Howarth, *Walden and Other Writings by Henry David Thoreau* (New York: Modern Library, 1981), viii. Robert Sattelmeyer, "Away from Concord: The Travel Writings of Henry Thoreau" (Ph.D. diss., University of New Mexico, 1975).

26. Shanley, *Making;* Sharon Cameron, *Writing Nature,* 23; Clapper, 7.

27. Michael West, "Scatology and Eschatology: The Heroic Dimensions of Thoreau's Wordplay," *Romanticism: Critical Essays in American Literature* (New York: Garland, 1986), 99–124.

2. FEEDING READERS

1. An early and still interesting discussion of Thoreau's attitude with respect to the railroad is G. Ferris Cronkhite, "The Transcendental Railroad," *NEQ* 24 (1951): 306–28.

2. Ray Angelo locates 270 references to huckleberry in Thoreau's collected works, *Botanical Index of Henry David Thoreau* (Salt Lake City: Peregrine Smith, 1984), 101–2.

3. Thoreau's disdain for the Horned Pout (or Common Bullhead) is stronger in another passage, quoted by David Starr Jordan and Barton Warren Evermann in *American Food and Game Fishes: A Popular Account of All the Species Found in America North of the Equator, with Keys for Ready Identification, Life Histories, and Methods of Capture* (New York: Doubleday, Page, 1902; Dover, 1969), 27: "The horned pout are dull and blundering fellows, fond of the mud and growing best in weedy ponds and rivers without current. They stay near the bottom, moving slowly about with their barbels

widely spread, watching for anything eatable. They will take any kind of bait, from an angleworm to a piece of tomato can, without hesitation or coquetry, and they seldom fail to swallow the hook."

4. Anonymous review of *Walden, Knickerbocker* 45 (March 1855): 235–41; reprinted in *Merrill Studies in Walden* (see chap. 1.4, n. 10), 8–14.

5. Perry Miller, *Consciousness in Concord: The Text of Thoreau's Hitherto "Lost Journal," 1840–1841, Together with Notes and a Commentary* (Boston: Houghton Mifflin, 1958).

6. Charles R. Metzger, *Thoreau and Whitman: A Study of Their Aesthetics* (New York: Archon Books, 1968).

7. Clapper, 462.

3. PARODIC *WALDEN*

1. Bradford Torrey, Introduction to *J*, 1:xix. E. B. White sees Thoreau like a cowboy, riding into town and shooting off his guns in all directions. Walter Harding calls Thoreau "the most erinaceous of American authors. Ideas stick out from his writings in all directions like porcupine quills," Foreword to *The Journal of Henry David Thoreau* (New York: Dover Press, 1962), 1:v. William Howarth notes the popular images of Thoreau as "the radical, the mystic, the naturalist" in *Book of Concord* (see chap. 3.2, n. 2), xiii. Edward Wagenknecht lists diverse celebrities from Bette Davis to Lin Yutang who admire different qualities in Thoreau's voices; *Thoreau: What Manner of Man?* (see chap. 3.2, n. 1), 6.

2. Edward L. Galligan, "The Comedian at Walden Pond," *SAQ* 69 (1970): 20–37; Stephen Fink, "Thoreau and His Audience in 'Natural History of Massachusetts,'" in *The Bucknell Review: The American Renaissance: New Dimensions,* ed. Harry R. Garvin (Lewisburg: Bucknell University Press, 1983), 65–80.

3. Gilmore, 44. As background to the following point about Thoreau's narrative "I," Robert D. Richardson's essay is useful: "The Social Ethics of *Walden*," in *Critical Essays on Walden.* Richardson counts 447 occurrences of "we," 1817 of "I," 310 of "me," and 727 of "my," against 106 of "us" and 294 of "our"; still, Richardson points out the rhetorical reality that his patently I-driven narrative "needs limits" (244), and that while the Walden experiences seem uniquely "his," yet they are also "ours" (245).

4. Shanley, *Making,* 6; Clapper, 23–25. Walter Benn Michaels, *"Walden's* False Bottoms," *Glyph I* (Baltimore: Johns Hopkins University Press, 1977), 136. Joseph Allen Boone marshals another roster of Thoreauvian quotations in rejecting Michaels's reading; "Delving and Diving for Truth: Breaking through to Bottom in *Walden,*" *ESQ* 27 (1981): 135–46. The rhetorical curiosity is that scholars had spotted Thoreau's bottomless style without raising scholarly hackles long before Michaels made it an issue. Back in 1968, for example, Thomas Woodson had revealed that finding *Walden*'s real bottom still re-

mains a mystery, "The Two Beginnings of *Walden:* A Distinction of Styles," *ELH* 35 (1968): 472.

5. I rely heavily on the theories of three critics, although none specifically studies Thoreau: Michel Foucault, *The Order of Things: An Archaeology of the Human Sciences* (New York: Vintage, 1973), particularly his discussion of *Don Quixote;* Linda Hutcheon, *Narcissistic Narrative: The Metafictional Paradox* (Waterloo, Ontario: Wilfred Laurier University Press, 1980; republished by Methuen, 1984), especially 25–28 and 51–69, and *A Theory of Parody: The Teachings of Twentieth-Century Art Forms* (New York: Methuen, 1985); Margaret A. Rose, *Parody // Meta-Fiction: An Analysis of Parody as a Critical Mirror to the Writing and Reception of Fiction* (London: Croom Helm, 1979), particularly part 2: "Theory of Parody," 59–114. Also valuable is Evan Carton's chapter "Parody and Possibility," in *The Rhetoric of the American Romance: Dialectic and Identity in Emerson, Dickinson, Poe, and Hawthorne* (Baltimore: Johns Hopkins University Press, 1985), 117–23. Of course, my debt to Jorge Luis Borges is incalculable.

6. Heinzelman, 74, emphasizes exchange rather than suspension. He also accents the violence that results from puns when disparate ideas are yoked together; for "violence" in Thoreau read "power."

7. Carton, *The Rhetoric of the American Romance,* 123.

8. John P. McGowan, *Representation and Revelation: Victorian Realism from Carlyle to Yeats* (Columbia: University of Missouri Press, 1986).

9. Torrey, Introduction to *J;* Gary Brenner points out that the parody does not integrate with the rest of the chapter, which otherwise makes perfect thematic sense, "Thoreau's 'Brute Neighbors': Four Levels of Nature," in *Twentieth-Century Interpretations of Walden,* 37–40; Joseph J. Moldenhauer comments that parody shows Thoreau in his mellowest mood, capable of poking fun at his idealism and reforms, "Paradox in *Walden,*" in *Twentieth-Century Interpretations,* 77; William Howarth believes Thoreau's self-parody is as severe as Melville's in *The Confidence-Man, Book of Concord* (see chap. 3.2, n. 2), 139; James McIntosh, however, denies the sketch is parodic and views it as a serious mystical meditation, *Thoreau as Romantic Naturalist: His Shifting Stance toward Nature* (Ithaca: Cornell University Press, 1974), 248; John C. Broderick's provocative essay asserts Thoreau's rhetorical emphasis on flux, flow, and freedom, but views parody's function to be a prelude to the theme of rebirth, "The Movement of Thoreau's Prose," in *Twentieth-Century Interpretations,* 64–72. One might also wish to compare this self-parody with Ellery Channing's larger project: a book of twenty chapters containing journal extracts from Emerson, Thoreau, and himself, whose working title matches the self-deprecating humor of "Brute Neighbors": "Walking in Addlebury, or Musings on the Piddlededees"; see Howarth, *Book of Concord,* 83.

10. John McPhee records how some living Concordians still view Thoreau as a woods-burner, even a "real bum," in *The Survival of the Bark Canoe* (New York: Farrar, Straus, Giroux, 1975), 41.

11. Thoreau did not put the final touches to the parody until *Walden*'s last draft (draft G); for example, he decided to delete archaic locutions such as "Methought I heard" and "dost thou."

12. A comparable attitude, although involving a very different rhetorical function, can be seen in other Thoreau texts, as in the first paragraph of "Walking, or The Wild," where he says he may make an "extreme statement" in favor of wildness because he presumes an antithetical audience of "champions of civilization" consisting of "the minister and the school-committee, and every one of you."

13. Sherman Paul, *Shores* (see chap. 2.2, n. 2), 321; Frederick Garber, *Thoreau's Redemptive Imagination* (New York: New York University Press, 1977), 200.

14. As testimony to the power of this primary voice, Walter Benn Michaels's analysis of Thoreau's uncertainty misses the countervoice and dismisses the parable as too flashy and portentous (see chap. 4.3, n. 4), 136; Galligan declines to discuss the sketch in his study of comedy in *Walden* (see chap. 3.2, n. 1), 20–37.

15. Paul, 321.

16. "Lies" and "Christ" quoted in Wagenknecht, 159; "Society," *Journal,* 9 February 1851; see also *Journal,* 27 February 1851 and 8 January 1842.

17. The paragraph on Cato was not part of "The Poet Buying a Farm" published in *Sartain's Union Magazine;* Cato, a rich Roman who decried luxury and extravagance, was known as cruel and niggardly. Richard Poirier offers an intriguing analysis of "the purchase of Hollowell Farm" in *A World Elsewhere: The Place of Style in American Literature* (New York: Oxford University Press, 1966), 84–91.

4. UNREADING "THOREAU"

1. *PJ2* has necessitated reconsideration of *Walden*'s genesis since it demonstrates that the *Walden* project had begun much earlier than previously supposed. Over twenty years ago, Thomas Woodson published a brilliant analysis of *Walden*'s styles, particularly the style that emphasized dialectics and polarities as contrasted with "the extra-vagant, mythopoetic style," "Two Beginnings of *Walden*" (see intro., n. 11), 440–73.

2. Lawrence Buell, *New England Literary Culture,* (see intro., n. 7), 62. Sacvan Bercovitch, *The American Jeremiad* (Madison: University of Wisconsin Press, 1978). Speech-act theory is most classically represented in the writings of J. L. Austin and John Searle.

3. Michael West, "Scatology and Eschatology," in *Romanticism: Critical Essays in American Literature,* 99.

4. *The American Notebooks by Nathaniel Hawthorne,* ed. Randall Stewart (New Haven: Yale University Press, 1932), 99.

5. For glosses on the horse-hound-dove parable, see Walter Harding, *The Var-*

iorum Walden (see intro., n. 3), 259–62, and Edward Wagenknecht, *Henry David Thoreau* (see chap. 1.1, n. 7), 178.

Conclusion: Thoreau's "Perfect Play"

1. Schneider, *Thoreau* (see chap. 2.2, n. 10), 93–108.

Index

About the Author

HENRY GOLEMBA is a professor of American literature and director of American studies at Wayne State University. He is associate editor of *Criticism,* has written books about George Ripley and Frank Stockton, and has contributed extensively to journals like *American Literature, ESQ, Modern Fiction Studies,* and *Midwestern Miscellany.*

9120396